CLOSE
CONNECTIONS

CLOSE
CONNECTIONS

THE BRIDGE BETWEEN
SPIRITUAL AND PHYSICAL REALITY

by
John S. Hatcher

Bahá'í
PUBLISHING
Wilmette, Illinois

Bahá'í Publishing, 415 Linden Avenue, Wilmette, IL 60091-2844
Copyright © 2005 by the National Spiritual Assembly
of the Bahá'ís of the United States —
All Rights Reserved. Published 2005
Printed in the United States of America on acid-free paper ∞

08 07 06 05   1 2 3 4

Library of Congress Cataloging-in-Publication Data

Hatcher, John, Dr.
    Close connections : the bridge between spiritual and physical reality / by
John S. Hatcher.
        p. cm.
    Includes bibliographical references and index.
    ISBN 1-931847-15-0 (softcover : alk. paper)
    1. Bahai Faith—Doctrines. 2. Life —Religious aspects—Bahai Faith. I.
Title.

    BP370.H373 2005
    297.9'322—dc22

                                                    2005045221

*If you read the utterances of Bahá'u'lláh and 'Abdu'l-Bahá
with selflessness and care and concentrate upon them,
you will discover truths unknown to you before
and will obtain an insight into the problems
that have baffled the great thinkers of the world.*

Contents

Acknowledgments

I would first like to acknowledge the assistance of my brother, William S. Hatcher. It was he who introduced me to the Bahá'í Faith, and our countless conversations about theology and philosophy assisted me in pursuing some of the avenues of investigation essential to this work.

I would also like to acknowledge my former secondary school teacher, Grady Randolph, a major influence in helping me realize that knowledge cannot be quantified. It was he who demonstrated for me the degree of dedication and sacrifice required to become a teacher capable of changing lives.

I also wish to express my eternal gratitude to my grandfather, William Benjamin Hardman, whom I never met but who provided me with an example of a life well lived and who bequeathed me the wherewithal to devote my own life to the craft of writing.

Additionally, I would like to thank my colleagues at the University of South Florida who awarded me a sabbatical to finish this ten-year project.

Finally, I would like to thank several individuals who contributed to the editing of this work: Raymond Vince, Duane Troxel, Lucia Hatcher, and, most strategically, Terry Cassiday and her assistants at the Bahá'í Publishing Trust, Christopher Martin and Bahhaj Taherzadeh.

- 1 -

The Value of Physical Existence for Essentially Spiritual Beings

Say: If ye be seekers after this life and the vanities thereof, ye should have sought them while ye were still enclosed in your mothers' wombs, for at that time ye were continually approaching them, could ye but perceive it. Ye have, on the other hand, ever since ye were born and attained maturity, been all the while receding from the world and drawing closer to dust. Why, then, exhibit such greed in amassing the treasures of the earth, when your days are numbered and your chance is well-nigh lost? Will ye not, then, O heedless ones, shake off your slumber?

—Bahá'u'lláh, *Gleanings*

Discovering the purpose of physical reality is possibly the most intriguing personal quest for anyone who has a belief in, or who wants to investigate the basis for a belief in, the existence of spiritual or metaphysical reality. Such a venture is especially challenging if one has come to believe that both physical and metaphysical aspects of reality have been created and organized by the design of a Divine Being, a Creator.

For those who follow the teachings of the Bahá'í Faith—and the teachings of various other world religions—discovering the purpose of physical reality is even more demanding because the Bahá'í scriptures assert that we human beings are essentially spiritual in nature and that all our "human" powers are actually powers and faculties of an essentially metaphysical reality—our soul.

1

Certainly we as human beings do not find it difficult to enjoy and appreciate physical reality, regardless of our religious views or scientific thought. Most of us find the reverse true—that we get so caught up in and attached to delights of sensual pleasures and our apparently insatiable need to acquire and "possess" physical things that we can scarcely afford a moment's leisure to meditate on matters of mind or spirit.

If we are judicious with our time, we may find a few moments now and then to reflect on the beauty of a flower, a landscape, a waterfall, a bird, a butterfly, or an occasional exotic beast. If we are more humanistic in our affections, we may delight in the recounting of noble deeds of heroes, in viewing great paintings or statuary, or in listening to the vast array of music that has emerged over time from so many different cultures. On a personal level, almost all of us have at one time or another experienced an overwhelming attraction to the physical aspect of another human being, what we sometimes allude to as the involuntary act of "falling in love"—a process most often followed sooner or later by what we consider to be the equally involuntary act of "falling out of love."

THE PROBLEM WITH PHYSICAL REALITY

But if we have come to believe in the existence of a just and loving Creator, we may well want to spend some "quality time" pondering why, if this God could have created anything He wished, why "for God's sake" did He decide it would be a good idea to fashion a creation that seems so persistently distracting and antithetical to any spiritual purposes? Furthermore, if physical reality is the product of such a Creator, why does this expression of reality seem so fraught with tribulation and injustice, so ostensibly devoid of inherent meaning or purpose, unless, somehow it is indeed "for God's sake"?

Perhaps the more philosophical and deep-rooted concern we have as human beings examining the possibility of believing in a Divine Creator is this: If God has created us as essentially spiritual beings (human souls operating temporarily through the instrumentality of a physical organism), and if God has ordained that we are destined to continue our existence beyond this "mortal coil" as spiritual beings operating in a nonmaterial reality, then why did this omnipotent, omniscient, and loving Creator

2

think it wise that we begin our eternal spiritual journey in an environment so contrary and confounding to all that He would have us become—namely, good or "Godly" individuals?

SOME FUNDAMENTAL RESPONSES

One justification for having us begin our eternal spiritual journey in a physical staging area—even if we are spirits operating through machines that inevitably deteriorate over time even with proper maintenance—is that our physical experience prepares us for birth into the next stage of our existence. In fact, if the Creator is loving and is also functioning in the capacity of a parent-teacher, we have to conclude that physical reality is not only *capable* of providing us with a foundational education, it necessarily provides the very *best* methodology that could possibly be devised.

And yet, even as a succession of horrible personal experiences erodes the naïve optimism of Candide in Voltaire's work of the same name—a satire on the philosophy and theology of Leibniz that since the world was created by a Perfect Creator, this must be a perfect world—so must our own experience in this world cause us to question why injustice and imperfection seem to abound. Furthermore, if somehow we can accept that physical reality is a complex classroom geared to teaching us and preparing us for our eternal future, why do not all human beings have an equal chance to benefit from this earthly experience? What is more, if the physical-foundational part of our education happens only once, then what is the fate of those souls who pass on to that next stage of reality as small children, or who spend the physical portion of their lives trying to function and develop through a defective brain or body? Likewise, what is the spiritual destiny of those who are abused, neglected, malnourished, or otherwise prevented from properly benefiting from the spiritual lessons this physical education is fashioned to provide?

WHERE DO WE GO FROM HERE?

The fundamental objective of the journey or "mind experiment" we are about to undertake is to approach these and other equally confounding issues about these apparently dual aspects of our reality so that by the end of our venture we can arrive at some conclusions that might prove practically useful for the time we have left in this formative and foundational stage of our development as human beings.

As we sally forth, we will use as primary guideposts passages from the authoritative writings of the Bahá'í Faith that seem to suggest solutions to the impediments that may block our passage from time to time. Our ultimate objective is to discover a bridge between what many believe to be two realities—one physical, the other metaphysical. Or if, during the course of our meandering we discover that reality is actually an inherently unified organism, then possibly we can figure out how the dual aspects of this single reality become bridged.

The method we will employ in our quest to discover the purpose of physical reality is similar to the process employed by Socrates in Plato's dialogue *The Republic*. After a lengthy and largely unsuccessful debate considering the various commonly held definitions of justice, Socrates suggests that they might succeed better were they first to define justice as it is manifest in society as a whole, and then, by analogy, see how these same attributes might help discover and define justice manifest in the individual. The basis for this method is his assertion that society is but a larger expression of the individual.

Employing this same analogical process, we will proceed to search for a bridge between spiritual and physical reality on two levels. Chapters 1 through 9 will examine this relationship "writ large" in the macrocosm— studying the theory that an essentially metaphysical being, a Creator, designed and fashioned physical reality for spiritual purposes. Chapters 10 through 16 will examine this relationship as it operates analogously at the microcosmic level—the theory that the human soul, also essentially spiritual in nature, employs an analogous process to run the physical body and direct the overall progress of our physical experience.

SOME IMPLICATIONS OF THIS STUDY

If we are successful in demonstrating that there are both a physical and a metaphysical aspect to reality and that there is a bridge between them, a number of important implications may follow. For instance, it may be that this connection or interpenetration occurs at various levels—at both the macrocosmic level of existence (the universe as a whole) and at the microcosmic level (the world of the individual self). For example, if we can demonstrate that there is an essentially spiritual God who effects creation and shapes human history, then clearly our understanding and interpretation of history would have to be completely revised, as would our understanding of cosmology and astrophysics. Likewise, if our own individual reality is essentially spiritual such that all our "human" faculties and powers (ideation, reason, will, consciousness, self-awareness, and memory) derive from metaphysical influence, then our understanding of our true nature and worth will be dramatically affected.

Stated succinctly, if there is interpenetration between physical and metaphysical aspects of reality, then science must in time consider the degree to which phenomenal events are affected and effected by non-physical causes. Conversely, those who avow belief in spiritual reality will have to consider the extent to which their spiritual condition is influenced by their daily regimen of physical activity (work, reflection, interaction with others, and so on).

A RATIONALE FOR EMPLOYING THE BAHÁ'Í PERSPECTIVE

I am predisposed to compare theories about reality to those presented in the Bahá'í teachings because the very means by which I became a Bahá'í was to test rigorously the foundational tenets of the Bahá'í Faith with whatever questions I could conceive and then compare the solutions it offered to those of any other theological, philosophical, or scientific explanation I could discover. That was forty-five years ago, and I am still employing this same approach to my various ventures into the realm of creative investigation of reality, most especially about the nature of physical reality.

Though the Bahá'í Faith is known primarily for its assertion that the world's revealed religions are all part of a single systematic attempt on the part of a Divine Creator to instruct humanity, of particular relevance to the subject of this study is the Bahá'í axiom that there is no inherent contradiction between science and religion. This verity is not intended to imply that there aren't contradictions between individuals studying in these two areas of interest or between the theories about reality that they propose—the ongoing debates about such vital issues as the theory of evolution or the question of abortion are but two examples that suggest no reconciliation between science and religion seems imminent. Rather, the Bahá'í teachings affirm that all study of reality can be valid if pursued with the logical tools with which human beings have been endowed, particularly when these faculties are employed in a well-conceived regimen such as the so-called "scientific method":

> God has endowed man with intelligence and reason whereby he is required to determine the verity of questions and propositions. If religious beliefs and opinions are found contrary to the standards of science, they are mere superstitions and imaginations; for the antithesis of knowledge is ignorance, and the child of ignorance is superstition.[1]

But the validity of the Bahá'í claim about the legitimacy of studying reality from either a scientific or religious perspective is not dependent on the use of similar methodologies. It stems from the Bahá'í belief that reality itself is a unified and organic system with various dimensions that can be reasonably studied from myriad points of view. Of particular relevance to this enduring conflict between science and religion is the Bahá'í view that there are both physical and metaphysical properties to reality. Therefore over time all the different valid studies of reality will come to discover and recognize the legitimacy of each other because the soundness or truth of one branch of learning will no longer be seen to nullify the validity of others.

Another Bahá'í axiom relevant to this study asserts that observations about reality, however accurate or true they may be, can never be final or complete. Inasmuch as reality itself is infinitely complex, all knowledge of reality must necessarily always be only relatively true. This axiom proffers to the student of reality the promise of inexhaustible delight. What is more, since the Bahá'í teachings also affirm that because our conscious mind is a power of the spiritual essence that is our soul, this

6

joy of study and discovery will persist in the continuation of our lives beyond the demise of our physical selves.

Akin to this revelation about the study of reality is what may well be the foremost principle espoused throughout the authoritative writings of the Bahá'í Faith—certainly it is the most foundational verity for this study—that reality has both physical and metaphysical properties, and, more to the point, that the physical properties of reality are the "outward" or sensually perceptible counterpart of the "inner" metaphysical properties of reality. By itself, this principle is not necessarily all that astounding— in some senses it might appear to be little more than a restatement of a form of Platonism. But coupled with this notion of a counterpart or metaphorical relationship between the physical and spiritual aspects of reality is the essential premise for all that we will discuss in the remainder of this discourse—that there is a prescribed, constant, and predictable interplay between these twin aspects of reality which, as the title of this work implies, requires a relentless bidirectional bridging of the gap between spiritual and physical reality.

Accordingly, the study of any part of reality from any perspective requires that we employ essentially the same tools of investigation. And since our quest here is to discover whether or not there are causal relationships between the metaphysical and physical aspects of reality, we might benefit as we proceed from considering statements by a system of belief or study which advocates that all observations and conclusions that do not employ scientific method are, by definition, tantamount to "superstitions and imaginations" and are, therefore, the "antithesis of knowledge."

FUNDAMENTAL BACKGROUND TO THE BAHÁ'Í FAITH

If we are going to pursue this subject from the perspective of the Bahá'í belief system, or at least by employing some of the methods and answers it suggests, it is essential that we prepare for our quest by considering some further background information about the Bahá'í Faith, its teachings and beliefs, that are particularly relevant to beliefs about the nature and purpose of physical reality. Much of this information will be apparent as we examine the relationship between the metaphysical and physical expressions of reality, but foundational principles of Bahá'í beliefs set the stage for our venture.

Sometimes called the world's most racially integrated religion, the Bahá'í Faith is, according to the *Encyclopaedia Britannica*, second only to Christianity in its diffusion of believers worldwide. Currently established in over 235 countries and comprising more than 5 million believers from 2,100 ethnic, racial, and tribal groups, the Bahá'í Faith is a world religion, not a cult, not a sect, not an offshoot of Islam or of any other religion. The Bahá'í Faith is neither synthetic nor syncretistic, but a world religion derived from the revealed teachings of Bahá'u'lláh (1817–92), its Prophet and Founder.*

At the heart of Bahá'í teachings is the belief—articulated throughout the writings of Bahá'u'lláh—that history is a spiritual dynamic proceeding according to progressive stages of guidance as revealed by God through the advent of divinely appointed Prophets or Messengers, whom Bahá'ís describe as Manifestations of God. These Manifestations, who appear approximately every five hundred to one thousand years, reveal in turn successively more complete descriptions of reality, together with updated laws and guidance for humankind. Their teachings provide governance that is meant to endure until the next Manifestation appears to advance further the systems that humankind must employ to foster an ever more spiritualized civilization—that is, a society run according to spiritual principles of justice, equity, freedom, education, and so forth.

From this perspective, all the world religions are viewed by Bahá'ís as one religion—the religion of God—revealed in progressively more complete expressions of knowledge and in evolving systems of governance to befit the ever-advancing needs and capacities of humankind. Bahá'ís thus believe that all the world's revealed religions are united in origin and purpose and that all the peoples of the world are members of one human family, a family that is proceeding through ever more expansive stages of social relationship and order.

---

* Bahá'u'lláh (Arabic for "the Glory of God") is the title bestowed on Mírzá Ḥusayn-'Alí, the son of a noble family from the district of Núr in the province of Mázindarán, Iran.

Critical to the Bahá'í view of this process is the assertion that humankind on planet earth has at long last evolved into one global community. Therefore it is a central theme of the Bahá'í teachings that each person is a citizen of a world community and that the nations of the world are thus obliged to assist in constructing a global commonwealth to administer this newly emerged reality. Shoghi Effendi, the great-grandson of Bahá'u'lláh, has written, "Unification of the whole of mankind is the hall-mark of the stage which human society is now approaching. Unity of family, of tribe, of city-state, and nation have been successively attempted and fully established. World unity is the goal towards which a harassed humanity is striving. Nation-building has come to an end."[2]

THE AUTHORITATIVE TEXTS OF THE BAHÁ'Í FAITH

The heart of the "sacred scriptures" of the Bahá'í Faith are the hundreds of volumes penned by Bahá'u'lláh, whom Bahá'ís consider to be the most recent, though not the last, Manifestation of God. One of the most weighty teachings of Bahá'u'lláh is that human history is the chronicle of an "ever-advancing civilization."[3] Thus there is no end point in history because humankind has the potential for infinite spiritual advancement, both in this world and in the afterlife, whether individually or collectively. For regardless how advanced we may become, we will never attain a state of absolute perfection, nor will we ever evolve to become anything other than a human soul, either in this life or in the afterlife.

Closely aligned with this concept of an ever-advancing civilization is the idea that there is an unrelenting and reciprocal relationship between belief and action, between faith and deeds. Bahá'u'lláh states emphatically in the preamble to the Kitáb-i-Aqdas, His Most Holy Book, that it is not enough merely to recognize and accept the truth revealed by the Manifestations of God (such as Krishna, Abraham, Moses, Buddha, Zoroaster, Christ, Muḥammad, the Báb, and Bahá'u'lláh). To become spiritually transformed, one must combine the recognition of the most recent Manifestation of God with a daily regimen as prescribed by the Manifestation, such as prayer, meditation, study, work, and service to humanity.

9

The other authoritative texts of the Bahá'í Faith are the works of the Báb (1819–50), the herald of Bahá'u'lláh and a Manifestation of God in His own right; the works of 'Abdu'l-Bahá (1844–1921), the son and authoritative interpreter of the works of Bahá'u'lláh as well as head of the Bahá'í Faith as designated in the will of Bahá'u'lláh; the works of Shoghi Effendi (1887–1957), designated by 'Abdu'l-Bahá as Guardian of the Bahá'í Faith and authoritative interpreter of the Bahá'í texts; and finally the decisions and commentary of the Universal House of Justice, a body established by Bahá'u'lláh, defined further by 'Abdu'l-Bahá, discussed in depth by Shoghi Effendi, and first elected in 1963 at the first World Bahá'í Congress.*

FOUNDATIONAL BELIEFS OF THE BAHÁ'Í FAITH

The Bahá'í Faith is often described succinctly as believing in three types of unity—the unity of God (there is only one Creator), the unity of religion (the foundation of all revealed religions is the same), and the unity of humankind (all people alike are the children of the same God).

At the heart of this concept is what Bahá'ís often term "progressive revelation," the belief in a deity who is at once Creator and Prime Mover of the universe and yet simultaneously a "personal" God who is aware of and concerned with each and every human being. From this cosmological perspective, Bahá'ís do not assume that the earth is the unique creation on which human life has evolved. Essential to the Bahá'í concept of the Creator is the concept of timelessness and limitlessness with regard to both physical and metaphysical realities. Furthermore, inasmuch as the Bahá'í authoritative texts state that the "fruit" of creation is bringing forth human life and an ever-advancing (ever more spiritualized) human society, the Bahá'í teachings confirm that there has never existed a time when this process was not occurring somewhere in the created universe.

---

* Bahá'u'lláh appointed 'Abdu'l-Bahá to succeed Him as head of the Bahá'í Faith after His passing, and 'Abdu'l-Bahá, prior to his own passing, appointed his eldest grandson, Shoghi Effendi, to succeed him. Shortly after Shoghi Effendi's passing, the Bahá'í world community for the first time elected the Universal House of Justice, composed of nine Bahá'ís, as head of the religion.

THE MANIFESTATIONS OF GOD

The method by which the Creator as an essentially spiritual Being effects physical creation is empowering specialized beings—the Prophets or Manifestations of God—who function as intermediaries or "Vice-regents" for God. Ontologically, the Manifestations are not ordinary human beings who have been temporarily inspired. The Manifestation preexists in the realm of the spirit, is aware of His special station from the beginning of His consciousness when He assumes an associative relationship with a human temple or persona, and of His own free will undertakes His mission as intermediary and spiritual teacher.

The Manifestations acknowledge the validity of one another, articulate the same essential spiritual verities, and provide for those who live during Their dispensation (the period that Their religion is intended to endure) the means designated by God through which all human beings can discover the most propitious path to spiritual development and can fulfill their individual purposes in life.

Because They appear in a systematic progression, each Manifestation builds upon what the previous Prophet taught and prepares the way for the advent of the succeeding Prophet. Therefore, the Manifestation changes those laws of His predecessor that need to be updated, abrogates those that are no longer necessary, and introduces new laws as they become appropriate.

From this perspective, it is easy to understand that a major source of conflict among religions has been the fact that while spiritual concepts of religions may agree, specific laws are not always in accord. For example, Moses allowed divorce, Christ forbade it, and Muḥammad permitted it. And yet the source of the most grievous conflict as discussed by Bahá'u'lláh in the Kitáb-i-Íqán (Book of Certitude)* is to misinterpret scripture in such a way as to create a type of chauvinism whereby a given religion may decide that it possesses the one and only valid path to God.

Bahá'u'lláh observes that one frequent source of this misinterpretation is a literalist approach to metaphorical passages of scripture, an approach

---

* Work revealed by Bahá'u'lláh that lays out the basic theological principles of the Bahá'í Faith.

that tempts religious authorities to take passages out of context and to misconstrue them as implying confusing or incorrect meanings.

THE SOUL AND THE AFTERLIFE

At the core of Bahá'í beliefs regarding the purpose of individual existence is the concept that the true reality of each individual is a spiritual essence, the soul. From the Bahá'í point of view, all distinctly human powers and faculties—such as reason, memory, imagination, will, and abstract thought—are but functions of the soul. Therefore the soul employs the physical capacities of the brain to channel ideas into physical action, but the soul is not *in* the body or *dependent on* the body for existence. Rather, the soul begins when it emanates from God to associate with the body at conception, though it endures infinitely beyond the body's deterioration and demise. To put it another way, the soul has a beginning, but it has no end.

However, the Bahá'í teachings explicitly deny the concepts of reincarnation (rebirth of the soul in another human body) and of metempsychosis (rebirth of the soul in the body of some other life form). The Bahá'í teachings also deny the belief in the afterlife as consisting of merely two possibilities—a heaven for those who have done well and a hell for those who have failed. Rather Bahá'u'lláh makes it clear that our physical existence is a period of preparation for our birth into a more expansive experience of reality, an experience in which reality will no longer be veiled or concealed in the guise of material forms.

In this sense, the afterlife is a continuation of the consciousness and identity that we have in this life. Yet, because the afterlife is a metaphysical or spiritual existence, the Manifestations admonish us to recognize and develop our spiritual faculties and capacities during our physical existence so that we will be prepared for the continuation of our existence, and the transition to this expanded reality will be felicitous and fruitful.

Bahá'u'lláh explains this relationship between these two parts of our existence by comparing our physical life to the gestation of the child in the womb of its mother. Every activity in that embryonic reality is geared to preparing the child for a productive and fruitful experience in a physical environment. In the same way, our lives in the physical world have the explicit purpose of preparing us for birth into the world of the spirit. The difference between these two experiences is that while we are in the womb, we have no conscious participation in our development, but we have free will in our physical lives to determine the extent to which we will become prepared for the transition to the afterlife and the continuation of our existence.

Therefore, while there is no physical heaven or physical hell in the Bahá'í belief system—since there is no physical reality for such places to exist—the Bahá'í texts state that there are explicit consequences to our actions in this life. We will never cease to exist or to remain human souls; our existence will always remain in a relative state of development. Consequently, if we ignore our opportunities and obligations in this life to prepare ourselves for our further development, we will experience remorse and regret when we evaluate our lives at the conclusion of our association with physical reality, as well as the existential sense of confusion and fear during our physical existence because we are not properly equipped to make propitious moral choices.

From this point of view, one can understand that the Bahá'í texts do not describe a specific point of spiritual development that would accord with some religious concepts of attaining "salvation." If we are capable of infinite progress both in this life and in the afterlife, there can be no single point of development or accomplishment that could be designated as a point where we have completed our purpose to become ever more perfected, nor do we reach a point of progress in physical existence when regression is not also a possibility.

The central emphasis of the Bahá'í teachings, however, is that spiritual progress or forward motion is rewarding in and of itself, both in the physical experience and in the spiritual world. To progress spiritually is an inherently blissful and empowering experience without regard to what such progress may yield in terms of reward or escape from punishment.

BAHÁ'Í SOCIAL TEACHINGS AND THE AGE OF MATURITY

While all Manifestations have the same capacity and are regarded as equal in spiritual station, the Bahá'í writings state that the spiritual evolution or progress of human society, like the development of an individual, has certain milestones, certain turning points in the process of advancement. During what the Bahá'í writings allude to as the Adamic or Prophetic Cycle—the period of time from the appearance of Adam through the dispensation of Muḥammad (about six thousand years)—humankind on this planet was being prepared for a turning point at which time the generality of humankind would understand that the world is one community, that all human beings are equal in the sight of God, that all religions derive from the same sacred source, and that the purpose of human society is to create institutions and relationships that are based on spiritual principles.

This period, Bahá'ís believe, the period of the maturation of humankind, has at long last arrived. So it is that the Bahá'í teachings proclaim that the time foretold in all the world's religions as the time of the end, as the Last Days, as the Day of Resurrection, has arrived, but not as a dire conclusion to the story of humankind—as some religious leaders have interpreted these scriptures—but rather as the point of our true beginning. For the stage of maturity for any organic life is not a period of conclusion or finality, but the true beginning of the period for which the organism has been created. It is the time for the fruit tree to bring forth fruit, for the rosebush to bring forth roses, and for the human being to be considered an adult and, therefore, ready to accomplish those special tasks for which human beings have been brought forth into creation.

In keeping with this belief in the maturation of humanity, the laws and teachings of Bahá'u'lláh focus on the critical nature of this time in human history, particularly on the necessity for humankind to create a global commonwealth to bring about creative governance for a world that has "matured" because it has become contracted into a single unified community. Among the features of this global community, as discussed in the Bahá'í writings, are the creation of a world auxiliary language, a world currency, a world system of weights and measures, and a world police force to ensure the security and sovereignty of all the constituent members. On a more personal level, the teachings of Bahá'u'lláh regarding this commonwealth call for the adoption of laws and policies to ensure the equality of men and women, the unity of science and religion, the abolition of all forms of prejudice, the establishment of a world peace, the establishment of universal compulsory education, and the securing of all basic human rights.

Yet however vast, encompassing, and idealistic this vision of a world community might seem, the foundational structures for this society are the home and the community, the successful creation of which are dependent on the universal recognition that the law which binds together all creation is the law of love in all its myriad forms: "Love is the most great law that ruleth this mighty and heavenly cycle, the unique power that bindeth together the divers elements of this material world, the supreme magnetic force that directeth the movements of the spheres in the celestial realms."[5]

It is in the context of these teachings and from my perspective as a Bahá'í that I undertake this attempt to respond to one of the most crucial personal issues one can deal with in coming to terms with any religious belief—the issue surrounding our proper relationship as essentially spiritual beings (human souls) with physical reality.

- 2 -

In Search of the Beloved:
The Mystery of the "Hidden Treasure"

I testify that Thou wast a hidden Treasure wrapped within Thine immemorial Being and an impenetrable Mystery enshrined in Thine own Essence. Wishing to reveal Thyself, Thou didst call into being the Greater and the Lesser Worlds, and didst choose Man above all Thy creatures, and didst make Him a sign of both of these worlds, O Thou Who art our Lord, the Most Compassionate!

Thou didst raise Him up to occupy Thy throne before all the people of Thy creation. Thou didst enable Him to unravel Thy mysteries, and to shine with the lights of Thine inspiration and Thy Revelation, and to manifest Thy names and Thine attributes.

—Bahá'u'lláh, *Prayers and Meditations*

Throughout the Bahá'í texts we find allusions to the Creator of the universe as an essentially spiritual, essentially unknowable, self-sufficient, omnipotent, and omniscient Being:

To every discerning and illuminated heart it is evident that God, the unknowable Essence, the Divine Being, is immensely exalted beyond every human attribute, such as corporeal existence, ascent and descent, egress and regress. Far be it from His glory that human tongue should adequately recount His praise, or that human heart comprehend His fathomless mystery. He is, and hath ever been, veiled in the ancient eternity of His Essence, and will remain in His Reality everlastingly hidden from the sight of men. "No vision taketh in Him, but He taketh in all vision; He is the Subtile, the All-Perceiving."[1]

As soon as we encounter these statements about the ontology of the Creator, somewhere inside us a core question spontaneously emerges, even if we are totally unaware that we have asked it: If God is truly self-sufficient, why would He find it desirable to create anything at all? Why isn't He satisfied to exist in a perpetual state of self-absorbed bliss? And even if we discover what we believe to be a rationale for this autonomous Being to create something, what possible motive could He have to fashion a reality so crass as to have physical properties, a reality that much of the time seems to contradict the very nature and attributes that are said to characterize the Creator—an essentially spiritual Being that is the source of an infinite array of spiritual attributes? After all, God is characterized in the scriptures of all the world religions as just, loving, a heavenly Father concerned with everything from the whole of humankind to the fall of a sparrow. Yet this environment He is said to have fashioned as an expression of His godliness much of the time seems to contradict any evidence that it has been fashioned by fundamental rules of justice and order, let alone by a heavenly Deity intent on demonstrating His exalted nature and lovable personality.

As with any question that presumes to consider the *modus operandi* of a Being who exists so infinitely beyond significant comprehension, a simple but thoroughly unsatisfying answer is always available. God created physical reality because He wanted to, and it sometimes appears to us a perverse environment because we just don't understand how the whole thing works: If God created it, it must be good!

An equally logical but no less unimpressive response is that the Creator creates because by definition and nature He is a creator. Creating stuff is precisely what a creator does, even as a master painter paints masterpieces.

These cryptic "solutions" may strike some as arrogant, even blasphemous, but what other answers are available to us? If we assert, as

Leibniz did, that because the Creator is perfect, His creation—even the physical aspect of it—must necessarily also be perfect, then what part of this created reality do we study to discover His perfection?

PERHAPS LOVE IS THE ANSWER

Though we may at first rebel against ascribing any implicit "requirements" to God, the Bahá'í Faith, like most other world religions, attributes a spiritual personality to the Creator, a character that would find a persistent state of self-absorbed delight logically untenable. For example, one of the essential attributes of the Creator is love, and love requires a love relationship, which requires more than one being.

It is most certainly logical and true that the Creator does appreciate and even "love" His own perfection. In a discussion of the "kinds of love," 'Abdu'l-Bahá observes that one category of love is "the love of God towards the Self or Identity of God." In other words, the Creator *does* love Himself, but not in some anthropomorphic sense of conceit or pride. Being intelligent, God is understandably aware of His own perfection. What is more—and this is the key to creation—as a loving Being, the Creator is aware of the joy other beings would have in coming to understand and benefit from the knowledge of His nature. Therefore He desires to create, but not because of any self-interest. He doesn't *need* someone to love or someone to love Him—this "wish" is entirely an altruistic intention, from which derives His will that such a being exist, and from that will derives creation itself: "Powerful is He to do that which He pleaseth. He saith: Be; and it is."[2] And yet, as we will discuss more completely in chapter 4, there is an understandable methodology by which the path of causality can be traced—from the Creator, across the bridge of the Intermediary, until the "wish" or will of God becomes gradually implemented in physical expression.

Does this make good sense? Does all of creation result from the Creator's desire to share the bounty of knowing Him? According to 'Abdu'l-Bahá it does: "This is the transfiguration of His Beauty, the reflection of Himself in the mirror of His Creation. This is the reality of love, the Ancient Love, the Eternal Love. Through one ray of this Love all other love exists."[3]

The implications of this passage are manifold because it not only suggests the divine rationale for creation, it also asserts that the logical consequence of this process is that everything in reality, be it physical or metaphysical, particular or composite, reflects or manifests the attributes of God's Essence to the degree that a given created thing is capable of doing so. Simply stated, all creation has as the core reason for its existence "the reflection of Himself in the mirror of His Creation." Therefore, not only human beings, but all created existence is made in God's image.

THE REQUISITES FOR A LOVE RELATIONSHIP

In one sense, then, this theological perspective implies that the act of creation, as well as all that is created, is an expression of the Creator's wish to share His love, and, accordingly, we are able to discern divine attributes or the Creator's imprint in every created thing, a subject we will later discuss in depth. But important as this observation might be in helping us discern some rational basis for creation, even for a physical creation, love in its more complete expression implies a reciprocal relationship; it is something more complex than a unidirectional act.

For example, we might say the masterpiece of the painter is an expression of his love—of beauty, of art, of reality, of the act of creating. In this sense, the painting bears the imprint of the painter's character and personality. But there is no relationship in a literal sense between the painter and his painting. The painting is not sensible or cognitive. It cannot decide to express to the painter how grateful it is for his having given it life, even though its beauty may proclaim the innermost thoughts and emotions of its creator.

But a love relationship that is an organic creation—capable of growth and development—requires two beings that possess several specialized capacities. First, each being must be capable of cognition and ideation in order to understand the nature of the beloved. For while infatuation or blind attraction to another is often portrayed as a kind of love, in truth it is but the initial stage of what may or may not be "love" in any important sense of the term. Second, in addition to possessing sufficient intelligence to comprehend and appreciate the attributes of the beloved, these beings must have the free will to decide whether or not to respond to this appreciation or love of the character of the beloved. For love, like learning, is necessarily an act that has value only when it is freely instigated. That which is coerced can never become authentic love or knowledge. Finally, having determined to respond to this understanding and love, the two beings must then carry out this response in action. However, if this love is to be worthy, the action cannot be a single event, but a systematic and ever more progressive and creative dramatization or expression of the internal condition.

God and the Tradition of the Hidden Treasure

Because the rationale for creation discussed thus far is such a crucial point of beginning for our entire study, it might be valuable to reiterate this same essential concept as it is depicted in a well-known Islamic *hadíth* (oral tradition) that both Bahá'u'lláh and 'Abdu'l-Bahá allude to in numerous passages. The simple but pithy poetic axiom states, "I was a Hidden Treasure. I wished to be made known, and thus I called creation into being in order that I might be known."[4]

In one of His revealed prayers, Bahá'u'lláh makes an allusion to this tradition that offers further insight into the divine rationale for creation implicit in this elliptical metaphor: "Lauded be Thy name, O Lord my God! I testify that Thou wast a hidden Treasure wrapped within Thine immemorial Being and an impenetrable Mystery enshrined in Thine own Essence. Wishing to reveal Thyself, Thou didst call into being the Greater and the Lesser Worlds, and didst choose Man above all Thy creatures, and didst make Him a sign of *both of these worlds*,* O Thou Who art our Lord, the Most Compassionate!"[5]

In this passage the purpose of creation is portrayed as bringing forth a being capable of "revealing Thyself" (that is, God's image) by becoming a "sign of both of these worlds," meaning spiritual and material reality. This allusion to man as being "above all Thy creatures" and a "sign of both of these worlds" confirms again the requisites for an authentic love relationship as we have portrayed it. Indeed, this passage implies that the

---

* Italics added.

creation of the human reality is the means by which the "wish" of the creator is fulfilled because the Creator has devised a means by which humankind is invested with the capacity to be a "sign" of God.

In short, this tradition seems to be a poetic expression of the explanation for creation we have already discussed, but it goes further by suggesting the creation of human beings fulfills the criteria essential for a reciprocal love and not mere emotional affect, infatuation, or blind attraction. Furthermore, this tradition works on many levels and demands extensive reflection. For example, this terse explanation for divine rationale is far less paradoxical and enigmatic than are the anthropomorphic explanations for creation articulated in the apologetic discourse of other theological and philosophical treatises.

PROBLEMS WITH SOME PREVIOUS ALLUSIONS TO GOD AS CREATOR

Any portrayal of God's will is logically puzzling when it attempts to embrace simultaneously a concept of a Creator that is an independent, infinite, omniscient, and omnipotent Lord of the Universe and, at the same time, a concept of a "personal" God that is aware of and concerned with each and every created thing.

Because we are largely incapable of imagining such a Being, religions of the past have understandably resorted to portraying God in anthropomorphic terms. We are all familiar with the Old Testament portrait of God as a tribal chieftain, as a liege lord of supreme power and authority, as a "jealous" ruler who often demonstrates His supremacy through miraculous and direct interventions in history. The New Testament portrayal of God as alluded to by Christ is a more approachable figure, a loving and forgiving Father who ransoms His only Son to effect the salvation of the human race: "Are not five sparrows sold for two pennies? And not one of them is forgotten before God. Why, even the hairs of your head are all numbered. Fear not; you are of more value than many sparrows."[6]

Ironically, even as Christ rejects the literalism of Jewish interpretations of Old Testament scripture, so Muḥammad denounces the literalism of what had become by the seventh century the Trinitarian deification of Christ. In the Koran, Muḥammad continually cautions His followers that God is a being so exalted as to be beyond allusion or comprehension except in the poetic terms devised by the Apostles of God (the Manifestations): "They do blaspheme who say: 'God is Christ the son of Mary.' But said Christ: 'O Children of Israel! Worship God, my Lord and your Lord.'"[7]

BAHÁ'U'LLÁH'S OBSERVATIONS ABOUT
ANTHROPOMORPHIC IMAGES OF GOD

While Bahá'u'lláh reiterates time and again this Koranic theme of the exalted and unique station of God, He also emphasizes throughout His many volumes that the nature or attributes of God are everywhere apparent to all who exercise their inherent capacities to perceive these signs.

For example, in the Kitáb-i-Íqán (Book of Certitude) Bahá'u'lláh explains that the station of entering the "presence of God" as promised in scripture does not signify entering the physical presence of God—whether in this life or in the next.[8] Instead, this metaphorical phrase indicates a process of perceiving the attributes of God as expressed through and explained by the Manifestations of God and then expressing this awareness in the systematic reformation of one's character.

Bahá'u'lláh writes, "No theme hath been more emphatically asserted in the holy scriptures. Notwithstanding, they [commentators] have deprived themselves of this lofty and most exalted rank, this supreme and glorious station. Some have contended that by 'attainment unto the Divine Presence' is meant the 'Revelation' of God in the Day of Resurrection. Should they assert that the 'Revelation' of God signifieth a 'Universal Revelation,' it is clear and evident that such revelation already existeth in all things."[9]

Reaffirming Muḥammad's insistent distinction between God and the Apostles of God, Bahá'u'lláh explains the distinction between God as Creator, as "unknowable Essence," and the Manifestations of God, who, by perfectly embodying all the attributes of God, enable human beings to perceive all the aspects of godliness dramatized in human actions, and who then exhort humankind to emulate Them.[10] Even as Christ states that to know Him is to know God, so Bahá'u'lláh affirms that to comprehend the spiritual character of the Manifestation is, effectively, to know God—or at least to know as much of God as we are capable of understanding.

According to Bahá'í scripture, the Manifestations embody *all* the attributes of God perfectly and, therefore, They also exemplify the same paradox of a dual nature. As we have already noted in chapter 1, They function in the station of essential unity, possessing the godly powers of omnipotence, omniscience, and all other divine attributes. On the other hand, They make Themselves directly accessible to humankind by deigning to appear in the guise of ordinary human beings in what Bahá'u'lláh designates the station of "distinction" (that is, as an individual personality in a particular society in the context of a particular point in history).[11] But the most critical gift They leave behind—in addition to modeling or exemplifying the behavior They wish us to emulate—is Their revealed utterance (*logos,* the Word of God).

The intention of the Deity to make Himself accessible, understandable, and intimate to us is demonstrated primarily by the subtle manner in which divine guidance is revealed through the Manifestations of God. They are no less than complete metaphorical or allegorical representations of godliness, at least to the extent that godliness can be made manifest in human expression at a given point in the evolution of human society.

This insight has astounding implications for our understanding of planetary history, for it signifies that the Manifestations are not merely teachers about God. Each is the perfect incarnation of all the attributes of God. Furthermore, as God's viceroys, or executors, They are, according to Bahá'í doctrine, the cause of creation itself, even as 'Abdu'l-Bahá notes in an often cited passage from *Some Answered Questions:*

> The enlightenment of the world of thought comes from these centers of light and sources of mysteries. Without the bounty of the splendor and the instructions of these Holy Beings the world of souls and thoughts would be opaque darkness. Without the irrefutable teachings of those sources of mysteries the human world would become the pasture of animal appetites and qualities, the

existence of everything would be unreal, and there would be no true life. That is why it is said in the Gospel: "In the beginning was the Word," meaning that it became the cause of all life.[12]

How Creation Fulfills God's Wish To Be Known

As we will discuss in detail in chapter 4, the Manifestations thus offer the pathway by which human beings can gain access to the "Hidden Mystery" that is the Creator. Yet, as we have already noted, the Bahá'í writings also repeatedly emphasize the theme that every created thing manifests recognizable attributes of the Creator. Thus we can correctly assert that because all creation emanates from God, all creation bears signs of its origin:

> Know thou that every created thing is a sign of the revelation of God. Each, according to its capacity, is, and will ever remain, a token of the Almighty. Inasmuch as He, the sovereign Lord of all, hath willed to reveal His sovereignty in the kingdom of names and attributes, each and every created thing hath, through the act of the Divine Will, been made a sign of His glory. So pervasive and general is this revelation that nothing whatsoever in the whole universe can be discovered that doth not reflect His splendor. Under such conditions every consideration of proximity and remoteness is obliterated. . . . Were the Hand of Divine power to divest of this high endowment all created things, the entire universe would become desolate and void.[13]

> Whatever is in the heavens and whatever is on the earth is a direct evidence of the revelation within it of the attributes and names of God, inasmuch as within every atom are enshrined the signs that bear eloquent testimony to the revelation of that most great Light. Methinks, but for the potency of that revelation, no being could ever exist. How resplendent the luminaries of knowledge that shine in an atom, and how vast the oceans of wisdom that surge within a drop![14]

While these passages allude primarily to physical reality, other passages make clear that the same relationship holds true between the Creator and spiritual reality: "No sign can indicate His presence or His absence; inasmuch as by a word of His command all that are in heaven and on earth have come to exist, and by His wish, which is the Primal Will itself, all have stepped out of utter nothingness into the realm of being, the world of the visible."[15]

THE SPECIAL PART HUMANKIND PLAYS IN THE PROCESS

The axiom that God is independent of His creation is extremely subtle. When properly understood and appreciated, this concept responds to the anthropomorphic portrait of God as a being in "need" of love. But as a Being of logic and love, of justice, mercy, and reason, God must have determined prior to His willing or wishing our creation that this would be a desirable act—"prior" in the path of causality, not in time—for the metaphysical realm is devoid of physical properties like time.

The tradition of the Hidden Treasure explains that God "wished to be made known." While all creation expresses that love, the creation of a human being capable of comprehending God's nature and then freely coming to love that nature is essential to His being known in any meaningful way. In this sense, God, like a parent, loved us even before our creation, perhaps similar to the way a parent loves an unborn child:

O SON OF MAN! Veiled in My immemorial being and in the ancient eternity of My essence, I knew My love for thee; therefore I created thee, have engraved on thee Mine image and revealed to thee My beauty.[16]

However, another verse from Bahá'u'lláh interjects an easily overlooked condition of that love—our own love of the Creator:

O SON OF MAN! I loved thy creation, hence I created thee. Wherefore, do thou love Me, that I may name thy name and fill thy soul with the spirit of life.[17]

Implicit here is something that is stated point blank in yet another verse:

O SON OF BEING! Love Me, that I may love thee. If thou lovest Me not, My love can in no wise reach thee. Know this, O servant.[18]

Our reception of God's love is conditioned on our love of God, a logically obvious but no less weighty axiom. God may be omnipotent, but He will not ordain or command that we love Him, because the very nature of love is such that it is a freely chosen response by beings who have independently discovered the worthiness of the beloved.

THE RECIPROCAL NATURE OF LOVE

This brings us back to a central metaphor in the tradition of the Hidden Treasure: God wishes for us to love Him authentically; however, we must freely discover His attributes and decide for ourselves that He is worth our affection and devotion. Then why has He concealed or hidden Himself and His nature from us? Why is that an essential ingredient in this process, in this love relationship?

One possible explanation is that once He reveals Himself through creation and through the Manifestations, He is no longer hidden. Likewise, if He has created us in His image, all we need to do to discover God is to follow the ancient Greek maxim "Know thyself."

Nevertheless, God is still concealed and hidden. Scientists cannot seem to find Him. Theologians think they have found Him, but they have a very hard time giving any sort of logical proof that He exists. His Manifestations who appear explicitly to dramatize godliness in human form and bring us the latest guidance from the Creator inevitably conceal Their identity during the early part of Their lives, and even after declaring Their station, appear as the most unlikely personages in the most unlikely of circumstances: Moses as a castaway child who grew up to stutter and slay an Egyptian; Christ as a fatherless child learning the trade of a carpenter and choosing as his first followers illiterate fishermen and others equally unlearned.

Those who are teachers can immediately perceive the wisdom in this indirect teaching method, in having students discover answers rather than simply having them memorize doctrine. True education is the acquisition of the tools for further learning, not the memorization of answers to a handful of questions. Therefore the Creator and His Manifestations are concealed so that human beings may freely discover what godliness is all about by penetrating the veils of physical appearance to comprehend the inner power of spiritual perfection.

In sum, God creates because He is aware that His "Treasures" (His attributes and powers) benefit the recipient. And while as a spiritual essence He is forever hidden from our complete comprehension, He has devised a most ingenious methodology for instructing us how to discover, appreciate, and benefit from His attributes.

THE FINAL REQUISITE FOR FULFILLING GOD'S WILL

So far we have touched on the fundamental properties implicit in the tradition of the Hidden Treasure. We have some sense of why the Creator creates. We have some degree of understanding of why human beings are the central focus of His education. We have defined what it is that the Creator desires of us—knowledge of Him that leads to a love that causes us to express that love in systematic action that, in turn, brings about the gradual reformation of our character. We further have determined that while the initial attraction to the Creator is everywhere available to us, our decision to seek out and understand the source of that attraction must result from a freely chosen course of action on our part. But we still lack one ingredient to complete the fulfillment of the "wish" of the Creator signified by this poetic verse.

Given the wish of the Creator that we come to know and love Him, and given the fact that we are created in His image and begin our eternal lives in an environment which, though ostensibly unspiritual, is replete with signs of the Creator, we still need further help—an educator to get us started, to give us clues about how to recognize in physical reality and in ourselves the image of the Creator. But this educator must provide something else as well: We need a systematic regimen that will at once deter us from doing anything that might damage our capacity to participate in this educational process, and at the same time direct us in a series of daily exercises that will help us to become and remain receptive, healthy, and self-motivated. What is more, since all human beings are ontologically the same and are thus equally in need, humankind requires an educator who is already aware of how this can best be accomplished, one who possesses an inherent understanding and wisdom beyond what an ordinary human being can attain—otherwise logic dictates that human society will fare no better than it presently does. Indeed, given that human society on this planet is effectively a closed system, the law of entropy implies that without an infusion of guidance from outside the system we will regress.

While further examination of this requirement and how it can best be fulfilled is the focus of the next chapter, we can observe at this point that, as beings who possess free will, we are unlike lesser beings whose capacities are inherent because they rely on instinct. For a human being to develop capacity, education is needed—whether from a parent or society. We human beings do not acquire knowledge spontaneously or intuitively, not before we have acquired foundational skills of language, logic, and love—skills that require training because by definition human beings are social beings. All our progress is dependent on our being nurtured by others, whether that nurturing be physical, intellectual, or spiritual. A child left on its own will not thrive or prosper. Even as rare examples of feral children raised among animals demonstrate, deprived of assistance, a human being does not develop its "human" powers. And if reintroduced into society after having been thus raised, the child is so damaged that it fails to thrive, and it dies.

At times in our development we feel strong, independent, self-sufficient. We may even reject society and decide to live a solitary life apart from the influence of others. Our heroic legends are replete with such characters. But such individuals are capable of accomplishing such a course of action only after they have attained a degree of physical and intellectual development with the assistance of others. Furthermore, more often than not, the most successful of such endeavors take place in a brotherhood or sisterhood of fellow monastics, within explicitly designed social environments. In addition, it is questionable how beneficial lives of solitude and denial ultimately are for inducing any sort of useful spirituality. Indeed, Bahá'u'lláh explicitly forbids monasticism for Bahá'ís, stating that now is the time when people of spiritual motivation and strength are needed in society: "Living in seclusion or practising asceticism is not acceptable in the presence of God. It behoveth them that are endued with insight and understanding to observe that which will cause joy and radiance."[19]

Logically, then, some "outside" force, some source of enlightenment and guidance beyond the human condition must help us devise both an environment for observing the "hidden" or "concealed" attributes of the Creator manifest in reality, and an educative process by which we can manifest this knowledge and love of the "beauty" of the Creator in creative action, or what might be properly termed a "metaphorical form." "Outside" in this context necessarily implies a source both "greater than" any ordinary human being and, if we accept the Bahá'í belief that the human being is the highest form of creation in physical reality, also "outside" or "other than" physical reality.

As we noted in chapter 1, a tenet of the Bahá'í Faith is that these "outside" Educators are the successive Manifestations who, as Beings superior to ordinary humans in nature and capacity and as divinely ordained educators, introduce the laws and daily regimen for our training. However, as the Bahá'í writings discuss at length and as the laws of all successive world religions demonstrate, the methodology embodied in the laws, admonitions, and guidance of these "outside" Educators must be progressive as humankind advances materially, socially, intellectually, and spiritually.

Therefore true religion must be progressive if it is to constitute a valid process by which humankind can achieve ever more complete expression in social structures and relationships the attributes of spiritual reality: "Religion is the outer expression of the divine reality. Therefore, it must be living, vitalized, moving and progressive. If it be without motion and nonprogressive, it is without the divine life; it is dead. The divine institutes are continuously active and evolutionary; therefore, the revelation of them must be progressive and continuous."[20]

This relationship between the Creator and the created through the intermediary of the Manifestation constitutes the completion of the "wish" or "will" of the Creator as expressed in the tradition of the Hidden Treasure. As a "loving Father," the Creator has provided a path to His Presence. He provides us with the education we need to discover that path. He requires that we freely recognize and choose this path, but He does not leave the opportunity for us to accomplish these objectives to happenstance, the chance that we might stumble upon evidence of God's existence and, by sheer intuition or instinct, discern His nature.

This, then, is the next step in our attempt to understand how an essentially spiritual Being runs an ostensibly physical enterprise: to examine more exactly how this interplay between spiritual reality and physical reality is systematically carried out by the intermediaries that are the Prophets or Manifestations of God. For it is only by means of Their assistance that we have the opportunity to understand the essential nature of our own reality so that we might then participate in preparing ourselves for the successive stages of our eternal existence.

- 3 -

The Bridge between Realities:
The Manifestation as Intermediary

*I have known Thee by Thy making known unto me that Thou art un-
knowable to anyone save Thyself. I have become apprised by the creation
Thou hast fashioned out of sheer non-existence that the way to attain the
comprehension of Thine Essence is barred to everyone. Thou art God, besides
Whom there is none other God. No one except Thine Own Self can
comprehend Thy nature. Thou art without peer or partner. From everlasting
Thou hast been alone with no one else besides Thee and unto everlasting
Thou wilt continue to be the same, while no created thing shall ever approach
Thine exalted position.*

— The Báb, *Selections from the Writings of the Báb*

To recapitulate briefly before we attempt to examine the bridge between spiritual and physical reality, let us note yet again that though the essence of God is beyond comprehension, His nature, character, or qualities are everywhere available: "Every created thing in the whole universe is but a door leading into His knowledge, a sign of His sovereignty, a revelation of His names, a symbol of His majesty, a token of His power, a means of admittance into His straight Path. . . ."[1]

Yet, as we noted at the end of chapter 2, obvious as the signs of the Creator may be theoretically, we are incapable of recognizing His spiritual imprint without the assistance of educators who are more advanced than we ourselves. Without such education we would remain ignorant of our own essentially spiritual nature and purpose.

We concluded that it is precisely because of our dependency on "outside" assistance, whether individually or collectively, that the Creator devised a "bridge" or pathway whereby we can gain access to His presence and an exemplary Teacher to lead us across that bridge. It is imperative, therefore, if we are to have any significant understanding of the Bahá'í theory of how a reciprocal relationship is devised and maintained across these two expressions of reality, that we gain some specific information about the nature and teaching methods of these Intermediaries.

DIVINE INTERVENTION

The concept of divine intervention has through the centuries been received by scientists and theologians alike as an archaic concept, an idea more akin to the legends of ancient Greece and Rome wherein deities periodically assume human shape to become involved in human history, either to rectify injustice or to impose their own preferences regarding the outcome of human conflict, such as the Trojan War or the founding of the Roman Empire. In the 1960s some Protestant theologians even posited the theory that the God of the Old Testament (who directly intervened to take revenge on the enemies of His chosen people or else to punish those who disobeyed His laws) was effectively dead. Some argued that God is now more subtle, or else has relinquished direct control of reality to His minions on earth.

Ever since science and religion parted company in the later Middle Ages, each field of study has left the other to do as it wished, unless and until the one seemed to encroach on the territory of the other. For example, the Roman Catholic Church felt the need to suppress Galileo's discoveries when his findings seemed to threaten the church's world view. There was a similar response on the part of various religious traditions to the Copernican model of a Sun-centered solar system, and to the Darwinian theory of evolution. And since human history was during the Middle Ages largely an admixture of legend and fact blended together, no one was much concerned about ancient tales of the interpenetration of supernatural reality and the "real" world of daily life, though Paul's caution about giving credence to the tales of Greek and Roman mythology* was commonly known as the "Pauline Precept" and made many medieval writers cautious about creating any stories that did not contain some explicit allusion to Christian doctrine.

But as we have also noted, it is a foundational tenet of Bahá'í belief that there is a systematic and even predictable influence in the history of physical reality by supernatural forces from spiritual reality. But if the Bahá'í teachings simultaneously affirm that science and religion are compatible—that they simply describe different aspects of the same reality—how can this concept of divine intervention, so disparaged by contemporary science and religion, be perceived as anything but a baseless, archaic, and anti-intellectual description of reality in general and of history in particular?

To begin with, the Bahá'í teachings in no way advocate a theory that asserts God, an essentially spiritual Being, directly intervenes in human affairs in the fashion symbolically portrayed in Michelangelo's famous fresco on the ceiling of the Sistine Chapel—God reaches out His finger to bestow life upon Adam, who represents humankind. To accept such a literal view of this process would be similar to envisioning a point in the physical evolution of humankind when we were ready to make the transition from the sea to the land and suddenly the vast arm of God reaches down from the sky, plunges into the waters, and nudges our lizardesque forms to the shore so that we might begin the next stage in our ascent to our present finished form.

These childlike anthropomorphic images of the interplay between spiritual and physical reality, together with all literalist interpretations of scriptural allegories, metaphors, and symbols found in all world religions through the ages, have alienated the vast majority of the scientific community and most other reasonable individuals from even attempting to participate in religious discourse.

This unfortunate division in the history of human thought has become particularly entrenched regarding the possibility of metaphysical influence in processes more artfully depicted by scientific research. Indeed, given a

---

* See 1 Tim. 1:4, 1 Tim. 4:7, and 2 Tim. 4:4.

choice between believing in the scientific model of creation or in a ludicrous concept of God's hands-on involvement in the process, one might well find a belief in science more rewarding spiritually and intellectually than many religious explanations.

If we are to accept the idea of divine intervention in the evolutionary process of creation, let alone in the course of human history, we must, according to our definition of *faith* as belief founded on rational investigation, find a rational explanation of how divine intervention occurs. This assumes that we accept the idea that creation occurs by design and, even more astounding, that human history is also designed and shaped by supernatural influence and intervention.

This question in one form or another—whether voiced aloud or concealed in silent angst—is at the heart of most people's consternation about belief in a spiritual or metaphysical reality, even when personal empirical evidence often seems to confirm its existence. Without a rational explanation of this process, accepting religious belief is to risk becoming internally divided, accepting one set of criteria for studying physical reality and quite another for studying metaphysical reality. This internal division creates conflict, wavering, and possibly a cynical rejection of learning in general.

The Critical Role of the Manifestation

As we have already implied, the Bahá'í concept of the bridging of spiritual and physical reality is not direct or physical (that is, literal), though it does involve interplay between the physical and the metaphysical. In this sense, the bare statement of the concept may be initially discomfiting to those unsure of a metaphysical reality. But for now, let us simply assume that there is a metaphysical reality, for if we are presently reading and considering these ideas (which are abstractions), we are giving some tacit approval to the notion that such a reality is worth considering. In this context and with this assumption, let us examine in sufficient detail the Bahá'í description of this indirect process, the path of causality by which the supernatural or metaphysical "wish" becomes translated into physical action.

THE NATURE AND INFLUENCE OF
THE MANIFESTATION OF GOD

According to the Bahá'í writings, the Manifestation of God exerts a positive influence on the human condition even *before* He appears on earth in human form to incarnate perfectly the attributes of God. In Their eternal station as "Vice-regents" of God, the Manifestations are the medium through which the First Will (the "wish" or "desire" portrayed in the tradition of the Hidden Treasure) is implemented in material form.

Most often it is only in retrospect—after the fact of Their historical appearance in human form—that we are able to discern and chronicle the influence of the Manifestations in shaping the course of human events. Even then, more sensational events are likely to be presumed to be the causal forces shaping history.

For example, no one can deny the incredible impact of Christianity as a religious, social, and political force. And yet the life, mission, and death of Christ went unnoticed as a historical influence until centuries after His death. In this same connection, we in the West are only now becoming the least bit aware of the nature and importance of Islam in shaping human history because it is suddenly having a dramatic impact on our lives. In spite of this fact, in discussing the critical influence of the spread of Islam in shaping Western history, Shoghi Effendi, Guardian of the Bahá'í Faith, observed that it will be the task of future American Bahá'í scholars to redeem the history of Islam in the Western world, because only in the light of this rewriting of history, this reexamination of the forces responsible for advancing human civilization, will the true positive influence of Muḥammad become apparent:

The mission of the American Bahá'ís is, no doubt, to eventually establish the truth of Islám in the West.

The spirit of Islám, no doubt, was the living germ of modern Civilization; which derived its impetus from the Islamic culture in the Middle Ages, a culture that was the fruit of the Faith of Muḥammad.[2]

THE PERSISTENT NEED FOR AN EDUCATOR

In chapter 2 we established a logical basis for the human need for education from "outside" the realm of human existence: Without guidance from one who is superior to ourselves, we can have little hope of ascending from our present condition of attainment.

But why is this so? Why do we need this "outside" divine guidance, not once or twice, but on a regular basis in our ascent from the mud to a glorious civilization? Have we not established that the exalted condition of the human being is the fulfillment of the wish or will of the "Hidden Treasure"? Have we not also established that a human being is fully capable of solving mysteries, of studying the world of being, of discerning its laws and relationships, and of profiting therefrom by fostering a civilized and just society that will advance eternally? Why is it not enough that the Creator has set in motion the evolutionary process as a continuum? Or if we must have an Educator as intermediary between the Creator and ourselves to instigate this process, to set us in motion, why isn't one such "Visitor" from the realm of the spirit sufficient?

This question might seem to allude to a Newtonian vision of the cosmos as a perfectly organized, self-sustaining, self-perpetuating machine that, once set in motion, contains all the laws necessary to keep everything in good order. It also seems to follow logically from the Bahá'í passages we have cited that refer to the need for us to develop a certain degree of autonomy in our progress, to discover the Manifestations independently, and to follow Their guidance as a result of our own free will.

Certainly the Bahá'í teachings do indeed assert that our study and search should be independent—that is, our study and search should not derive from coercion or degenerate into dogma. The discovery of the existence and influence of each Manifestation, as well as the utilization of the knowledge and guidance each one brings to us at God's behest, is certainly a personal obligation. But we have also noted the Bahá'í texts establish that if the Manifestation as intermediary did not exist—both to exemplify human virtue in action and to articulate these concepts in understandable language and laws—our autonomy would gain us nothing. We would be free to wander aimlessly and accomplish nothing of lasting worth. We would fare no better than infants without parents or children in a school without teachers. But the further point is that we are never finished in our education, never beyond the capacity for further development, never beyond the ability to increase our capacity itself!

In other words, a single Manifestation is sufficient for us individually so long as He is the most recent Emissary and thus provides the guidance appropriate for the age in which we live. But humankind collectively needs a succession of such teachers to befit its ever-changing, ever-evolving, ever-advancing capacity. We never reach a point where further progress is not possible, where further improvement cannot be imagined.

THE PERSISTENT NEED FOR AN INTERMEDIARY

One of the most profound and little appreciated observations we can make about the intermediary relationship by which the Creator effects creation and steers the course of human progress is that the need for a bridge between the Creator and the created is not confined to earthly life.

We might assume that once we have ascended from the physical realm, we will be capable of progress without need for assistance or intermediaries. This assumption is particularly understandable in light of the many passages in the Bahá'í texts as well as in the scriptures of other religions that the "afterlife" or continuation of our lives in the spiritual realm is no longer an indirect spiritual experience. It is designated as the world of "vision" where the concealed or hidden mysteries of earthly existence will no longer be veiled in symbolic or metaphorical form: "the Kingdom is the world of vision, where all the concealed realities will become disclosed."[3] Nevertheless, if the Creator is essentially unknowable, He will ever remain essentially unknowable. In this sense He must ever remain beyond our direct knowledge.

In an authoritative description of the Bahá'í teachings on this subject, Shoghi Effendi interprets and confirms the implications of Bahá'u'lláh's statement about the eternal nature of this intermediary relationship between the Creator and the human soul. Shoghi Effendi explains in a letter written on his behalf that the station of the Creator is so lofty that this *indirect* method by which we come to "know" God and "come into

39

His Presence" persists after death, in the continuation of our lives in the realm of the spirit: "We will have experience of God's spirit through His Prophets in the next world, but God is too great for us to know *without this Intermediary.** The Prophets know God, but how is more than our human minds can grasp."[4]

ESSENTIAL INGREDIENTS IN AN INTERMEDIARY PROCESS

This intermediary process, then, is how we are educated, both intellectually and spiritually, in both this world and in the continuation of our lives beyond this realm. Thus we would do well to probe the fundamental ingredients of this "close connection" if we are to understand and more adequately traverse the bridge or "interconnectedness" between spiritual and physical reality and, in the afterlife, between ourselves and the Creator.

First, any sort of intermediary process obviously involves two or more entities between which the intermediary operates. Second, any intermediary process requires some means by which the entities are conjoined. For example, between the viewer of a television program and those who are actually performing before a television camera are devices that translate physical images into electronic impulses and other devices that receive those electronic impulses and translate them into forms that can be seen and understood.

The camera begins the process by capturing an image and digitalizing it into segments that are registered as colors of varying intensity. These segments are translated into electronic information, which is transmitted through a cable or through the air by an electronic signal. A television receiver then reverses the process by translating the signal back into electronic segments, which show up as pixels on the television screen. The screen then registers the same color or combinations of colors with the intensity equivalent to that which was conveyed by the physical image the camera originally captured.

---

* Emphasis added.

THE RECIPIENT'S PARTICIPATION

If the sender of the television image wants the recipient to participate in the process of receiving the message, the segments of the picture might be sent randomly so that the recipient would have to reconstruct the picture, much as one might put together a jigsaw puzzle. But a more instructive way to involve the recipient in the intermediary process would be to send an image containing some subtle, concealed, or symbolic meaning that requires interpretation to be correctly understood. The recipient would then have to reflect on what was being conveyed, much as we might try to interpret the levels of concealed meaning in a poem by Yeats, a painting by Picasso, or a film by Ingmar Bergman.

A slightly more complicated intermediary process is required if the communication is bidirectional; the same procedure required for one-way communication must be replicated in the opposite direction. And yet the more sophisticated the intermediary process becomes, as with the modern telephone, the more transparent the intermediary sequence becomes—that is, the less we are aware of the process and the more we focus on what is being communicated.

For example, with older telephones, sound waves (vibrations of air) caused pulsations of a diaphragm in the telephone receiver. The vibrations of the diaphragm would then cause an attached electromagnetic device to translate these vibrations into electronic signals. These signals would be sent through wires or through the air with the same pitch and frequency as the original vibrations that occurred in the sound waves. At the other end, the receiver contained an electromagnetic device that would cause a diaphragm to vibrate with the same frequency and pitch as the electronic impulses so as to create sound waves for the listener. Each participant in this process of communication thus possessed a sending system (the mouthpiece) and a receiving system (the earpiece).

Today this intermediary process is so familiar and so accurate (transparent) that we have become oblivious to the technology involved—the intermediary system has become transparent to us. The sophistication of telecommunications technology today enables us to focus on the quality of the discourse and on what ideas are being exchanged. In effect, we have lost any sense of awe at this technology—after all, the telephone was patented long ago in 1876. But if we examine the entire process taking place in a conversation, whether or not it employs an explicit intermediary process, we will soon discover that communication during our physical existence is much more complex than we commonly realize and reveals much that will assist us in our objective of discovering the bridge between realities.

LANGUAGE AND THE MIND

A field of study that has recently emerged as a distinct academic discipline is communication. Formerly studied within the purview of mass media, speech and forensics, linguistics, and speech pathology, communication is now recognized as a distinct field at major universities.

While the nature of study in this discipline varies widely from university to university, the validity of such a discrete area of academic interest seems obvious: What could be more fundamental to and indicative of our humanness than our ability to communicate with one another? Yet, involving our conscious will as it does, what could be more mysterious and elusive than the intermediary process that occurs when we attempt to convey thoughts, feelings, and other abstract notions to the mind of another human being?

As we implied in our discussion of the telephone as intermediary, what we are conveying over that phone are not merely vibrations, but words. And words are ultimately not arbitrary sounds, but symbols in the context of an entire language system of symbols. A language system, in turn, is an intermediary by which human beings are capable of sharing ideas, feelings, theories, and an infinite array of abstractions.

What is more, we can hardly discuss the intermediary process of human communication without also being aware of how the human mind translates the ephemeral reality of thought into language. In this sense, the physical intermediary of language is not nearly as astonishing as the process by which the ideas emanate from the conscious mind.

THE ENTIRE INTERMEDIARY PROCESS IN COMMUNICATION

We have thus far alluded to several components in the causal pathway of a relatively simple intermediary process—speaking with someone on the phone. These components are: (1) the reality (idea or thought) being discussed, (2) the language describing that reality, (3) the vibrations in the air from the words, (4) the vibrations of the diaphragm, (5) the creation of electromagnetic impulses, (6) the transmission of the impulses through the air or a wire, (7) the transforming of electromagnetic impulses into diaphragmatic vibrations, (8) the translation of those vibrations into language, (9) the recipient's mind, which analyzes, envisions, and reflects upon the idea, (10) and, finally, the recording of the idea in the repository of the recipient's memory.

Therefore, even if we decide not to concern ourselves with exactly how the brain causes the mouth to utter sound or how it translates noises back into ideas, we must include the brain itself as an essential part of the intermediary system; surely the most critical ingredients in this pathway of communication are the minds of the individuals involved.

Common sense would dictate, then, that we should consider at this point in our analysis how human consciousness and ideas are formed in the brain. This step assumes particular importance in the context of Bahá'í thought because an absolutely essential understanding of the Bahá'í perspective about the bridge between spiritual and physical reality is the assertion that the conscious mind is not in itself the ultimate source of thought, but that the mind is a function, a power, or a faculty of the soul (a spiritual, not a physical, essence). If this assertion is correct, then we should enhance our description of this causal pathway to include a bridge across the gap between spiritual reality and physical reality.

After all, if conscious thought derives from a spiritual essence that is the soul and is then through the intermediary of the brain translated into physical forms of speech, and if that physical sound of speech is then translated back into metaphysical form in the conscious mind of the recipient (also a faculty of the soul), then the gap between spiritual and physical reality is bridged not once, but repeatedly, bidirectionally, and constantly in any given communication.

THE INTERMEDIARY PROCESS AND THE MANIFESTATION

But let us set aside temporarily our analysis of the gap between realities and how that gap might be bridged on a personal or interpersonal level.

For now, let us return to our larger concern, which is issues of creation and the macrocosmic relationship between spiritual and physical reality. For we need first to grasp how the gap between realities is bridged at a macrocosmic level if we are to understand more precisely what is occurring at the individual level.

Once more, let us reaffirm the Bahá'í theological doctrine about the Manifestation as intermediary between the Creator and the created. Each Manifestation is immaculate, a perfect incarnation of divine attributes to the extent that essentially spiritual abstractions can be manifest in human terms: "His Manifestation can adduce no greater proof of the truth of His Mission than the proof of His own Person."[5] And yet, though all the Manifestations exhibit a perfection and possess powers beyond our understanding, They repeatedly confirm that They in no wise should be confused with or even associated with the Essence of the Creator. Shoghi Effendi states emphatically that there should never be any sense of identifying the physical personage or human persona that the Manifestation assumes while on earth, either with the Holy Spirit itself or with the essence of God:

> The divinity attributed to so great a Being and the complete incarnation of the names and attributes of God in so exalted a Person should, under no circumstances, be misconceived or misinterpreted. The human temple that has been made the vehicle of so overpowering a Revelation must, if we be faithful to the tenets of our Faith, ever remain entirely distinguished from that "innermost Spirit of Spirits" and "eternal Essence of Essences"—that invisible yet rational God Who, however much we extol the divinity of His Manifestations on earth, can in no wise incarnate His infinite, His unknowable, His incorruptible and all-embracing Reality in the concrete and limited frame of a mortal being. Indeed, the God Who could so incarnate His own reality would, in the light of the teachings of Bahá'u'lláh, cease immediately to be God. So crude and fantastic a theory of Divine incarnation is as removed from, and incompatible with, the essentials of Bahá'í belief as are the no less inadmissible pantheistic and anthropomorphic conceptions of

God—both of which the utterances of Bahá'u'lláh emphatically repudiate and the fallacy of which they expose.[6]

The "will," or "wish," or "first mind" thus emanates from God and becomes manifest in the world of creation through the intermediary of the Manifestation, whose own person, as we have noted, perfectly exemplifies the attributes of that Divine Emanation and whose utterances infallibly convey the command of God, the laws of God, and the Word of God in all its forms.

Since we know that human language is inexact and liable to various interpretations, we might question the extent to which the utterances of the Prophets might be considered "perfect" or "flawless" or "infallible." Bahá'u'lláh alludes to such issues in several passages where He explicitly acknowledges that He must shape the ideas He has to share into words and concepts according to human capacity at a given time in our history. He goes on to state that were He to describe reality according to His own capacity, we would be so dumbfounded as to be bereft of the benefit of the wisdom He is trying to impart:

> These words are to your measure, not to God's. To this testifieth that which is enshrined within His knowledge, if ye be of them that comprehend; and to this the tongue of the Almighty doth bear witness, if ye be of those who understand. I swear by God, were We to lift the veil, ye would be dumbfounded.[7]

> By My spirit and by My favor! By My mercy and by My beauty! All that I have revealed unto thee with the tongue of power, and have written for thee with the pen of might, hath been in accordance with thy capacity and understanding, not with My state and the melody of My voice.[8]

As these passages make clear, in what we have previous referred to as the Prophet's station of distinction, the Manifestation assumes an ordinary human persona, conveys information about reality, and adopts a language suitable to human capacity for a certain stage or era in our collective human development. At the same time, because the Manifestation is capable of carrying out this dramatic operation flawlessly, there is for us no effective distinction between God and these Expressions of God personified and articulated by the Manifestation. It is because of this exalted state that Bahá'u'lláh alludes to the Manifestations of God as "Sanctified Mirrors":

> The door of the knowledge of the Ancient of Days being thus closed in the face of all beings, the Source of infinite grace, according to His saying: "His grace hath transcended all things; My grace hath encompassed them all" hath caused those luminous Gems of Holiness to appear out of the realm of the spirit, in the noble form of the human temple, and be made manifest unto all men, that they may impart unto the world the mysteries of the unchangeable Being, and tell of the subtleties of His imperishable Essence. These *sanctified Mirrors*,* these Dayprings of ancient glory are one and all the Exponents on earth of Him Who is the central Orb of the universe, its Essence and ultimate Purpose. From Him proceed their knowledge and power; from Him is derived their sovereignty. The beauty of their countenance is but a reflection of His image, and their revelation a sign of His deathless glory. They are the Treasuries of divine knowledge, and the Repositories of celestial wisdom. Through them is transmitted a grace that is infinite, and by them is revealed the light that can never fade. Even as He hath said: "There is no distinction whatsoever between Thee and them; except that they are Thy servants, and are created of Thee." This is the significance of the tradition: "I am He, Himself, and He is I, myself."[9]

---

* Emphasis added.

- 4 -

The Manifestation as
All-Knowing Physician

The All-Knowing Physician hath His finger on the pulse of mankind. He perceiveth the disease, and prescribeth, in His unerring wisdom, the remedy. Every age hath its own problem, and every soul its particular aspiration. The remedy the world needeth in its present-day afflictions can never be the same as that which a subsequent age may require. Be anxiously concerned with the needs of the age ye live in, and center your deliberations on its exigencies and requirements.

—Bahá'u'lláh, *Gleanings*

In light of our observations thus far about the manner in which the Manifestation serves as intermediary between the macrocosm and the microcosm, between the Primal Will and the human heart, we might understandably consider His principal role as a type of communication system. And in that capacity He may at first appear to us as a mostly passive functionary, as God's mouthpiece or messenger, with little creative part to play in this function as an intermediary.

The images we have used might seem to support such a conclusion. We have likened the Manifestation to a perfect mirror capable of reflecting flawlessly the attributes of God so that we might perceive these abstract realities reflected in physical forms of speech and comportment—a poetic and meaningful comparison, but an image that seems to portray a mostly passive participation. Similarly, we have employed the metaphor of telecommunication to understand the Manifestation as the means by which the spiritual essence that is God enables His "wish" or "will" to become accessible to humankind.

What we now need to examine are those passages in the Bahá'í texts indicating clearly that the Manifestation is not passive, not solely an example of godliness translated into human terms—lofty as such a station is—nor solely a vehicle through which God speaks to humankind to influence the course of human history. The Manifestation is an active participant, a creator, an artist, and an innovator in determining exactly what process will be employed in translating God's "wish" or "will" into human speech.

Consequently, before we can advance in our examination of the bridge between spiritual and physical reality, let us first understand a little more about the creative function the Manifestation plays in this process so that we can later understand how a similar intermediary process operates on the individual level.

THE MANIFESTATION AS PHYSICIAN

Knowledge of reality can be defined in part as possessing the ability to see the end in the beginning. Such knowledge is demonstrated in the wisdom a parent exercises by establishing strict rules for a child, not as an arbitrary exercise of authority, but as a safeguard for the child. What might seem from the child's perspective as a restriction on freedom is, in reality, the parent's expression of love because the parent sees the end result of these rules (the child's well-being) in the instigation of this guidance.

Bahá'u'lláh employs the metaphor of the "Physician" in such a context to describe the teachings of each Manifestation. Because of His omniscient perspective, the Manifestation knows precisely what has gone wrong with human society during a given period in history, and because of His divine wisdom, the Manifestation has the knowledge and wisdom to prescribe the precise remedy for both short- and long-term healing and rehabilitation of the human body politic.

But to what extent does the Manifestation merely carry out divine command, ordaining that which He is told by God to ordain, and to what extent does He Himself exert a creative influence in the process of directing the affairs and ministering to the ills of humankind? For example, Bahá'u'lláh asserts that each Manifestation knows precisely how to respond to the needs of humankind for the particular age in which He appears. It was perhaps in this context that Bahá'u'lláh ordered some of His writings destroyed; He foresaw that humankind would not be capable of utilizing these insights or this advice during the course of His dispensation.

Thus we are tempted to ask whether Bahá'u'lláh Himself, after witnessing the degree of defiance and obstinacy on the part of humankind, decided He would not reveal as much as He had intended or had hoped to reveal, or was this act merely a dramatic means by which He could demonstrate to humankind that (1) revelation is continuous and never-ending and (2) that humanity's response to the revelation determines the extent to which we will have the bounty of receiving more knowledge? Or was Bahá'u'lláh simply following instructions from God without understanding the "end in the beginning" of this action?

Let us make our question a bit more specific regarding the intermediary process. Does the Manifestation receive from the First Mind (the will of God) through the medium of the Holy Spirit a sense of the objectives He is to bring about (His "mission"), and then decide how best to achieve this objective? Or is the Manifestation told on a daily, or even on a moment-by-moment basis, exactly what to do and what to say?

We know the Prophets communicate with the Creator through prayer. In some of the prayers Bahá'u'lláh has bequeathed humankind in His writings, He praises God, expresses concern about the state of human receptivity to the gift of His revelation, and beseeches God for assistance to carry out His mission, much as did Christ in His well-known prayers in the Garden of Gethsemane. However, we do have solid evidence in each revelation that the Manifestation does play a creative role in His function as intermediary and emissary. He is not merely following instructions or repeating verbatim what He is told to say, an act that any inspired individual might be capable of performing.

The importance of this distinction cannot be overstated because it is strategic evidence that the Manifestation as intermediary is neither an ordinary human being whom God has transformed, nor is He God incarnate. He receives the information as thought, but He Himself must devise the exact language and the precise laws that will best effect the remedy in the healing and education of humankind.

One indication of the extent to which the Manifestation designs His own methodology is found in a description of Bahá'u'lláh's own creative plan. Shoghi Effendi states in unequivocal terms that we cannot yet begin to fathom the ultimate wisdom in all that Bahá'u'lláh has created. In riveting poetic language, Shoghi Effendi alludes to the creative role that Bahá'u'lláh plays in the destiny of the Bahá'í teachings to awaken humankind to the relationship between spiritual reality and every aspect of physical creation:

> Not ours, puny mortals that we are, to attempt, at so critical a stage in the long and checkered history of mankind, to arrive at a precise and satisfactory understanding of the steps which must successively lead a bleeding humanity, wretchedly oblivious of its God, and careless of Bahá'u'lláh, from its calvary to its ultimate resurrection. Not ours, the living witnesses of the all-subduing potency of His Faith, to question, for a moment, and however dark the misery that enshrouds the world, the ability of Bahá'u'lláh to forge, with the hammer of His Will, and through the fire of tribulation, upon the anvil of this travailing age, and in the particular shape His mind has envisioned, these scattered and mutually destructive fragments into which a perverse world has fallen, into one single unit, solid and indivisible, able to execute His design for the children of men.[1]

The tribute to Bahá'u'lláh's "Will" as a primary source of change—together with Shoghi Effendi's allusion to the "particular shape His [Bahá'u'lláh's] mind has envisioned" as the outcome of this creative force—clearly indicates that according to Bahá'í belief, the Manifestation is not merely a functionary, not merely a divinely inspired factotum, and most certainly not a temporarily inspired ordinary human being reiterating what he has been inspired to say.

We have already noted that the Manifestation is ontologically not an ordinary human being. The Manifestation occupies a station and performs a function quite beyond our comprehension. For example, this same theme of the creative power of Bahá'u'lláh concerns His blueprint for a world commonwealth as set forth in the primary repository of Bahá'u'lláh's laws and ordinances, the Kitáb-i-Aqdas (Most Holy Book). Shoghi Effendi explicitly attributes the genius of this plan to the creative mind of Bahá'u'lláh, stating that this work "whose provisions must remain inviolate for no less than a thousand years, and whose system will embrace the entire planet, may well be regarded as the brightest emanation of the mind of Bahá'u'lláh, as the Mother Book of His Dispensation, and the Charter of His New World Order."[2]

Causality in the Macrocosm

The intermediary between realities at the macrocosmic level, then, is not merely a series of passive metaphysical connections between the sender of guidance (God) and the recipient (humankind). Instead, this gap is bridged by a complex process whereby the idea, will, or wish emanates from the sender (God) and is received by the intermediary (the Manifestation) through the metaphysical force (the Holy Spirit). The Manifestation then creatively translates "wish" and "idea" into specific language, laws, and actions that He conveys to humankind. The most obvious means through which He communicates these various kinds of guidance to humankind is by appearing in the guise of an ordinary human being who, through example and utterance, unveils the plan of God for the next stage in the progress of human civilization.

It is important to note in this connection that the influence of the Manifestation occurs in three distinct conditions. The Manifestation perfectly reflects the will of God *before* assuming a human persona— before His earthly appearance. Then, having assumed a human persona, the Manifestation reveals God's will and exemplifies or dramatizes the attributes of God in a manner accessible to those to whom He appears. But He then continues to function as intermediary or bridge between the Divine Will and humankind after He ceases to associate with a human temple—after His death, or ascent. In that third condition, He empowers and assists us to execute the plan He has set forth for His followers to administer and coordinate for the benefit of human social and spiritual progress.

Thus, while the metaphor of the "perfect mirror" is an accurate analogy inasmuch as it demonstrates how the power of the Holy Spirit reaches us unchanged and untrammeled even as the rays of the sun might reach us without alteration through a perfect mirror. In this sense, the Manifestation is a perfect or clear channel through which we receive the image and knowledge of God and the specific guidance to assist us during a given era in human history. But now we can understand that the analogy is not adequate to explain the station of the Manifestation or all the powers that emanate from Him. As we have noted, the analogy fails to portray the complexity of the process by which the two aspects of reality are bridged, and it fails to express fully the Manifestation's creative participation in carrying out His intermediary function.

FOUNDATIONAL STEPS IN BRIDGING THE DUAL ASPECTS OF REALITY

From the parts of the intermediary process we have discussed thus far, let us now attempt to rehearse as best we can the entire path of causality as it seems to occur at the macrocosmic level.

THE CREATOR AS DISTINCT FROM THE MANIFESTATION

First there exists God, the Hidden Treasure, the source of all creation, the Essence of Essences. One revealing allusion to the station of the Creator as compared to the intermediary role played by the Manifestations can be found in the following statement by Shoghi Effendi:

> The human temple that has been made the vehicle of so overpowering a Revelation must, if we be faithful to the tenets of our Faith, ever remain entirely distinguished from that "innermost Spirit of Spirits" and "eternal Essence of Essences" that invisible yet rational God Who, however much we extol the divinity of His Manifestations on earth, can in no wise incarnate His infinite, His unknowable, His incorruptible and all-embracing Reality in the concrete and limited frame of a mortal being. Indeed, the God

Who could so incarnate His own reality would, in the light of the teachings of Bahá'u'lláh, cease immediately to be God.[3]

'Abdu'l-Bahá, in an equally powerful statement, describes the same distinction between God (or the realm of the Creator) and the Manifestations (or Their function as intermediary for the Holy Spirit). In this passage 'Abdu'l-Bahá is responding to the tendency on the part of some religions to deify the Prophets or to perceive them as an incarnation of the essence of God rather than to understand that They are actually perfect incarnations of the attributes of God: "But that Essence of Essences, that Invisible of Invisibles, is sanctified above all human speculation, and never to be overtaken by the mind of man. Never shall that immemorial Reality lodge within the compass of a contingent being. His is another realm, and of that realm no understanding can be won. No access can be gained thereto; all entry is forbidden there. The utmost one can say is that Its existence can be proved, but the conditions of Its existence are unknown."[4]

THE DIVINE WILL OR WISH

From this essentially unknowable but cognitive Creator emanates His will or wish to be known. Again, while all language utterly fails to convey this process with exactitude, suffice it here to note that the first emanation from God in the chain of causality is the "First Will": "Therefore, all creatures emanate from God—that is to say, it is by God that all things are realized, and by Him that all beings have attained to existence. The first thing which emanated from God is that universal reality, which the ancient philosophers termed the 'First Mind,' and which the people of Bahá call the 'First Will.' This emanation, in that which concerns its action in the world of God, is not limited by time or place; it is without beginning or end—beginning and end in relation to God are one."[5]

We might compare the emanation of the First Will to an idea, desire, or thought that occurs in the human consciousness, an analogy we will explore more fully when we analyze how the soul runs the body. This "will" or "wish" is not a single event, but a constant flow of creative power, an eternal emanation from the Creator. Yet 'Abdu'l-Bahá is careful to note that this will or wish is distinct from the Creator Himself, not identical with God. In other words, the First Will is a product or an effect of the Creator, not a cause of its own existence: [The First Will] "does not become a sharer in the preexistence of God, for the existence of the universal reality in relation to the existence of God is nothingness, and it has not the power to become an associate of God and like unto Him in preexistence." This distinction becomes even clearer when we consider other passages in which the concept is conveyed through the term "wish" of God. For example, in describing His own function as a Manifestation, Bahá'u'lláh states, "Behold, We have hearkened to His call, and now fulfill His wish." In another passage Bahá'u'lláh asserts a similar distinction between His own will or thought and that of God, who has empowered Him to speak on God's behalf and act at His behest: "And We assented to His wish through Our behest, for truly We are potent to command."[6]

Likewise, in *Epistle to the Son of the Wolf*, Bahá'u'lláh states, "For the will of God can in no wise be revealed except through His will, nor His wish be manifested save through His wish. He, verily, is the All-Conquering, the All-Powerful, the All-Highest."[7] In another passage distinguishing between God and the Primal Will and discussing how the terms "wish" and "Primal Will" denote the same emanation, Bahá'u'lláh writes,

No tie of direct intercourse can possibly bind Him to His creatures. He standeth exalted beyond and above all separation and union, all proximity and remoteness. No sign can indicate His presence or His absence; inasmuch as by a word of His command all that are in heaven and on earth have come to exist, and by His wish, which is the Primal Will itself, all have stepped out of utter nothingness into the realm of being, the world of the visible.

Gracious God! How could there be conceived any existing relationship or possible connection between His Word and they that are created of it?[8]

In this passage we see that "His Word" is described by Bahá'u'lláh as synonymous with the "wish" and "Will" of God.

When we speak about concepts of causality occurring in the spiritual or metaphysical aspect of reality, we are not dealing with the constraints of time and space that are essential in analyzing causal processes in the temporal world. Implicit in this sequence of cause and effect is that, while the sequence occurs in a causal relationship, it is taking place simultaneously even as it has been occurring eternally. Thus it would be incorrect in one sense to say first God existed, then God had an idea, then God conveyed that idea to the Manifestations He had created, and then They assumed a human persona and began to teach humankind about God.

This lack of temporal limitation in such a causal relationship is endlessly fascinating, but for our present purposes it can be adequately illustrated by our own prayers regarding the outcome of certain events. For example, we might pray that, if it be God's will, a certain individual be healed. Unknown to us, the event has already taken place and the healing has occurred. We might thus assume that the prayer had no effect: It would appear that it was too late to have an effect. However, from the perspective of a realm not limited by time and presuming a God with foreknowledge and omniscience, the event could still have been influenced by the prayer inasmuch as God would have foreknown that the suppliant was going to pray for this outcome. God could thus take into account this prayer or wish in influencing the outcome of the healing, if He thought it best to do so.

THE MANIFESTATION AS INTERMEDIARY

We would be hard put to make a useful distinction between the will or wish and the Holy Spirit as conveyer of that wish—effectively they are one and the same force for us. Perhaps we could liken the Holy Spirit to the rays of light emanating from the sun, and we could liken the attributes or "message" contained in those rays (heat, light, and nourishment) to the will of God. In effect, the Holy Spirit is the medium and the will is the message.

Nevertheless, the power of the will of God (or the Holy Spirit containing that will) reaching the Manifestation enables this preexistent spiritual being to plan how much of that wish to convey at a given point in the progress of human history. He also devises the best methodology by which it can be delivered. This methodology might include both the teaching technique (for example, Christ used parables almost exclusively) as well as the human condition in which He might appear to have the most strategic impact on those whom He will teach.

In the human condition, the Manifestation is described in some scriptures as the "Word" of God or the "Word made Flesh." As we have noted, these appellations are appropriate inasmuch as the Manifestation takes the ideas latent in the Holy Spirit (First Will) and transforms that ineffable wish into meaningful increments of actions as portrayed in utterance. The Manifestations have a creative role to play in this part of the sequence of causality, though They are effectively subjugating Their own will to the will of God. That is, the Prophet *chooses* to take on human form and to forgo His own personal will or desires to carry out what will be conducive to the education and assistance of the very people who He knows will reject His help and persecute Him in spite of His attempt to provide them benign assistance. For example, before His crucifixion Christ exemplified His willingness to accept the will of God over His own will: "And he was withdrawn from them about a stone's throw, and He knelt down and prayed, saying, 'Father, if it is Your will, remove this cup from Me; nevertheless not my will, but Yours, be done.'"[9]

In a similar situation Bahá'u'lláh showed the same willingness to accept God's will over His own will. At one point in His life, Bahá'u'lláh had retreated from Baghdad to the mountains of Kurdistán to avoid creating disunity among His followers. There He was free for a time from the onslaught of the enemies who were intent on destroying His Faith. As time passed, tensions within the community mounted to the extent that even His most inveterate opponent, Mírzá Yahyá, pleaded for Him to return. Realizing that if He did not return, all the blood of the Bábí martyrs would have been sacrificed in vain, He agreed to return to Baghdad, though He knew full well that the rest of His life would involve suffering countless hardships, perverse attacks, and betrayals: "The tragic situation that had developed in the course of His two years' absence now imperatively demanded His return. *'From the Mystic Source,'* He Himself explains in the Kitáb-i-Íqán, *'there came the summons bidding Us return whence We came. Surrendering Our will to His, We submitted to His injunction.'*"[10]

Through this episode in Bahá'u'lláh's life we can glimpse that the Manifestation, though infinitely below God in rank, is categorically above the station of an ordinary human being. He is charged with devising a plan through which the will of God can be implemented by degrees in human society for a given period in history. He therefore determines what measure of progress is necessary, appropriate, and timely. For if the raw power of the will of God were released without restraint, without consideration for human capacity, without gradualness and thoughtful application, humankind would would be dumbfounded and destroyed rather than nurtured and assisted.

Explaining this need for gradualness in the process of human education, Bahá'u'lláh writes,

> Know of a certainty that in every Dispensation the light of Divine Revelation hath been vouchsafed unto men in direct proportion to their spiritual capacity. Consider the sun. How feeble its rays the moment it appeareth above the horizon. How gradually its warmth and potency increase as it approacheth its zenith, enabling meanwhile all created things to adapt themselves to the growing intensity of its light. How steadily it declineth until it reacheth its setting point. Were it, all of a sudden, to manifest the energies latent within it, it would, no doubt, cause injury to all created things. . . . In like manner, if the Sun of Truth were suddenly to reveal, at the earliest stages of its manifestation, the full measure of the potencies which the providence of the Almighty hath bestowed upon it, the earth of human understanding would waste away and be consumed; for men's hearts would neither sustain the intensity of its revelation, nor be able to mirror forth the radiance of its light. Dismayed and overpowered, they would cease to exist.[11]

THE AUTHORITY AND POWER OF THE MANIFESTATIONS

The Manifestations frequently state that They do nothing on Their own authority, that They do only that which God commands Them to do. These assertions might seem contrary to the role we have just examined in which the Manifestations appear to play an active and creative part in determining how best to administer the will of God. Therefore we might ask whether these statements are merely examples of self-effacement by which the Manifestations try to deter any attempt on the part of Their followers to make Them the object of adoration, instead of the intermediary by which we are enabled to know and to worship God.

For example, Christ says, "The words that I speak to you I do not speak on my own authority; but the Father who dwells in me does the works." Likewise, Bahá'u'lláh states in His letter to the shah, "This thing is not from Me, but from One Who is Almighty and All-Knowing. And He bade Me lift up My voice between earth and heaven, and for this there befell Me what hath caused the tears of every man of understanding to flow."[12]

These statements might understandably lead some to view the Manifestations as ordinary individuals whom God has inspired. But Their function as intermediaries of the Holy Spirit is ultimately explained most fully if we return to the analogy of the rays of the sun. Unless we examine the bright light of the sun with a spectrometer, we cannot begin to discern the complex nature of that light. The sun and the life it provides are effectively one and the same thing for us.

By the same token, we cannot usefully distinguish between the Holy Spirit emanating from God and reflected to us through the intermediary of the Manifestation and the Manifestation Himself. Likewise, we cannot distinguish between the will of God and the translation of that will into language and action by the Manifestation. The wisdom, power, and authority for us come from one unified source, the Manifestation. They are, for us, correctly designated as the Word of God.

Indeed, when we examine the exalted terms with which the Manifestations allude to each other, we are astonished by the epithets of love, power, and ascendancy They employ, but we must realize They are referring to the will of God unleashed through Them and to the heroic sacrifices They have made to convey that will to humankind. For example, in proving that the Báb is the Qá'im* of Islamic prophecy in the Kitáb-i-Íqán (Book of Certitude), Bahá'u'lláh gives the following eloquent testimony to the divine station of the Primal Point (the Báb): "And among the evidences of the truth of His manifestation were the ascendancy, the transcendent power, and supremacy which He, the Revealer of being and Manifestation of the Adored, hath, unaided and alone, revealed throughout the world. No sooner had that eternal Beauty revealed Himself in Shíráz, in the year sixty, and rent asunder the veil of concealment, than the signs of the ascendancy, the might, the sovereignty, and power, emanating from that Essence of Essences and Sea of Seas, were manifest in every land."[13] Alluding to the Manifestation for whom the Báb is the Forerunner and Herald (Bahá'u'lláh), the Báb states that the sole purpose of His revelation is to prepare people for the coming of "Him Whom God shall manifest," though He also observes that They are emissaries of one and the same Spirit and, in the station of essential unity, are indistinguishable:

It behooveth you to await the Day of the appearance of Him Whom God shall manifest. Indeed My aim in planting the Tree of the Bayán hath been none other than to enable you to recognize Me. In truth I Myself am the first to bow down before God and to believe in Him. Therefore let not your recognition become fruitless, inasmuch as the Bayán, notwithstanding the sublimity of its station, beareth fealty to Him Whom God shall make manifest, and it is He Who beseemeth most to be acclaimed as the Seat of divine Reality, though indeed He is I and I am He. However, when the Tree of the Bayán attaineth its highest development, We shall bend it low as a token of adoration towards its Lord Who will appear in

---

* Literally *He Who Arises:* in Shí'ih Islam, a reference to the Twelfth Imam, the Mihdí, who was to return in the fullness of time and bring a reign of righteousness to the world. The Báb declared Himself to be the Qá'im and the Gate to a greater Messenger, "Him Whom God shall make manifest"—Bahá'u'lláh.

the person of Him Whom God shall make manifest. Perchance ye may be privileged to glorify God as it befitteth His august Self.[14]

Confirming the Báb's statement about the unity of the Prophets— "He is I and I am He"—Bahá'u'lláh delineates in the Kitáb-i-Íqán the powers and attributes of these Vice-regents of the Almighty: "Thus, viewed from the standpoint of their oneness and sublime detachment, the attributes of Godhead, Divinity, Supreme Singleness, and Inmost Essence, have been and are applicable to those Essences of being, inasmuch as they all abide on the throne of divine Revelation, and are established upon the seat of divine Concealment. Through their appearance the Revelation of God is made manifest, and by their countenance the Beauty of God is revealed. Thus it is that the accents of God Himself have been heard uttered by these Manifestations of the divine Being." In the context of the same discussion, Bahá'u'lláh states that the Manifestations, when in a state of immersion "beneath the oceans of ancient and everlasting holiness," assert that Their words are nothing less than "the Call of God Himself": "Thus in moments in which these Essences of being were deeply immersed beneath the oceans of ancient and everlasting holiness, or when they soared to the loftiest summits of divine mysteries, they claimed their utterance to be the Voice of divinity, the Call of God Himself."[15]

In such a condition of complete and utter servitude to the command of God, the Manifestations attain a state of total obliviousness to Themselves as anything other than functionaries of the divine will: "Were the eye of discernment to be opened, it would recognize that in this very state, they have considered themselves utterly effaced and nonexistent in the face of Him Who is the All-Pervading, the Incorruptible. Methinks they have regarded themselves as utter nothingness, and deemed their mention in that Court an act of blasphemy. For the slightest whispering of self, within such a Court, is an evidence of self-assertion and independent existence. In the eyes of them that have attained unto that Court, such a suggestion is itself a grievous transgression."[16]

As Divine Physician, the Manifestation thus implements the "idea," "will," or "wish" of God into actions and utterances suited to the capacity of humankind. We have already observed that when Bahá'u'lláh determined the "patient" was not ready for some of the "remedies" He had devised, He destroyed the medicine:

> A vast, and indeed the greater, proportion of these writings were, alas, lost irretrievably to posterity. No less an authority than Mírzá Áqá Ján, Bahá'u'lláh's amanuensis, affirms, as reported by Nabíl, that by the express order of Bahá'u'lláh, hundreds of thousands of verses, mostly written by His own hand, were obliterated and cast into the river. "Finding me reluctant to execute His orders," Mírzá Áqá Ján has related to Nabíl, "Bahá'u'lláh would reassure me saying: 'None is to be found at this time worthy to hear these melodies.' . . . Not once, or twice, but innumerable times, was I commanded to repeat this act."[17]

With these capacities as God's vice-regents, the Manifestations are both flawless sources of the Holy Spirit and active, creative beings "filled with" the Holy Spirit: "For the Holy Spirit is the divine bounties and lordly perfections, and these divine perfections are as the rays and heat of the sun. The brilliant rays of the sun constitute its being, and without them it would not be the sun. If the manifestation and the reflection of the divine perfections were not in Christ, Jesus would not be the Messiah. He is a Manifestation because He reflects in Himself the divine perfections. The Prophets of God are manifestations for the lordly perfections—that is, the Holy Spirit is apparent in Them."[18]

In another discussion of this same concept of the Holy Spirit as the intermediary power between God and the Manifestation, 'Abdu'l-Bahá uses the appellation *Holy Spirit* to allude to the Manifestations Themselves, since for us there is no effective distinction because They are both message and messenger, the power by which the Word of God is both generated and conveyed: "This Holy Spirit is the mediator between God and His creatures. It is like a mirror facing the sun. As the pure mirror receives light from the sun and transmits this bounty to others, so the Holy Spirit is the mediator of the Holy Light from the Sun of Reality, which it gives to the sanctified realities. It is adorned with all the divine perfections. Every time it appears, the world is renewed, and a new cycle is founded."[19]

HUMANKIND: RECIPIENTS AND EXECUTORS OF THE WILL OF GOD

Finally, at the end of the causal pathway in the macrocosmic bridge between spiritual and physical reality is humankind, individually and collectively. The Manifestation prescribes the remedy for what ails us, but He does not impose that remedy on us. The ultimate efficacy of the remedy thus depends on our individual and collective free will to recognize the True Physician and to accept His prescription for healing our ills.

Here again the paradigm for success is knowledge coupled with action. As with any procedure for rehabilitation and healing, we must follow the guidance with rigorous dedication over time. The training or education of the human collective is, therefore, a subtle process. As we have noted, the goal of the process is to bring about a voluntary response on the part of humankind, a response based on recognition of the essential justice and love inherent in the guidance itself.

Within this context Bahá'u'lláh admonishes humankind with the following counsel about the attitude that must accompany compliance with His guidance: "'Observe My commandments, for the love of My beauty.' Happy is the lover that hath inhaled the divine fragrance of his Best-Beloved from these words, laden with the perfume of a grace which no tongue can describe. By My life! He who hath drunk the choice wine of fairness from the hands of My bountiful favor will circle around My commandments that shine above the Dayspring of My creation."[20] True obedience, then, is obedience carried out not with grudging deference to authority, but with an understanding of the benefits to be derived from compliance and with loving appreciation of the Physician's timely remedy and for His sacrificial dedication in delivering this cure.

As with any medicine, we may not enjoy the medical procedure that ultimately induces health unless we have developed the knowledge to see the "end" in the "beginning," but if we have faith in the physician and, even better, if we acquire understanding of the rationale governing the medicinal procedures, we happily accept any short-term discomfort in anticipation of the long-term benefit.

We can conclude that the causal pathway in the macrocosm of this intermediary process is neither automatic nor simple. It requires creativity from its inception, during the intermediary stage of conveyance, and at the final stage of reception and implementation. For this reason the Creator fashions beings capable of participating in such a complicated process, beings capable of understanding and anticipating the benefits of His love and also capable of responding to His guidance out of their own free will.

So it is that creation is not a single event. It is, as we will observe in succeeding chapters, a constant dialogue between God and humankind, between the Creator and the created, a dialogue that becomes ever more refined as we implement the transformative remedies prescribed by the Divine Physicians.

- 5 -

The Genesis Myth

As to thy question concerning the origin of creation. Know assuredly that God's creation hath existed from eternity, and will continue to exist forever. Its beginning hath had no beginning, and its end knoweth no end. His name, the Creator, presupposeth a creation, even as His title, the Lord of Men, must involve the existence of a servant.

—Bahá'u'lláh, *Gleanings*

Thus far we have considered three major questions that deal with the bridge between spiritual and physical reality as a whole: (1) Why would a Creator choose to create something physical? (2) How can we fulfill the Creator's wish that we love Him? and (3) How is this pathway from the Creator to us established through a bridge between spiritual reality and physical reality?

Now that we have some idea of "why" and "how" the bridging between these realities takes place, we are ready to pursue three related and somewhat less abstract questions: When did this process begin? What is the method by which human beings emerged from what was once a molten mass? What exactly is the relationship between ourselves and that from which we seem to have emerged?

Let us begin with the first of these questions, one that is still at the heart of controversy between science and religion: When did the creation of physical reality begin? Or put in a slightly more intriguing way, what existed prior to reality as we normally understand it?

We have dealt with this question to a certain extent: If God wishes to be "known," can there be a point at which that wish began, or has He always wanted to be known? If He always has wished to be known, how could there be a point in time when the effects of this wish first became manifest in physical reality?

Contemporary physicists are now hotly debating the idea of absolute "nothingness" and the possibility of an absolute "void"—two concepts of physical reality that were readily accepted less than a century ago. If we contemplate the idea of a "beginning" of creation, simple logic would seem to dictate that the universe cannot be limited with regard to time or space. For how can space be contained unless something contains it, and if there was a "Big Bang," what preceded it and caused it?

Of course, proving empirically that the universe is infinite would be difficult. We might attempt to travel in a straight line until we either reach the end of the universe (possibly falling off the edge of it or bumping into whatever contains it), or else we might never reach an end, in which case we could report that we cannot find an end and that, therefore, there must not be one (an equally ludicrous proposition).

Or if space is curved, as Einstein contended, we might come back to the starting point or take a wrong turn and bump into ourselves, having grown incredibly large because we would be approaching the speed of light. Perhaps some civilization more advanced than ours on another planet has such a mission in progress at this very moment. Or perhaps we may conclude, as indicated by the epigraph at the beginning of this chapter and as common sense would seem to confirm, that any beginning in regard to time is unfathomable, except in terms relative to our own limited perspective.

Curiously, however, we confront myths about how the world got started in virtually every religious and cultural tradition. Therefore, before we delve into the scientific discussions of beginnings, let us first examine the background of some religious traditions as they portray the origin of creation.

THE TRUTH ABOUT MYTHS

The word *myth* is replete with meanings and applications. In the context of history, literature, and religion, myth often refers to a symbolic or allegorical statement of reality. In the latter sense a myth can be considered true so long as it is understood to be an allusion to reality and not a representation of reality itself.

The most familiar indirect method of presenting truth is teaching children about abstract concepts through allegorical stories, although myth is also capable of being so complex and layered with meaning as to test and stretch the capacity of the most erudite scholars. For example, Christ almost exclusively employed parables (analogical methodology) to explain extremely complex theological concepts such as the nature of spiritual reality, the nature of God, humanity's relation to God, the purpose of material existence, and the concept of justice in the afterlife.

Christ did not employ this methodology because His followers were unlearned. On the contrary, this methodology was just as challenging to the learned Pharisees in His audience as it was to the untutored masses.

CHRIST'S USE OF NOURISHMENT ANALOGIES

Christ consistently used metaphors taken from the parallel relationship between physical nourishment and spiritual nourishment. Describing the nature of His own appearance, He stated, "'I am the bread of life. Your fathers ate the manna in the wilderness, and they died. This is the bread which comes down from heaven, that a man may eat of it and not die. I am the living bread which came down from heaven; if anyone eats of this bread, he will live for ever; and the bread which I shall give for the life of the world is my flesh.' The Jews then disputed among themselves, saying, 'How can this man give us his flesh to eat?'" Even His own disciples could not always understand the symbolic or metaphorical nature of Christ's teaching: "Many of his disciples, when they heard it said, 'This is a hard saying; who can listen to it?'"[1] Certainly various Christian religions today are in great disagreement about the extent to which one can "interpret" the scriptures figuratively, as opposed to accepting the words "literally" at face value.

Myth as analogy is thus useful because it defies a single authoritative interpretation, is capable of yielding a variety of meanings, can also produce multiple levels of meaning, and requires creative effort on the part of the listener if any meaning is to be discovered. When thus understood, myth is not a falsehood, not a "dumbing down" of truth, and not a distorted portrayal of reality—unless one violates its very nature by taking it as literal fact when it is intended to be symbolic.

Properly understood and explained, myth can be described as truth translated into art—abstract thought expressed in images that enable the imagination to grasp highly abstract concepts. Through myth, truth can be made accessible to everyone. In Christ's parable of the vineyard (Matthew 20:1–16), the lord of the vineyard pays all of the workers the same wage even though some worked the entire day while others came at the eleventh hour. This parable can be understood very simply as Christ's statement that spiritual salvation is available to all alike, or it can be seen as a very taxing and complex allusion to divine justice.

Perhaps Christ employed the parable to break through the literalistic, legalistic, and fundamentalist mentality of the Pharisees. Thus He responded with myths or stories to those learned clerics who dared to test Him, thereby forcing the Jewish scholars to think for themselves rather than respond with memorized legalisms.

The poets who wrote the books contained in what we call the Old Testament wrote from and for societies steeped in the mythological context of an oral storytelling tradition similar to that of all indigenous tribal cultures. In the oral tradition of these cultures, no precise intellectual distinction is made between myth and the reality it portrays. All know on some level that the stories have both an "outer" meaning that fascinates and entertains and captures the imagination of the hearer, and an "inner" meaning that teaches a moral lesson. Furthermore, in such societies virtually everyone is expected to become adept at employing these narrative analogies to teach their offspring the ethical lessons that describe social expectations regarding the character and conduct of the people. Only in later generations when a culture has lost touch with the ethical content and shared moral perspective transmitted through such narrative myths do the myths lose their power to teach—or worse, become accepted as factual history.

THE MYTH OF NOAH AND THE ARK

Was there a great flood? Was there a man named Noah who built a great ship and gathered all the animals on earth to save them from destruction? The ancient mythology of many cultures seems to confirm such an occurrence. Modern science sometimes connects these narratives with identifiable geological events such as the end of the Ice Age. Perhaps there actually was a great flood to which the scriptures allude.

Logic dictates that the fundamental story of Noah must be fiction. Certainly it is hard to imagine that, during the age in which Noah would have lived, a small group of individuals could construct a sizable seagoing vessel, or if they could, that it would have ventured outside a very small portion of the eastern Mediterranean world. How, then, could Noah have obtained male and female animals of every species from remote parts of the world?

Almost every aspect of the story of Noah and the ark seems to defy rational acceptance. We can imagine that there may have been some figure with such a name who attempted to teach spiritual principles to his people and who, according to the scripture of Judaism, Christianity, Islam, and the Bahá'í Faith, was rejected and scorned for his efforts. But did such an individual actually build a huge boat onto which were placed male and female animals?

For decades explorers have attempted to discover the remains of the craft, which some claim to have spied within the glacial ice on Mount Ararat. But could the boat be a metaphor, a symbol of Noah's covenant with his followers? Could his teachings represent the "ark" as the means by which the faithful could be saved from the tumultuous storms of iniquity and strife that afflicted the people? If so, then perhaps the animals in the story represent the male and female aspects of all the human virtues, since it is traditional in most "folk" literature to create various forms of bestiaries—allegorical stories in which animals exhibit various human traits or attributes.*

Certainly the interpretation of the ark as symbolic would seem to be corroborated in the Bahá'í texts with Bahá'u'lláh's use of the ark symbol in His Tablet of the Holy Mariner.† Clearly the ark in this tablet is not to be taken literally. The craft in this highly allegorical work represents the Covenant of Bahá'u'lláh as a refuge for believers. At the very least we can be sure the story of Noah is quite hyperbolic, as are almost all folk myths. They employ extraordinary characters who perform extraordinary feats to make the message of the story unmistakably clear. In Western literary tradition, for example, we have figures such as Hercules, Beowulf, and King Arthur.

Shoghi Effendi himself observes that the story of Noah and the ark and the flood "are symbolical."[2] Therefore, whether or not some historical fact may be behind the story, the allegorical story behind the myth is most certainly true, and that is the critical issue addressed in all scriptural allusion to Noah—that the Prophets come from God with guidance for the well-being of humanity. Yet inevitably They are scorned by the very people whom They have come to save, a phenomenon that Christ laments in the following diatribe against the scribes and Pharisees:

"Therefore I send you prophets and wise men and scribes, some of whom you will kill and crucify, and some you will scourge in your synagogues and persecute from town to town. . . .

"O Jerusalem, Jerusalem, killing the prophets and stoning those who are sent to you! How often would I have gathered your children together as a hen gathers her brood under wings, and you would not! Behold your house is forsaken and desolate. For I tell you, you

---

* In Taoism, each action has a male and female aspect to it. Breathing, for example, consists of the male aspect of expiration and the female aspect of inhalation. Similarly, a virtue such as courage could imply the male aspect of aggressive attack or the female aspect of forbearance.

† A tablet of Bahá'u'lláh in which the Faith of God is symbolized as an ark.

will not see me again, until you say, 'Blessed is he who comes in the name of the Lord.'"[3]

CREATION MYTHS

Keeping the concepts of myth and metaphor in mind, let us turn our attention to the myth of Adam's creation as recounted in the book of Genesis and in Súrih 2, the Koran's Súrih of the Cow. Western literary tradition is influenced most prominently by the story of Adam and Eve as depicted in Genesis: God created the world, fashioned Adam in God's image, and, when Adam was lonely, fashioned for him a woman as a companion and helpmate from one of Adam's ribs.

Like the story of Noah, the story of Adam's creation is an ancient myth that is rich with symbolic meaning, yet common sense cannot accept it as a factual account of human history. 'Abdu'l-Bahá comments, "If we take this story in its apparent meaning, according to the interpretation of the masses, it is indeed extraordinary. The intelligence cannot accept it, affirm it, or imagine it; for such arrangements, such details, such speeches and reproaches are far from being those of an intelligent man, how much less of the Divinity—that Divinity Who has organized this infinite universe in the most perfect form, and its innumerable inhabitants with absolute system, strength and perfection."[4] Yet 'Abdu'l-Bahá further observes that the story has great value in the truth it conveys through the symbolic story or myth, and he explains in some detail what he describes as one of its many possible meanings.

But even if we dismiss the Adamic myth as having no historical value for elucidating the process by which humankind was created on this planet, we still know that there was a creative process capable of bringing about human beings and human society, and we also know that this process required millions of years to achieve completion. Therefore, though the creation story is mythological and allegorical, we do know that at some point in time this planet had a beginning.

THE PROBLEM OF LITERALISM AND MYTHS

Perhaps the most prominent point of interest in the creation story as told in Genesis is the conjoining of the male and female progenitors of humankind. This union we interpret as possibly alluding to the dual nature of the human being—the Adamic or physical self, and the Evian or intellectual and spiritual aspect of self—that is, how the soul and its powers express themselves in this life through the intermediary of the body.

However, since both the Koran and the Bahá'í scriptures also allude to Adam as a historical figure and as a Prophet, or Manifestation (the Arabic term *Rasúl,* used by Muḥammad in the Koran to allude to the Prophets of God, is often translated as "Apostle"), we can also find in this story the probability of some allusion to a point of major transition in the evolution of collective human understanding or human social achievement. One possible meaning could be that Adam, as empowered by God to "name" things, may have been a Manifestation who, among other achievements, explained to His followers that spiritual attributes are latent in every part of creation,* or as we noted earlier, that everything in creation bears the "imprint" of the Creator.

While the story of Adam doubtless describes some point of development in human self-awareness or human appreciation of the essentially spiritual nature of creation as a whole, the Adamic dispensation represents a beginning only in this relative sense. The advent of each Manifestation can be similarly understood as a point of beginning, a revolutionary change in human history, a point of such significance that we feel the need to start counting years anew as a symbol of our realization that humankind has once again been reborn or rejuvenated.

The concept of the *Word* thus marks the beginning of the Revelation of the Manifestation, and His revelation marks the beginning of a new Era. Bahá'u'lláh states in a prayer,

I testify that no sooner had the First Word proceeded, through the potency of Thy will and purpose, out of His mouth, and the First

---

* The concept of "names" in the context of Bahá'í scripture relates to the spiritual attribute manifest in a physical entity. Hence physical reality is sometimes called the "Kingdom of Names."

Call gone forth from His lips than the whole creation was revolution-
ized, and all that are in the heavens and all that are on earth were
stirred to the depths. Through that Word the realities of all created
things were shaken, were divided, separated, scattered, combined
and reunited, disclosing, in both the contingent world and the
heavenly kingdom, entities of a new creation, and revealing, in the
unseen realms, the signs and tokens of Thy unity and oneness.[5]

The myth of Adam clearly does not denote the point at which humankind
attained the distinguishing attributes of humanness, nor, as strict
Darwinists would have it, a point when humankind emerged as a species
distinct from those that preceded human beings. We also know that
human society is much older than six thousand years, the period when
some biblical scholars date the appearance of Adam.

A figurative interpretation of the Adamic myth does not make the
process of creation any less mysterious or spiritual, as we will discover
later. Neither does such a figurative understanding of the myth exclude
the possibility of divine intervention. But the symbolic nature of the
myth does reveal that an anthropomorphic view of creation and of the
Creator may be appropriate when figuratively interpreted, even if
traditional understandings derived from literal interpretations of the myth
defy rational thought and foster anti-intellectualism within the religious
community.

Alluding to literal interpretations that engender misunderstanding and
distortion of the Prophets' utterances, Bahá'u'lláh explains that the learned
in every age have failed to recognize the advent of the Manifestation
because of their "misapprehension" of the metaphorical and symbolic
nature of scripture: "Had they sought with a humble mind from the
Manifestations of God in every Dispensation the true meaning of these
words revealed in the sacred books—words the misapprehension of which
hath caused men to be deprived of the recognition of the Sadratu'l-
Muntahá, the ultimate Purpose—they surely would have been guided to
the light of the Sun of Truth, and would have discovered the mysteries
of divine knowledge and wisdom." In a more general assessment of the
misunderstanding of scripture, Bahá'u'lláh states that the mere act of

reading or reciting scripture has little value unless one attempts to understand its meaning: "Again and again they read those verses which clearly testify to the reality of these holy themes, and bear witness to the truth of the Manifestations of eternal Glory, and still apprehend not their purpose. They have even failed to realize, all this time, that, in every age, the reading of the scriptures and holy books is for no other purpose except to enable the reader to apprehend their meaning and unravel their innermost mysteries. Otherwise reading, without understanding, is of no abiding profit unto man."[6]

THE FEAR OF INFINITY

If we accept that all stories about creation and beginnings are mythological representations of points of change relative to the evolution or progress of a particular sequence of events, then we can readily accept the truth inherent in creation stories and narratives from every culture. In some instances these stories may be related to points within the history of a people—perhaps a famed leader or a heroic battle. Given the Bahá'í view of human history as successive cycles of Manifestations, these narratives often allude (however obliquely) to the appearance of a Prophet or Manifestation and the subsequent influence of His revelation on the progress of human society and history.

Mythological and archeological evidence of such appearances can be found in the indigenous cultures of Africa and the Americas. Similarly, allusions to Prophets about whom we know virtually nothing can be found in various scriptures. For example, Húd and Ṣáliḥ, who appeared in the Arabian peninsula, are alluded to in the Koran.

But whether within the context of a tightly structured tribal community or within the context of a modern global community, we human beings have an understandable tendency to create universal perspectives that are only slightly expanded replications of local experience. God may be portrayed as a great Father or as a tribal Chieftain. The universe may be perceived and portrayed as being focused exclusively on this planet, or this planet may be portrayed as centered around a particular society, or tribe, or holy place.

This tendency has existed throughout human history and has caused various nations and peoples to view themselves or their communities as special, as blessed, as the focal point of existence, as the chosen people of God. This tendency arises from the fact that our view of the world is formed within a personal context—whether as individuals, families, tribes, nations, or races. Therefore this inclination does not demonstrate an inherent chauvinism so much as it illustrates that we do not live in the universe at large. Our everyday world is the microcosm of our personal lives.

THE DESIRE FOR BOUNDARIES

Taken to an extreme, local thinking about reality may foster chauvinism, which can produce tribalism at one level, or it can produce individuals such as Alexander the Great, Caesar, Napoleon, or Hitler on another. This same reduction or contraction of the world into the realm of self has induced leaders of thought throughout human history to war against the notion of creation as infinite. After all, to consider that there could be an endless number of planets and, consequently, an endless number of human beings, or to imagine that all human beings are equally precious in the sight of an omniscient Deity seems tantamount to a diminishment of self, most especially to those who aspire to fame.

There is an inherent conflict in trying to maintain belief in an eternal, omnipotent, omniscient, omnipresent Deity while simultaneously asserting that the reality created by this infinite Being is focused on producing only a handful of individuals (relatively speaking). Theoretically this conflict is resolved by accepting the notion of a "personal God," a Being so complex, so far beyond any Being our imagination might conceive, that He is capable of concern for the fall of a sparrow while remaining the infinite Creator and Omnipotent Ruler of the universe.

Our minds cannot imagine such a Being any more than we can logically accept that an elf in a red suit lives at the North Pole and delivers presents to children over large portions of the earth in a single evening. Therefore, many people either cease to believe in a personal God or resort to blind faith—the very sort of belief that 'Abdu'l-Bahá says is inevitably doomed to failure: "If religious beliefs and opinions are found contrary to the standards of science, they are mere superstitions and imaginations."[7]

It is only natural that we tend to conceive of God by extrapolating an exponential increase in our own capacity. But while our own love can develop and expand without bounds—from love of ourselves to love of family, progeny, and community—these personal emotions do not enable us to envision a Deity that is aware of, concerned with, ministering to, and assaying the merits of each and every human being and human action while simultaneously responding to the needs of an entire planet, let alone to the needs of all possible planetary societies in an infinite universe.

Any student of human thought is aware of this enigma. This "fear" or sense of the implausibility of infinity is not limited to those who long to maintain belief in a just and loving Creator or in the existence of spiritual reality. Scholars through the ages have found it difficult to accept the notion of a boundless universe. Gradually, and often painfully, they have managed to surpass the limitations of the Ptolemaic geocentric notions of the medieval and early Renaissance periods in favor of a less anthropomorphic heliocentric solar system. With modern instruments, we can now view other worlds within our own galaxy and other galaxies at a distance at the borders of present human observation. Yet many cosmologists and physicists still choose to assert that creation is a closed system, that at some point it stops, or is confined, or folds back on itself. Even at this very moment, scientists have come forth with pictures of what they believe to be the outermost reaches of reality: images of the "Big Bang" itself—the first celestial entities that emerged from that primal burst of creation and time.

THE LOVE OF WALLS

We can identify this need to impose limits most clearly in retrospect. For example, we can note the fear the ancients in the Mediterranean region had of passing beyond the bounds of the Pillars of Hercules. The world of the Mediterranean was all they knew and all the world they wished to deal with. Beyond Gibraltar was the mysterious "other," the undefined and possibly "uncreated" realm of chaos. We might also cite the example of various cultures that have used literal walls as strategic boundaries to keep out the "other"—walls to fortify cities (Jericho, Jerusalem, Avila, Acre), walls to fortify countries (the Great Wall of China, Hadrian's Wall in northern England, the Maginot Line in France).

In the poem "Mending Wall," Robert Frost portrays the building of fences between neighbors as a symbol of our desire to confine reality to our own microcosm. While providing us with the illusion of autonomy or security, more often than not these walls serve an ulterior motive of excluding the "other" and reinforcing the sense of ourselves as the center of our microcosm.

The poem depicts a sort of spring ritual in New England farmland in which neighbors pass together on either side of a stone wall, stacking the stones that winter has displaced. The speaker concludes with the observation that some mysterious force seems to find such walls and boundaries "unnatural" to have torn them down:

> Something there is that doesn't love a wall,
> That wants it down. I could say "Elves" to him,
> But it's not elves exactly, and I'd rather
> He said it for himself. I see him there
> Bringing a stone grasped firmly by the top
> In each hand, like an old-stone savage armed.
> He moves in darkness as it seems to me,
> Not of woods only and the shade of trees.
> He will not go behind his father's saying,
> And he likes having thought of it so well
> He says again, "Good fences make good neighbors."[8]

Frost seems to be alluding to the idea that the literal boundaries people employ to define or contain reality are nothing more than symbols of subtle but pervasive and often more austere "walls" meant to exclude those who might tamper with our ordered existence.

Ironically, in most revolutionary movements, leaders of thought and intellectuals are usually the first victims of the tyranny and fervor chauvinism induces. In the Spanish Civil War, the fascists (the *Falange*) promulgated the motto *Que muerre la intelegencia!* (Death to the intellectuals!)—the implication being that those who thought independently posed a threat to those who wished to marshal the might of mob mentality among the disenfranchised masses. This phenomenon occurred under the Nazi regime in Germany, especially in the suppression of Jewish intellectuals, even as it had three hundred years before during the reign of the Spanish Inquisition.

THE HEART OF THE PROBLEM

Let us attempt a mental experiment to get to the heart of the problem. Let us imagine we are attending a sports event at a stadium, and we are sitting among tens of thousands of others. We survey the faces around us—the men and women, the young and old, the beautiful and the ugly, the varied colors, shapes, and sizes. As we sit, we consider our theory that each and every one of these human forms is associated with and empowered by an eternal soul.

Like us, each of these people believes that he or she is the center of his or her universe. All alike may sincerely think themselves to be under the watchful eye and loving care of the Creator. And if this supposition be true, then each of these human beings is capable of evolving into a wonderful and admirable person. Each has some degree of capacity, some chance at magnificence.

Possibly this mental exercise may disturb us. If it does, we should want to know why, since we are merely extending logically the ideas we have already established. We can maintain a belief on a theoretical level more easily than we can endure those among us who are overtly ugly, boisterous, crude, crass, or generally obnoxious. We can more easily love "humankind" than we can endure each other individually.

In fact, we can hardly manage to achieve meaningful intimacy among our family and a few close friends. We can scarcely imagine extending our affection to all those gathered at the stadium, nor can we imagine a Being capable of doing so. For if we cannot even accurately assess or judge our own moral condition, our own spiritual progress, how can we conceive of a Being knowledgeable about, concerned with, or having love for each and every one of these individuals, let alone the countless individuals not in the stadium?

We may find temporary comfort in imagining that some of these individuals just don't matter much—that they are simply "set decorations" the Creator has provided for our entertainment or instruction. For instance, we may think the paunchy drunk behind us sloshing beer down our shirt as he bares his chest and screams about "his" team should be counted as no more significant than an undomesticated farm animal we see in the fields as we go for a drive.

Of course, the other extreme may also concern us. We may consider how many in the crowd easily surpass us in intelligence, talent, wealth, or importance. How many in the stadium might consider *us* unworthy occupants of *their* microcosm? Perhaps we are *their* set decorations!

COMPETITION AS OUR ENEMY

Let us imagine that we do *not* consider ourselves to be in competition with these other human beings—certainly a mature and healthy attitude. Let us say that we are only trying to be the best human beings we are capable of becoming, that we are in competition solely with our own potential. After all, to imagine that there is no competition, that all are truly equal in the estimation of God, frees us from the limiting assumption perpetrated by modern social norms that our sole value derives from the number of people we consider below us according to accepted standards of wealth, power, physical appearance, and car model.

However, while such a belief may release us from the escalating frenzy of competition, it may not remove our "fear of God." For if we accept that there exists a Being who is capable of taking into account the infinite variables at work in a given life and determining the extent to which one has wielded sufficient free will to make the most of a given set of circumstances, we still have to evaluate ourselves constantly to determine whether we will merit a favorable assessment by this Being.

In such a context Bahá'u'lláh offers the following admonition: "Bring thyself to account each day ere thou art summoned to a reckoning; for death, unheralded, shall come upon thee and thou shalt be called to give account for thy deeds."[9] We must then ask according to what criteria we should we assess our performance.

The answer to this question takes us to another level of understanding at which we begin to see that competition is our enemy as well as our solace: The acquisition of attributes is, by definition, almost entirely dependent on interaction with other individuals. Thus, to realize that we are in competition with no one or nothing but our own potential *does not* free us from the obligation to involve ourselves with others. When we recognize that our own potential can be realized almost exclusively through acquiring social virtues (love, justice, kindness, and so forth), we also must accept that all the "others" in our world are not merely set decorations fashioned to enhance the reality of our individual lives. Each of them, however unbeautiful or downtrodden, however uncouth or apparently unimportant, represents an individual soul with spiritual capacity, with an essentially divine nature, and with unique gifts, because one of the eternal laws of creation is that no two beings are created exactly the same. 'Abdu'l-Bahá states,

> The material world corresponds to the spiritual world. Now observe that in the sensible world appearances are not repeated, for no being in any respect is identical with, nor the same as, another being. The sign of singleness is visible and apparent in all things. If all the granaries of the world were full of grain, you would not find two grains absolutely alike, the same and identical without any distinction. It is certain that there will be differences and distinctions between them. As the proof of uniqueness exists in all things, and the Oneness and Unity of God is apparent in the reality of all things, the repetition of the same appearance is absolutely impossible.[10]

THE INSIDIOUSNESS OF SUCCESS

Let us try another mental exercise regarding our latent fear of infinity, one that is particularly valuable for those who might aspire to some degree of rank, status, or achievement. Take any encyclopedia with thumbnail pictures of people of note. Casually page through any given volume.

Stop periodically and note how many of these individuals you have never heard of. Read why they deserve to be remembered in this chronicle of human achievement.

Now consider how proud you and your progeny would be if you were to merit your own small picture there. Think how startled and pleased you would be at this very moment to call your friends and show your family, even though those individuals whose pictures also appear in the encyclopedia are sufficiently numerous to comprise a sizable telephone book.

This exercise illustrates that all attempts at accomplishment for the sole purpose of being distinguished, for the objective of being set apart from the rank and file of other human beings, or to attain a type of worldly immortality by living on in the collective memory of society, are ultimately futile and, if we are to be honest with ourselves, even a bit unseemly. This observation is especially worth considering when we note that the best among those so remembered accomplished what they did in the pursuit of truth or the betterment of the human condition and not for the purpose of being remembered in a massive book. A good many of those included in the book would be shocked to know they achieved recognition when, during their earthly existence, their peers considered them abysmal failures.

The ironic futility of striving for greatness is the poignant message of the so-called *ubi sunt* theme of lyric poetry,* the plaintive question about what happens to those who *did* achieve rank and acclaim in the past. The answer is ever the same—they have passed from the scene, together with all but fragmentary evidence of their lofty accomplishments. This refrain is especially true for those who sought material status—the empire builders and conquerors—perhaps less so for those whose ideas stimulated progress in human thought.

---

* The entire Latin phrase is *ubi sunt qui ante nos fuerunt,* meaning *where are those who lived before us.*

But let us forget the crowded stadium and disregard the seemingly endless supply of notable personages in the encyclopedia. Consider that in any competitive relationship with other human beings, you are ultimately doomed to lose because you are pitting yourself against insurmountable odds. You are forced to conclude that your chance of attaining immortality through accomplishments is not great, especially if such status is your primary goal and not an incidental reward of the joy you find in what you do.

But what if immortality is an inherent property of human existence? If this be the case, then there may occur another sort of fear of infinity—the fear of the afterlife. If we are enjoying life and feel we are striving to become an increasingly spiritual and worthy human being, the possibility of immortality may well be quite appealing, providing it amounts to something like the continuation of an existence at least as nice as the one we are presently experiencing. But as we have noted, according to the Bahá'í teachings, this physical stage of our existence—to which Bahá'u'lláh alludes as "the earliest days of my life"—is but a formative stage of an eternal existence.[11] And as we have also noted, this life is virtually programmed to become uncomfortable, at least physically. Our bodies are doomed to become increasingly dysfunctional until they cease to work at all. In other words, the final stages of our "earliest days" are certain to become so stressful, so sorrow-filled that we may not find the anticipation of the continuity of existence very appealing at all.

Even if we are convinced that there is life after death, we may find small solace if, on the one hand, we believe we may be punished for having failed to live well or if, on the other hand, we believe the same anguish (be it physical, mental, or spiritual) we are experiencing here will continue in the afterlife experience.

SOME RESOLUTIONS OF THE FEAR OF INFINITY

Accepting that the creation story found in Genesis alludes to a relative point of beginning, while also accepting that our personal genesis is quite explicit, need not induce anxiety or fear concerning our existence in this life or in the afterlife. In fact, one of the primary goals of this discussion is to disabuse ourselves of the notion that we are accountable for forces over which we have no control, and further, to distinguish between our true "self" (those aspects of self that are eternal and enduring) and those aspects of self that are derived from the experience of abiding in a physical or associational relationship with a human temple.

WE ARE A WORK IN PROGRESS

The first and most profound balm for the fear of infinity is the realization that "salvation," or succeeding in life by any standard, is not a fixed point of achievement or progression. We are now and will ever remain a work in progress. But far from implying that any sense of joy or success must ever remain beyond our grasp, this axiom implies that the very act of being in motion is rewarding in and of itself, that the existential delight of discovery and enlightenment and growth never ceases, and that we never exhaust the possibilities of spiritual development and ascent. It would seem logical, therefore, that instead of fearing infinitude, we should embrace this sense of our own continuity as being on an endless journey of ever-expanding knowledge and usefulness.

JUDGMENT AS A PREPARATORY EVALUATION

A second resolution to the fear of infinity naturally follows from the idea that we are a work in progress. According to many belief systems, including the Bahá'í Faith, when we pass from this realm to the next, we may be required to assess how well we have fulfilled the mandate for our physical existence—to prepare ourselves for this transition from the illusory world of names into the spiritual world of "vision."*

While this process of evaluation may be correctly described as a type of judgment, it is obviously not a point beyond which redemption and transformation are impossible. Were this the case, our physical experience would be "real" life, and the "afterlife" experience merely a reflection about and reaction to how well we succeeded during this relatively brief period of testing.

---

* A term sometimes employed by 'Abdu'l-Bahá to allude to "spiritual reality" where reality is no longer perceived indirectly.

From the perspective of the Bahá'í Faith and other belief systems that view physical experience as preparation for a more expansive and important experience, our death (or dissociation from physical experience) represents another genesis: our birth into that realm wherein reality is no longer veiled, where our nature and purposes are no longer concealed, and where further spiritual progress beyond our imagining becomes available to us.

If this perspective is correct, and if our experience of death is governed by a just authority, doubtless the birthing process we go through and the initial emotions we experience will be tailored to how we as individuals have performed in the physical stage of our existence. The "just" response to our performance and our emotional experience of that judgment will not be a final or interminable condition, but rather an evaluation geared to assist us in proceeding to the next stage in our eternal development and education.

Such a view does not imply that we will feel no remorse or consternation as we review our efforts, but it would seem to indicate that we will never be bereft of the assistance of a loving and forgiving God so long as we actively *seek* that divine assistance.

THE JOY OF UNITY

A third—and for many the most important—remedy for the "fear of infinity" regards a point we have already made: There is no competition. The foremost objective in this educative process is an ever-expanding sense of "self," a state of being in which we ever more gradually cease to regard our individual progress as separable from or independent of the unified purpose of other beings.

We discover this concept of the positive emotion associated with a sense of the loss of self in the Arabic mystical tradition of *faná,* or "nothingness." In this poetic tradition, the experience of nothingness refers to the loss of selfishness and of the perception of our own progress as independent of how everyone else is doing. It is a state that is, in reality, a fulfillment of self that occurs when we experience a sense of unified purpose with all the other human souls and with the rest of creation as a whole.

To understand this sense of harmony and unity, let us imagine ourselves participating in a vast choir in which each of our individual voices harmonizes with all the other voices. Certainly anyone who has experienced such a bounty or who has participated in any similar cooperative enterprise knows that in such an endeavor one does not feel the least "diminished" because "individuality" is sacrificed to the unified purpose or because the success of the conglomerate in creating beautiful music assumes greater significance than our own aggrandizement. On the contrary, instead of sensing a loss of self, we experience an enhanced power and joy within ourselves that can only be derived from sharing and experiencing this unity of purpose.

Any "team" effort where true accord and fellowship produce something worthwhile tends to produce this sense of elation, wonderment, and fulfillment—the very antithesis of diminishment. Therefore, correctly understood, the notion of our physical demise resulting in the union of ourselves with an infinity of other souls should cause neither trepidation nor dread, but comfort and solace.

WE HAVE ONLY JUST BEGUN

But all of these fears and resolutions are predicated on the vision of a universe that we have as yet neither portrayed nor proven. Our mere assertion that the physical universe is a metaphorical counterpart of the unseen spiritual world offers little consolation if we are simultaneously asserting that we are all obliged to investigate reality for ourselves. Therefore, before we take comfort in the notion of an infinite universe, a reality with both physical and spiritual dimensions, we will deal with several of the principal questions that must be answered before we can be consoled by a theology, cosmology, or philosophy that presents us with immense and as yet unanswered questions and paradoxes—all of which beg for resolution.

- 6 -

How the Creator Creates:
Evolution as Divine Process

We have now come to the question of the modification of species and of
organic development—that is to say, to the point of inquiring whether
man's descent is from the animal.

This theory has found credence in the minds of some European
philosophers, and it is now very difficult to make its falsehood understood,
but in the future it will become evident and clear, and the European
philosophers themselves will recognize its untruth.

—'Abdu'l-Bahá, *Some Answered Questions*

As we have previously noted, if it is the Creator's purpose to bring
forth a system whereby individuals are constantly produced and
whereby all of these individuals have the capacity for infinite
progression, then what must be devised is not an event but a process.
From this perspective, genesis is not a point in time or a beginning of
time, but a law of generation that is divine in origin, timeless, ceaseless,
and governed by predictable laws.

What Darwin discovered, however imperfectly he understood it, was
the evidence of such a system. If we are to understand more about bridging
the gap between physical and spiritual reality, it is well worth noting
what has happened to our understanding of this system since Darwin's
heroic first attempt to unveil the laws of origin and change.

EVOLUTION AND THE MODERN ERA

The theory of evolution is now so commonly accepted as to be no more "theoretical" than the roundness of the earth or the heliocentric view of our solar system. Fossilized remnants testify in their muteness to the various forms of life that once occupied this wonderfully rich globe. We can date these archaic remains with accuracy. We can set before ourselves our own special visions of how life began, how this global entity that is our home might have appeared as it emerged through countless ages of gradual change.

Every child now gleefully conjures in his mind's eye fields and forests teeming with reptilian Titans, with the seas, shores, and skies filled to overflowing with forms so exotic that even now, millions of years later, we still miss them and their trumpeting voices booming through canyons and heralding from hilltops.

Yet, less than a century ago in Dayton, Tennessee, a high school teacher named John Scopes was charged with violating state law when he taught this same theory. Less than two centuries ago even the thought of such a theory was deemed blasphemous. But time and science since Darwin's "second Copernican Revolution"* have radically altered our perspective about ourselves and our origins.

Because of the incalculable advances made since the dawn of the Industrial Revolution in the early nineteenth century, traditional faith in the role of God in our lives has been lost for many, or else it has degenerated into entrenched dogma. At the same time, the faith of others has been restored, as those who wish to maintain belief in creation by design have gradually come to realize that a Creator capable of a single act of instantaneous magic—fashioning a universe in six days during the course of which He had time to make a man from clay, a woman from a rib, and then spend a seventh of His time resting—could also be powerful and creative enough to fashion a complex system capable of accomplishing this same task for Him, and in fascinating, magical, mysterious ways! Furthermore, many can also now find solace in the logic that this same

---

* An appellation sometimes employed to convey the astounding effect of this revised view of cosmology.

Being set in motion this process not once, but constantly throughout the limitless universe from the beginning that has no beginning, and that He will continue to do so until the end that has no end!

Yet what is becoming for many the birthplace of the necessity for metaphysical belief—the rapidly changing fields of science and scientific thought—was at the time of Darwin's discoveries considered by most of the "faithful" as the archenemy of all that was deemed sacred about creation and distinctly noble about human reality, at least from the perspective of Western Christendom.

THE DAWN OF THE MODERN AGE

Darwin's vision of human beings as just another life form was not the sole cause for consternation as the "modern" age began, nor did modernism devastate only those bound by fundamentalist Christian thought. In 1829, some thirty years before Darwin published *On the Origin of Species by Means of Natural Selection,* American poet Edgar Allan Poe wrote a sonnet to science, a plaint decrying the ruination of our wonder at the majesty of the universe caused by the cold, calculating, analytical eye of science:

Sonnet—To Science

Science! True daughter of Old Time thou art!
    Who alterest all things with thy peering eyes.
Why preyest thou thus upon the poet's heart,
    Vulture, whose wings are dull realities?
How should he love thee? Or how deem thee wise?
    Who wouldst not leave him in his wandering
To seek for treasure in the jeweled skies,
    Albeit he soared with an undaunted wing?
Hast thou not dragged Diana from her car?
    And driven the Hamadryad from the wood
To seek a shelter in some happier star?
    Hast thou not torn the Naiad from her flood,
The Elfin from the green grass, and from me
    The summer dream beneath the tamarind tree?[1]

Even if we have never personally enjoyed the shade of a tamarind tree, we can imagine exactly how Poe felt. As the century progressed, the poet Walt Whitman expressed a similar sentiment in an 1885 piece indicting the impersonality of scientific research:

When I Heard the Learn'd Astronomer
When I heard the learn'd astronomer,
When the proofs, the figures were ranged in columns before
    me,
When I was shown the charts and diagrams, to add, divide,
    and measure them,
When I sitting heard the astronomer where he lectured with
    much applause in the lecture-room,
How soon unaccountable I became tired and sick,
Till rising and gliding out I wander'd off by myself,
In the mystical moist night-air, and from time to time,
Look'd up in perfect silence at the stars.[2]

The power of Whitman's poem is in what is left unsaid—the implicit joy, peace, and comfort the speaker finds in contemplating the endless skies and countless stars, the worlds beyond measure, a reality capable of transcending human control, comprehension, or calculation.

For poets and many others, the mystery and wonder of creation seemed somehow diminished by the attempt to replace mystical awe with formulae, theorems, quantification, and data. But in spite of poets' pleas, the century proceeded apace with truly miraculous inventions, amazing discoveries, and revolutionary changes, not the least of which was the urbanization of Western civilization and the birth of crass materialism.

Ideas of the divine origins of the human soul, of the brotherhood of humankind, and of the Platonic forms of nature—all that the Romantic poets earlier in the same century had lauded and set forth as the basis for revolutions against tyranny,* for the adoration of nature, for the assertion

---

* For example, the French and American Revolutions.

90

of the inalienable rights of the common man—seemed quickly dashed to pieces in favor of vast factories, endless railroads, and worldwide trade.

Science was not the sole culprit. Wars and the decline and dying of empires and emperors were having their effect. Attitudes embracing stark realism and mechanistic determinism were replacing all that had been perceived as the stable and imperishable ideal of social elegance and decorum. The aspiration to social refinement was being overwhelmed by a society running on the grease of laws of cause and effect and the drive for wealth beyond measure.

How noble could we be, sprung not from Eden's blissful rapture but from the bubbling mud like gothic bugs? In the emerald isle of England, the pleasant, idyllic countryside villages were depopulated as rich landowners forced lowly tenant farmers into the cities to search for the wherewithal to survive. The Neoplatonism of Wordsworth and the noble savage of Rousseau succumbed to Darwin's laws of natural selection: We are what we are because of forces quite beyond our control and beyond the creative urges of a benign heavenly Father. We just happened to be the ones that grew an opposing thumb and learned to speak, not because God ordained us sacred, not even through divine assistance or dogged determination, but because of random chance.

No longer was there a need for mystery, for a passionate crucifixion to save us, because we could save ourselves, were we to accrue sufficient wealth or power. Every historical fact could be explained and described by pure circumstance of cause and effect, or else by a faceless and impersonal determinism operating through chance or through the equally impersonal laws of hereditary, environmental, or other equally volitionless "subalterns," as Thomas Hardy described natural law in an 1898 poem.

Hardy's poem, written on the brink of the "modern age," did not decry science as a villain. Science, after all, had served only as a tool to reveal to us the stark reality of the operation of the universe, the sad truth of our solitude, and the awful realization that our sole enemy, mere happenstance, is impervious to either our victories or our defeats:

Hap

If but some vengeful god would call to me
From up the sky, and laugh: "Thou suffering thing,
Know that thy sorrow is my ecstasy,
That thy love's loss is my hate's profiting!"

Then would I bear it, clench myself, and die,
Steeled by the sense of ire unmerited;
Half-eased in that a Powerfuller than I
Had willed and meted me the tears I shed.

But not so. How arrives it joy lies slain,
And why unblooms the best hope ever sown?
—Crass Casualty obstructs the sun and rain,
And dicing Time for gladness casts a moan. . . .
Those purblind Doomsters had as readily strewn
Blisses about my pilgrimage as pain.[3]

This growing angst was not exclusively the result of advances in science and technology, nor even the onset of industrialization, but of wars, disease, and the sudden collapse of a staid but predictable way of life.

By the end of World War I in 1918, emerging fears and an infectious cynicism had produced an atmosphere of fatalism and nihilism among many Western thinkers and writers, a tenor captured well in a quaintly cynical poem penned by the "modern"* American poet Archibald MacLeish in 1926:

The End of the World

Quite unexpectedly as Vasserot
The armless ambidextrian was lighting
A match between his great and second toe

---

* The term "modern" insofar as literature is concerned has come to designate 1914–65.

And Ralph the lion was engaged in biting
The neck of Madame Sossman while the drum
Pointed, and Teeny was about to cough
In waltz-time swinging Jocko by the thumb–
Quite unexpectedly the top blew off:
And there, there overhead, there, there, hung over
Those thousands of white faces, those dazed eyes,
There in the starless dark the poise, the hover,
There with vast wings across the canceled skies,
There in the sudden blackness the black pall
Of nothing, nothing, nothing—nothing at all.[4]

This bitterly ironic poem portrays our life on earth as a self-made illusion in which our actions are no more meaningful than the nonsensical acts of a bizarre circus. It brilliantly captures in a succinct metaphor what so many had come to view as futile distractions we create to conceal from ourselves the awful truth about reality—that behind all our imagined goals and the sheer busyness of our lives is . . . nothing!

There is no sure-handed Creator at the tiller carefully eyeing how well each of us performs his or her part, only a perverse deception that our lives and efforts have value and purpose. The same tone pervades Hemingway's quintessentially brief short story "A Clean, Well-Lighted Place" when the stoic waiter parodies the Lord's Prayer: "Our nada who art in nada, nada be thy name thy kingdom nada thy will be nada in nada as it is in nada. Give us this nada our daily nada and nada us our nada as we nada our nadas and nada us not into nada but deliver us from nada; pues nada. Hail nothing full of nothing, nothing is with thee."[5]

In literature, then, the term *modern* did not imply improvement, advancement, reform, or renewed faith in human potential because of our exponentially expanding capacity for material advancement. We would not be saved by electric lights, telephones, cars, and airplanes. It was not the Renaissance with a hope-filled humanism—a renewed faith in human potential unleashed by the rediscovery of the accomplishments of the classical age. Instead there emerged a view of humanity as lonely, hopeless, alienated, and purposeless, a somewhat higher form of animal dwelling in despair in a world of complex forces impervious to purpose or will. William Harmon writes in his *Handbook to Literature,* "*Modern* implies a historical discontinuity, a sense of alienation, loss, and despair. It not only rejects history but also rejects the society of whose fabrication history is a record. It rejects traditional values and assumptions and it rejects equally the rhetoric by which they were sanctioned and communicated. It elevates the individual and the inner being over the social human being and prefers the unconscious to the self-conscious."[6]

In light of this definition we come to appreciate the dark and pessimistic mood in perhaps the best-known poem capturing the tenor of the modern age. T. S. Eliot's "Wasteland" (1922) sets forth in a lengthy and complex pastiche of symbolic allusions the notion of a land that is not only devoid of hope or the capacity to redeem or heal itself, but also lacks even the wherewithal to discover such a capacity. Likewise, in a more succinct metaphor W. B. Yeats, in his 1920 poem "The Second Coming," portrays the modern age as betokening some dire upheaval that will render the same sort of vast historical change as did Christianity, except this transformation will result in a spiritual regression, a reversal of the cycle of advancement that was grinding to a halt.

Yeats's image of the "Second Coming" is thus the imminent birth of a hideous beast, not a boy savior. The opening passage of the poem captures all that the term *modern* signaled to many people of thought:

> Turning and turning in the widening gyre
> The falcon cannot hear the falconer;
> Things fall apart; the center cannot hold;
> Mere anarchy is loosed upon the world,
> The blood-dimmed tide is loosed, and everywhere
> The ceremony of innocence is drowned;
> The best lack all conviction, while the worst
> Are full of passionate intensity.[7]

RELATIVISM AND POSTMODERNISM

The period since 1965 is designated in various fields (literature, history, communications) as the postmodern period, a term that is amorphous because it alludes to a dissolution of any shared moral assumptions or imperatives. The result has been a period that some scholars portray as a freedom from standard ("received") perspectives about the human condition and about society as a whole. Indeed, the concept of "objectivity" itself is perceived by many postmodern writers and theorists as an illusion wrought by the inevitably subjective nature of perception and communication.

Consequently, instead of attempting to construct objective views that are appropriately qualified, the tendency of postmodern thought is to discard the attempt at neutral or objective constructions of reality. According to some postmodern thinkers, it matters not whether a verity can be proven by standards of logical discourse (by "proofs"). Logic itself is perceived as suspect, as a specialized language constructed largely by white European males to disenfranchise those not submissive to its rules and cant.

For the scholar employing postmodern methodologies, the assertion of a proposition is sufficient proof of its validity, so long as the assertion is properly qualified as a "suggestion" or "proposition." For if there is no objective reality (no reality that can be portrayed without bias according to how reality is portrayed in language), then all common assumptions about everything are mere assumptions. One can describe, or propose, or suggest personal theories about math, physics, or morality, but no proof is needed or required because it would not be respected even if it were properly executed, and no contradiction needs to be responded to with anything much more substantial than "Well, that's just *your* opinion."

The end result of this academic vogue has been a return to the apotheosis of rhetoric, often at the expense of logical discourse. A similar milieu existed when Socrates waged his war against the Sophists in Periclean Athens, where the political power of rhetorical panache was perceived as superior to the search for truth (that is, accurate knowledge and description of reality).

The critical focus of this postmodern perspective is on language, the medium of communication, the tool by which any given perception of reality is portrayed and conveyed to others. And because language is necessarily imprecise and subjective, insofar as what a given word connotes (let alone entire sentences or a complete discourse), descriptions of reality can never be completely objective or accurate because each new statement creates a context all its own, a reality that someone not possessing the speaker's consciousness can never precisely understand.

On the one hand, such a theory "validates" all individual opinions. On the other hand, such a theory is self-refuting by virtue of proving that reality is never perceived without personal bias. Therefore no objective reality can be discovered or articulated with total accuracy. Consequently, the argument of postmodern thought itself—that no objective reality can be discovered or articulated—is itself merely an assertion posited by an inherently biased individual, or worse, by a whole group of biased individuals who think and write under the illusion that they are describing the same process. Obviously, then, the theory that no proof or perception is objectively accurate is itself necessarily flawed: The theory cannot be objectively proven and is, therefore, merely opinion and conjecture.

RATIONAL DISCOURSE IN THE QUEST FOR REALITY

Obviously perceptions of reality may be flawed, skewed, or biased according to the perceiver. But this fact in no way diminishes the capacity of reality to exist independent of the perception and portrayal of reality by others.

According to Bahá'í texts, rational discourse (the activity of the "rational faculty") is an inherent capacity designed by the Creator specifically to enable us to discover reality, and in particular to discover the "names" of God—the divine imprint manifest in every aspect of reality. For instance, 'Abdu'l-Bahá states, "Beyond and above this, God has opened the doors of ideal virtues and attainments before the face of man. He has created in his being the mysteries of the divine Kingdom. He has bestowed upon him the power of intellect so that through the attribute of reason, when fortified by the Holy Spirit, he may penetrate and discover ideal realities and become informed of the mysteries of the world of significances." 'Abdu'l-Bahá further states, "This human rational soul is God's creation; it encompasses and excels other creatures; as it is more noble and distinguished, it encompasses things. The power of the rational soul can discover the realities of things, comprehend the peculiarities of beings, and penetrate the mysteries of existence. All sciences, knowledge, arts, wonders, institutions, discoveries and enterprises come from the exercised intelligence of the rational soul."[8] In short, were it not for the accuracy of the rational faculty, how could those who wish to deny the reliability of rational thought even present (let alone presume to "prove") that these faculties are unreliable, since such a process requires logical discourse?

It is no coincidence that the attitudes and tenor expressed in the poems we have examined parallel the path of thought about creation that stemmed from Darwin's publication of his research and the conclusions that this research seemed to unveil. We leave in the dust the Romantic notion of human beings as infused with divinity, of Nature as corresponding to eternal metaphysical forms, and we end up in the present with the solipsism of postmodern thought that leaves off where Descartes began—that the only evidence of reality is the internal consciousness of self.

THE EVOLUTION OF EVOLUTION

Obviously we cannot attribute what we might perceive to be the present state of cynicism, amorality, or social instability to Darwin. Many other transformative movements in philosophy and religion, together with our collective human experience during the past century, have brought us to our present circumstance. What is more, the concept of evolution did not suddenly spring forth with the publication of Darwin's findings in 1859.

The question of our origins is as ageless as human thought. And not surprisingly, as we examine the progression of theories about this subject, we find that most often they are influenced by the tenor of religious and philosophical attitudes dominating the period or culture in which they are articulated. But because these ideas did not "evolve" in a strict chronological sequence, it is useful to categorize some theories of teleology according to theoretical paradigms rather than according to chronological order, at least until we arrive at Darwin's theory and can note the sequence of reactions that have occurred since his monumental work.

MATERIALIST VIEW OF CREATION

First, let us consider the strict materialist view of creation. From such a view, the emergence of all forms of life on this planet, though produced by discernible laws of cause and effect, is merely an accident. Perhaps such an accident has occurred elsewhere in the universe, given infinite time and infinite solar systems, though many materialists assert that the universe is finite in both space and time.

But whether or not other such accidents have occurred, this one occurred because of the favorable position of this planet, which contained all the strategically necessary elemental ingredients and various forms of energy as catalysts. Furthermore, it just so happened that all of these ingredients and forces interacted propitiously, though through explicit and successive violations of the law of probability.

THE PROBLEM WITH CHANCE

Creation from a materialist perspective violates scientific law because laws of probability are themselves scientific descriptions of predictability based on the fact that we should accept the simplest or most likely explanation for an event. The most scientific explanation for successive violations of natural law is that *probably* some as yet undiscovered or undetected force has brought about this deviation from the straight path— which in the case of a planet would be chaos degenerating into more chaos by virtue of the law of entropy, the second law of thermodynamics.

Nevertheless, strict materialists still hold that while improbable, this accident among accidents has occurred, the sufficient proof of which is the earth itself and all its inhabitants. And for materialists, the fact that we have as yet discovered no other such "accidents" in scanning the heavens lends further credence to the theory. We happen to be a part of a most rare and possibly unprecedented occurrence—the evolution of higher forms of life because of pure dumb luck.

CREATION FROM DESIGN

Is such a proposition entirely untenable? After all, given infinite time and infinite configurations, anything is possible. But wait! According to

98

most modern physicists, there has not been infinite time or infinite configurations. But for the sake of the materialist theory, let's assume that there have been an infinite number of chances. And then let's recall the old saw that with an infinite number of monkeys at an infinite number of keyboards (one per monkey), the monkeys (or one particularly lucky monkey) would eventually write *Hamlet*.

The problem is that this propitious accident could not happen. That's where design comes in. Necessary for the writing of *Hamlet* is an idea derived from a mind. Prior to particular words and carefully conceived images is an idea, a concept in Shakespeare's (or the monkey's) mind. Without any such external input towards order and meaning, any process will degenerate into disorder and meaninglessness. This is also scientific law.

Darwin concluded that all beings proceed in a chain or sequence of mutations derived from the advantageous mutations of other species. While not intended to deny the existence of design or of God, his theory had the effect for some thinkers of making God unnecessary in the process of physical creation. Darwin himself saw no denial of God in the process of natural selection. Somewhat like the watchmaker image of God proposed by the Deists a century earlier, Darwin's idea presumed that God set the process in motion and let His own natural laws do the rest. After all, what could be blasphemous or sacrilegious in any methodology God employed, so long as it produced the results we see around us— beings capable of thought, self-awareness, and the ability to discover God and God's laws, like the law of evolution? Proponents of this theory are called "essentialists," and more often than not, their theories derive from a monotheistic belief in a Creator whose plan preceded creation.

Some of the most stringent opponents of Darwin in the mid-nineteenth century also believed that an idea or plan preceded creation. These were Neoplatonists who believed that the idea, form, or essence—the ultimate goal or vision of what was to be created—necessarily preceded the evolutionary process by which beings or species became manifest. Disputing this belief, Darwin claimed that chance variations or mutations, when propitious, allowed one form of a species to survive but caused another not so endowed to expire. This process of natural selection thus brought about a new creation, but this new creation derived from chance or mutation or innovation, not divine Will.

SOME PROBLEMS WITH DARWIN'S UNDERSTANDING OF EVOLUTION

One problem in Darwin's concept of evolution is the lack of evidence for the gradualness of variation, mutation, and change. As scientists have paid increasingly more attention to sedimentary fossilized remains, it has become apparent that new species appeared relatively suddenly. Periods of stasis were followed by periods of rapid change and transformation. There is little evidence of a consistent gradual intermediary condition of transformation among species that one would expect to discover according to Darwin's explanation of change.

NATURAL SELECTION

Another problem with Darwin's understanding of evolution is his belief that organisms mutated in order to increase their chances of survival. There was only slight evidence that might have seemed to support some transitional stage. For instance, some specimens that seemed to be intermediary between reptiles and birds had appendages (the predecessor of wings?) during a period in which these appendages afforded them no strategic advantage whatsoever. They were not responding to any known or even to any anticipated condition in which the wings would be essential for survival.

Consequently, how could there be a "selection" in this process? According to Darwin, the winged reptile would have survived and prospered because the wing offered the beast a strategic advantage. But the wing simply appeared as what we must presume was part of the natural or inherent progression of the evolutionary progress of that species. Certainly we cannot attribute some collective will to those reptiles that began growing the wings—as if some group decision were made through which the beasts, after appropriate consultation, decided to sacrifice their acceptance among their nonwinged contemporaries to serve the greater good of the generations yet unhatched.

WILLFUL CHANGE

The logical extension of such a theory belabors the point. We would have to believe that plants and animals of various degrees of capacity could discern a problem, conceive of a solution, determine to change their physical shape or capacity to fulfill that objective, and finally—and this is the clincher—agree to begin this process not for their own benefit, but for the benefit of descendants hundreds or thousands of years in the future.

In other words, we are asked to accept that these plants and animals could accomplish what we now have a difficult time trying to convince our fellow human beings to accomplish—to sacrifice some degree of self-gratification in order to cease damaging our environment so that future human beings will have an inhabitable planet. How can we believe that a plant, bug, or beast was more intellectually and spiritually advanced than we have yet become?

This ironic observation is not intended to disparage the factual observations that changes did occur and that some of the changes were advantageous. The point is that, from a Bahá'í perspective, mutation or transformation is not an accident. Evolution is an inherent and scientifically demonstrable process appropriate to any form of organic life.

STASIS

There is also the problem of stasis as regards Darwin's understanding of evolution. The remains of cats and other animals from ancient Egyptian tombs have the same appearance and anatomy as do their present-day counterparts. Having become a cat, a cat seems to have remained a cat. Likewise, whether or not the birds evolved from their intermediary forms as dinosaurs, once a bird became a bird in all its myriad shapes, sizes, colors, and classifications, it remained a bird.

In other words, it would seem plausible to infer from this fact of apparently achieved stasis that there is a certain point in the development of an organism at which evolution stops, at least in terms of fundamental physical properties. If so, then the idea of one species evolving into another would seem disproved. We must assume it was the destiny all along of a certain form of life to become a cat, or a bird, or a human being. The fact that certain parallel forms of life became, and are still becoming, extinct may mean that not all forms of life on the planet are intended to endure. Instead, perhaps they serve a certain purpose in the process of the planet's development; then, having served that purpose, they disappear.

It would seem more accurate, consequently, to say that what Darwin perceived to be changes from one species to another through random mutation and natural selection was really evidence of the developmental stages of a species before it had achieved its final or mature form.

THE CONCEPT OF "SPECIES"

Part of the problem in any discourse about evolution is the term *species*. Viewed inside the womb, a fetus might be said to be migrating through a series of forms or *species*, emulating at first a fish, then a reptile, then a mammal. And yet we know these various appearances are but stages in the evolving of a human being—from its beginning with the conjoining of two cells until its final stage of physical development as a human adult. Were we to assemble the pictures of fossils from a single species and arrange these images into a time-lapse display, possibly we could discern a similar sequence of change—evolution in the sense of gradual growth or development of a single "species" from its incipient form until its final stage of fruition or mature development.

EVOLUTION AS A DIVINE PROCESS

Since the Bahá'í view of creation and evolution incorporates systematic metaphysical influence, we need to conclude this discussion about evolution with a sense of how this view of "divine intervention" accords logically with an equally plausible scientific concept of evolutionary development.

PARALLELISM THROUGHOUT

We have already discussed the Bahá'í cosmogonic concept of creation, how the Primal Will begets creation through the intermediary of the Manifestations. Later we will discuss more completely the particulars of that causal pathway. But first, let us review the parallelism that exists throughout this process of systematic creation we allude to as evolution. For example, 'Abdu'l-Bahá draws a parallel between the evolution of the human species and the evolution of the embryo into a human being, an analogy also employed by Bahá'u'lláh:

So also the formation of man in the matrix of the world was in the beginning like the embryo; then gradually he made progress in perfectness, and grew and developed until he reached the state of maturity, when the mind and spirit became visible in the greatest power. In the beginning of his formation the mind and spirit also existed, but they were hidden; later they were manifested. In the womb of the world mind and spirit also existed in the embryo, but they were concealed; afterward they appeared. So it is that in the seed the tree exists, but it is hidden and concealed; when it develops and grows, the complete tree appears. In the same way the growth and development of all beings is gradual; this is the universal divine organization and the natural system. The seed does not at once become a tree; the embryo does not at once become a man; the mineral does not suddenly become a stone. No, they grow and develop gradually and attain the limit of perfection.[9]

Continuing this illuminating description of evolutionary development as applied to all forms of life, 'Abdu'l-Bahá states explicitly that the divine plan as applied to creation always employs this methodology of gradualness. Yet the inherent destiny of each creation is latent in its beginning. From its conception an inherent "idea" of its destiny precedes the evolutionary process and dictates each stage in the progress of every created thing:

All beings, whether large or small, were created perfect and complete from the first, but their perfections appear in them by degrees. The organization of God is one; the evolution of existence is one; the divine system is one. Whether they be small or great beings, all are subject to one law and system. Each seed has in it from the first all the vegetable perfections. For example, in the seed all the vegetable perfections exist from the beginning, but not visibly; afterward little by little they appear. So it is first the shoot which appears from the seed, then the branches, leaves, blossoms and fruits; but from the beginning of its existence all these things are in the seed, potentially, though not apparently.[10]

'Abdu'l-Bahá concludes this passage with an another allusion to the human embryo, the usefulness of the image here being its demonstration of how all the future potential of the created being is latent in its beginning, however concealed that fruition might be to the uneducated observer:

In the same way, the embryo possesses from the first all perfections, such as the spirit, the mind, the sight, the smell, the taste—in one word, all the powers—but they are not visible and become so only by degrees.

Similarly, the terrestrial globe from the beginning was created with all its elements, substances, minerals, atoms and organisms; but these only appeared by degrees: first the mineral, then the plant, afterward the animal, and finally man. But from the first these kinds and species existed, but were undeveloped in the terrestrial globe, and then appeared only gradually. For the supreme organization of God, and the universal natural system, surround all beings, and all are subject to this rule. When you consider this universal system, you see that there is not one of the beings which at its coming into existence has reached the limit of perfection. No, they gradually grow and develop, and then attain the degree of perfection.[11]

EVOLUTION AS A TEACHING DEVICE

Evolution, as we have portrayed it from a Bahá'í perspective, is not only the best means by which the Creator can bring about a ceaseless fulfillment of the Hidden Treasure, but it is also an essential tool for our education. First, studying evolution as a divine process—one of the important tools by which the gap is bridged between spiritual and physical reality—teaches us that in terms of our own experience in this life, growth and development are predicated on energy and effort expended over time. Consequently, we learn from this axiom to acquire the virtues of patience, persistence, and determination.

Second, from this axiom we also discover that while we—like all other created beings—have an inherent or essential destiny, the human goal of acquiring spiritual attributes—to become "good" or "Godly"—derives from two different sorts of energy or effort. One is our own willful energy applied consistently and constantly as a result of discovering what is the most propitious, meritorious, and rewarding objective for our lives. The other source is the unremitting energy and assistance from outside us in the form of guidance and energy from the Holy Spirit as channeled to us through the Manifestations. As we have noted, one of the inherent laws governing this external assistance is that it is unfailingly available to us, but only if we willingly seek it by being receptive—that is, by actively desiring it and asking for it.

Third, because there is for human beings no final point of intellectual or spiritual attainment, the higher aspect of our evolution requires that we constantly evaluate and monitor our present performance and status. We are and always will be in a state of evolving.

A "PERSONAL" GOD AT THE HELM

From some passages about the evolutionary process that we discover in the Bahá'í writings, we might understandably conclude that there is no need for "outside" assistance. Since 'Abdu'l-Bahá describes evolutionary growth as an inherent property of everything that exists in material reality, we might concur with the Deist image of God as the great "clockmaker" who, having fashioned the perfect mechanism to produce and maintain physical reality, has no need for further direct intercession in the process.

Yet as we have noted, this image itself is inaccurate or inadequate as a portrayal of evolution, particularly the evolution of humankind. There is still required a preexistent will or idea to set the process in motion. Second, without the continuous influx of energy and guidance, the "clock" would eventually cease to run, or else begin to run erratically over time. Consequently, scientific law itself contends that it would be improbable beyond calculation that our present society evolved from random chance, inasmuch as systems tend to decline toward entropy and chaos unless further energy and guidance are introduced.

This is the crux of what the evolutionary process has to teach us—that a system which tends toward order cannot run itself or become more sophisticated and complex. There must be some organizing force, some source of energy and guidance from outside the system. And since the "system" we are discussing consists of the entire physical universe, then the only source of energy and guidance truly "outside" that system would have to come from another reality—a metaphysical or "spiritual" reality.

SCIENCE, RELIGION, AND EVOLUTION

If this proposition is true—that outside or external influence is required to produce the ever more refined planet that is our home—we can presume that science is destined in time to discover that force or cause, and probably sooner than later. Certainly we will not discover a faded photo of the hand of God reaching out to the limp finger of Adam, but there most certainly will emerge obvious, clear, and irrefutable proofs of a metaphysical relationship in this process.

As with the Copernican theory, science will in time accept the interrelationships between physical and metaphysical expressions of reality because this thesis, if true, will offer the simplest (that is, most scientific) explanation for a process that will otherwise remain clouded in "mystery." The evolution of human society as presently portrayed ultimately flies in the face of all other reasonable material explanations.

The corollary of this future course of study will be confirmation on the part of religion and metaphysics that science is not the enemy of religion, but the very means by which the foundation of religious belief can be firmly established and upheld. For to the extent that science ultimately is self-correcting (though often haltingly), it will in time by its own tools of rational investigation be forced to recognize the undeniable evidence of the interpenetration between scientific law (natural forces) and spiritual law (supernatural forces). Likewise, at the heart of true religion and authentic religious belief is not the love of mystery or "blind faith" but the love of discovering the pearls of wisdom that explain reality, resolve mysteries, and make clear the divine rationale for natural law and for the integration of these dual, reciprocal aspects of reality.

WHEN DOES THE MANIFESTATION "DESCEND"?

If at the heart of human ascent spiritual reality becomes revealed as being manifest in physical reality via the intermediary of the Manifestation, at what point in the evolutionary educational process does the Manifestation take on a human persona to help guide humankind? Or stated more aptly, at what point do human beings reach a state of evolutionary development such that divine emissaries would be able to have any educative influence on them?

If the Manifestations appeared early on in this process when human beings had the form and capacity of something like a tadpole, did a Manifestation appear as one among them urging these embryonic human beings towards the shore as they swam about in primordial pools, but starting to show evidence of incipient arms or legs? And if these Educators functioned this early and in this direct manner, how was information imparted?

In direct response to this question, Shoghi Effendi says, ". . . Though we cannot imagine exactly what the Manifestations of the remote past were like, we can be sure of two things: They must have been able to reach their fellow-men in a normal manner—as Bahá'u'lláh reached His generation, and They were sent from God and thus Divine Beings."[12] While Shoghi Effendi does not explain exactly what he intends by the phrase "normal manner," the phrase would seem to imply that the Manifestations appear as ordinary human beings only after the point when human beings have achieved some condition of maturity peculiar to the human species. He observes that this "manner" is comparable to the way in which "Bahá'u'lláh reached His generation"—through speech and example.

This conclusion, if correct, should not be interpreted to mean that the Manifestations had to await some point of evolutionary development before They exerted influence. After all, we have already asserted that propitious guidance was needed from the beginning in order to produce an environment capable of bringing forth the human being in a physical form. Therefore we can conclude that this early influence may well have been exerted directly from the spiritual realm long before it was needful or useful for the Manifestation to incarnate divine attributes in the form of a human persona in order to communicate in a "normal manner."

Once the human being had achieved fruition physically, we can imagine that the earliest Manifestations could have suggested forms of law or behavior, or practical tools, like fire or the wheel, without getting into complex ideas and concepts, just as a parent establishes laws, boundaries, and behavioral norms. The parent teaches useful skills to a child who doesn't yet understand the principles underlying these patterns of action. Even this early in human evolutionary intellectual and spiritual development, we can envision foundational concepts of "correct" or "good" behavior being exhibited as a part of the instruction.

We can envision, then, that Manifestations in a similar fashion at the very dawn of human consciousness could have introduced fundamental guidance regarding safety, health, the nurturing of children, and other fundamental capacities that other animals perform instinctively. Of course, as we have already noted, the Manifestation provides guidance both prior to and after He assumes a human aspect in the physical world. His creative influence could thus have been effective whether or not it was yet time for these Teachers to become incarnate in a form familiar to the evolving human being.

But we can certainly afford to let the specifics of these early stages of this creative process remain veiled or concealed from us for now, so long as we glimpse the integration between the "scientific" descriptions of evolutionary laws and the Bahá'í description of the laws of divine guidance. In short, we have now arrived at some relatively respectable vision of the close connection at work in creation, the "how" of it, if you will. What we can now consider is how the close connection between these twin expressions of reality becomes expressed in terms of "what" is created, the fact that each and every created thing is expressive in a unique way of the union of spiritual and physical properties.

- 7 -

What the Creator Creates:
The Great Chain of Being

As the degrees of existence are different and various, some beings are higher in the scale than others. Therefore, it is by the will and wish of God that some creatures are chosen for the highest degree, as man, and some others are placed in the middle degree, as the vegetable, and some are left in the lowest degree, like the mineral.

—'Abdu'l-Bahá, *Some Answered Questions*

The system that unites, organizes, and orders all existent beings is subtle, pervasive, and integral to the process of bringing forth and sustaining human life. To a certain extent, knowledge of this system is now common because of modern studies in ecology and related sciences. But as we have noted, from a Bahá'í perspective all species exist first in the mind of God as an essential idea or form before being created in the world of existence.

As we noted in the previous chapter, the idea that each created entity is a divine emanation and has a divine purpose is quite distinct from various materialist views of the variety of creation emerging by pure chance. Early in our discussion we alluded to the usefulness of the rest of creation. Now let us consider how the rest of creation relates to us and to physical reality as a whole.

THE CONCEPT OF THE CHAIN OF BEING

If each created thing has a special value, should we not, like ardent environmentalists, be extremely concerned if one of these manifest signs of divine attributes is endangered or becomes extinct? Would that not mean that some part of our education, however minuscule, might be lacking or that the educational system that is physical reality would become an incomplete expression of the Creator's attributes?

Another question looms even larger as we consider the rest of creation. As we have already observed, even though human beings may be the "fruit" of creation, surely it is specious to assert that one part of creation is superior to another. How can there be competition among the integrated parts of a system? The engine of a car is not in competition with the drive shaft—the car is useless without either one.

We might correctly assert, however, that the engine is superior in complexity and design to the drive shaft. Similarly, the component parts of one's body are not in competition with each other. Yet there is a sense of rank or order in the degree of their importance that is related to one's survival and well-being. We consider our heart and our brain superior in importance to our fingers. Therefore, while we can consider "nature" (material creation) as one integrated system geared to the education of human beings, we are also correct in presuming that each part is important, even though there may be a systematic rank or relative subordination of one part to another in this organic unity.

For this reason, philosophers through the ages have employed various metaphors to indicate the concept of unity coupled with the concept of rank or degree. The most frequently employed and possibly the most useful metaphor to express the concepts of integration and degree is the Great Chain of Being.

The particular value of this metaphor is that it expresses several different aspects of the relationship among the diverse components of the integrated system that is material creation. It demonstrates that every created entity— every link on the chain—is subordinate to the links above it but superior to the links below it. Creation may thus be considered a hierarchical arrangement. Furthermore, since a chain is only as strong as its weakest link, we also derive from this analogy the idea of the value of creation at every level of existence.

This is the notion of "plenitude" or "sufficiency"—that there are no "missing links" in creation. For if material creation has as its animating purpose to mimic or manifest in physical terms the infinite varieties and degrees of spiritual attributes, then there must be an infinite number of variations in creation as a whole and also within each level of creation. Indeed, as we have already mentioned, there is no replication in creation. Yet this fact does not imply that the earth is populated by an infinite assortment of random entities, each with its own special destiny, purpose, and self-interest. The Chain of Being analogy implies that this infinitude of variety possesses an inherent order, all of which is conjoined by a sequence of connections. 'Abdu'l-Bahá describes the metaphor of the chain as follows:

> [A]ll these endless beings which inhabit the world, whether man, animal, vegetable, mineral—whatever they may be—are surely, each one of them, composed of elements. There is no doubt that this perfection which is in all beings is caused by the creation of God from the composing elements, by their appropriate mingling and proportionate quantities, the mode of their composition, and the influence of other beings. For all beings are connected together like a chain; and reciprocal help, assistance and interaction belonging to the properties of things are the causes of the existence, development and growth of created beings.[1]

SOME BACKGROUND ABOUT THE CHAIN OF BEING

In Western philosophy the concept of the Chain of Being has persisted since Plato's time as an image of hierarchical order and as an analogy for the interconnectedness of phenomenal reality. It also demonstrates symbolically the relationship of the material world to the spiritual world in some versions of the analogy. For example, with some Christian conceptions of the chain analogy, the celestial world is included in the hierarchical system, as in Renaissance philosophy.

MEDIEVAL VIEWS

Though the exact origins of the analogy are uncertain, the concept has been constantly revised and reshaped to articulate the beliefs and attitudes of various world views through the ages. The Great Chain of

Being metaphor gained favor in Europe with medieval scholars. Chaucer alludes to the idea in *The Canterbury Tales* as the "Great Chain of Love," applying the idea of "love" in its most expansive sense of the force that ties the Creator to the Created.

The Chain of Being concept was also used to support medieval notions of the divine right of kings whereby hierarchical social authority was bestowed by God on the monarch parallel to the spiritual authority bestowed by God on the church. This replication of macrocosmic order in microcosmic society thus implied divine sanction to social stratification, even the bondage or quasi slavery inherent in feudalism.

When thus applied to social order, such a theory can be taken to assert that society requires all degrees in order to be complete—from the lowest "bondman" (slave) to the monarch. Furthermore, instead of upholding affluence as a worthy goal, such a view denigrates aspirations as hubris, as tampering with "natural" social order. The monarch's authority was thus thought to be a divine sanction derived implicitly from natural order and explicitly from God.

Perhaps the single most important dictum to be derived from the concept of the Chain of Being during the medieval period was the idea that such a theory sanctions the rejection of all that is considered to be among the lower appetitive nature of the human being. In short, the theory upheld a rejection of the world, the flesh, and the devil by advocating a disdain for the things of this world and for the human faculties associated with worldly activities. When coupled with the monastic ideal of *contemptu mundi** (aspiring to become as spiritual as possible by disdaining all earthly and material considerations), the Chain of Being concept became integrated into Christian Neoplatonism as set forth in the works of St. Augustine.

The attitude expressed by this application of the chain analogy was quite appropriate to the wretched physical conditions of the medieval

---

* In 1140 the monk Bernard de Morlaix articulated his Neoplatonic disdain for the material world in *De Contemptu Mundi (Concerning Contempt for the World)*. In this work he maintains the commonly held view of medieval scholasticism that the only reality worth our concern is the world of forms ("ideas"), which we will encounter in the afterlife.

era after western Europe's emergence from the so-called "Dark Ages,"* during which the "Black Death" eliminated close to half the population. Likewise, the Manichean influence in the Neoplatonic works of St. Augustine described well a life that had little expectation of health, wealth, or felicity. Thus developed the monastic or ascetic ideal, the *vita contemplative*, a tacit recognition that the mutable nature of the world—both material reality itself and the immoral society with its perverted values— renders physical life an unfit environment for willful development of the soul. Consequently, the most responsible course recommended by many Christian writers of the period was to aspire to spiritual ascent by disdaining worldliness in all its forms.

RENAISSANCE VIEWS

The Renaissance employed the Chain of Being analogy in a different manner. With the rising influence of humanism, the Renaissance adopted a more classical view of the duality of the human condition. The human being is half reasonable and half passionate because each entity (or "link" on the chain) is a composite of the attributes it shares with the link that is immediately beneath it in rank and the link that is immediately above it. Furthermore, in the Renaissance application of this analogy, the human being is not at the top of the chain but in the middle—halfway between the lowest element and the Creator. The various orders or degrees of angelic hosts comprise the intervening links between man and God.

According to the Renaissance view, humankind thus possesses the appetites and senses common to the animal kingdom and the reason and spiritual sensibilities associated with the angelic hosts. From this Renaissance perspective, neither aspect of self is negative or evil. Both aspects of our composition are inherent and therefore "natural." To deny either of these dual aspects of the self is thus unnatural and unhealthy.

However, these two aspects of self are not equal in rank. Clearly the "higher" self is the rational or spiritual self. Therefore, in accordance

---

* This term is now rarely used because historians informed by archeological findings have discovered that the same tribes that conquered the Roman Empire and its colonies (for example, Britannia), were in many ways quite as learned and sophisticated in thought as those materially advanced Roman communities.

with natural order, the rational-spiritual self must ever hold sway over the "lower" physical-appetitive self. Conversely, the lower self must ever accede to the dictates of the higher self. An important accompaniment to this doctrine in Renaissance thought is the notion of "right reason" or the concept of "degree." Not only was it considered "unnatural" for the higher self not to rule over the lower self or for the lower self to aspire to overrule the higher self, it was also viewed as a violation of divine order and natural law.

Thus the classical dictum of *mens sana in corpore sano* ("a healthy mind in a healthy body") reemerged in the Renaissance as the concept of the ideal human, a well-rounded individual, the "Renaissance man," one who might be equally adept at riding a horse, at writing a sonnet, or, better still, at doing both simultaneously.

A subsidiary doctrine associated with the concept of the Chain of Being during the Renaissance was that hierarchical order persists throughout existence. The concept of degree is not confined to the more encompassing categories of creation but persists through every sub-category of creation. The diamond might be considered the highest expression of the mineral kingdom, the rose the most precious flower, the lion the king of the beasts.

We find examples of this Renaissance concept of cosmology in relation to social order incorporated in Milton's *Paradise Lost* when the poet, following the biblically based Pauline tradition of subordinating women to men in matters of governance, has Eve eat of the forbidden tree because she is told by the guileful Satan that it will offer her a rank or status equal with or even superior to that of Adam. Her sin is thus a type of hubris in which she tries to rise above her "natural" station on the Chain of Being. Adam's sin relates to the same violation of degree because he allows Eve, who is by nature beneath him in rank and capacity, to decide the course of action they should take, even though it is his inherent responsibility to make such decisions.

Therefore, though their sins are distinct in one sense, both sins relate to a violation of the Renaissance concept of degree or right order in relation to the Chain of Being. Consequently, as they discuss their transgressions, Eve states that she is guiltier than Adam because while

Adam sinned against God, she has sinned against both Adam and God: "Both have sinned, but thou / Against God only, I against God and thee. . . ." Adam responds that, in truth, all was his fault because he did not respond sufficiently to the responsibilities of his station:

> If prayers
> Could alter high decrees, I to that place
> Would speed before thee, and be louder heard,
> That on my head all might be visited,
> Thy frailly and infirmer sex forgiv'n,
> To me committed and by me exposed.[2]

We discover a more encompassing allusion to the Chain of Being in another English Renaissance work, the often-cited speech by the character Ulysses in Shakespeare's *Troilus and Cressida*. Bemoaning the lamentable state of the Greek forces, who are quarreling among themselves and who are in general disarray, Ulysses, who ultimately leads them to victory against Troy, makes a memorable speech on "degree." In the speech he asserts that once we tamper with that decorum which belongs to the concept of right order, whether in the world of nature or in the context of human social relationships, all order is undone because the integrity of the whole is affected negatively when the function of a single part is impaired:

> The specialty of rule hath been neglected:
> And look, how many Grecian tents do stand
> Hollow upon this plain, so many hollow factions.
> When that the general is not like the hive
> To whom the forager shall all repair,
> What honey is expected? Degree being vizarded,
> The unworthiest shows as fairly in the mask.
> The heavens themselves, the planets and this centre
> Observe degree, priority and place. . . .
> Take but degree away, untune that string,
> And, hark, what discord follows![3]

THE UNIQUE STATION OF THE HUMAN BEING ON THE CHAIN

The most obvious implication of the Chain of Being analogy in relation to Bahá'í thought is that the lower something is on the chain, the simpler it is in its expression of metaphysical reality. A rock, for example, might express tenacity, endurance, and reliability. Something higher on the chain within the mineral kingdom—a diamond, for example—might express brilliance, effulgence, loftiness, and a myriad other virtues because of its ability to refract light and thereby demonstrate the variety of colors and attributes that are otherwise concealed within the light.

This relativity of capacity shows the concept of degree or hierarchy within a category of existence as well as among different categories. Thus as we ascend from the lesser realm of the mineral into the kingdom of plants and animals, the complexity of composition increases and, accordingly, so does the ability of an entity to manifest ever more completely in metaphorical form the abstract or spiritual concepts of metaphysical reality. In short, we can assert the following axiom: The more complex a composition, the higher it is on the Chain of Being, and the higher on the Chain of Being a composition is, the greater the variety of virtues it can manifest and the more completely it can manifest them. A second crucial axiom expressed in this hierarchical relationship is that while there is the possibility of infinite perfectibility within state or category, one category or "kingdom" of existence cannot ascend to become another:

> When you reflect deeply, you discover that also outwardly the perfections of existence are also unlimited, for you cannot find a being so perfect that you cannot imagine a superior one. For example, you cannot see a ruby in the mineral kingdom, a rose in the vegetable kingdom, or a nightingale in the animal kingdom, without imagining that there might be better specimens. As the divine bounties are endless, so human perfections are endless. If it were possible to reach a limit of perfection, then one of the realities of the beings might reach the condition of being independent of

God, and the contingent might attain to the condition of the absolute. But for every being there is a point which it cannot overpass—that is to say, he who is in the condition of servitude, however far he may progress in gaining limitless perfections, will never reach the condition of Deity. It is the same with the other beings. A mineral, however far it may progress in the mineral kingdom, cannot gain the vegetable power. Also in a flower, however far it may progress in the vegetable kingdom, no power of the senses will appear. So this silver mineral cannot gain hearing or sight; it can only improve in its own condition and become a perfect mineral, but it cannot acquire the power of growth, or the power of sensation, or attain to life; it can only progress in its own condition.[4]

Accordingly, at the top of this chain in the material world is the human being, which is the most complex and complete expression of divine attributes in the created world. As we have noted, the human being is capable of manifesting all divine attributes. And yet we misunderstand this idea if we accept the materialist view that man is no more than the sum total of the system that is beneath humankind and of which the human body is both a product and an integral part.

Recalling a conversation he had with an Egyptian intellectual on this very issue, 'Abdu'l-Bahá hints at this distinction:

> I was once conversing with a famous philosopher of the materialistic school in Alexandria. He was strongly opinionated upon the point that man and the other kingdoms of existence are under the control of nature and that, after all, man is only a social animal, often very much of an animal. When he was discomfited in argument, he said impetuously, "I see no difference between myself and the donkey, and I am not willing to admit distinctions which I cannot perceive." 'Abdu'l-Bahá replied, "No, I consider you quite different and distinct; I call you a man and the donkey but an animal. I perceive that you are highly intelligent, whereas the donkey

is not. I know that you are well versed in philosophy, and I also know that the donkey is entirely deficient in it; therefore, I am not willing to accept your statement."[5]

The point of this anecdote is that in spite of the apparent agreement between the Bahá'í concept of the human being and the materialist view, there is an inescapable distinction. True, the human being is an integral part of materiality, and, insofar as his body is concerned, a material composition, the human being can incorporate and manifest all the powers and capacities of the entities beneath him on the Chain of Being.

Yet, as 'Abdu'l-Bahá notes in this same discussion, human beings possess a power that does not derive from nature, nor can it be found in nature. Furthermore, this power is greater than the sum total of these attributes derived from those entities beneath humankind on the Chain of Being:

> Man possesses certain virtues of which nature is deprived. He exercises volition; nature is without will. For instance, an exigency of the sun is the giving of light. It is controlled—it cannot do otherwise than radiate light—but it is not volitional. An exigency of the phenomenon of electricity is that it is revealed in sparks and flashes under certain conditions, but it cannot voluntarily furnish illumination. An exigency or property of water is humidity; it cannot separate itself from this property by its own will. Likewise, all the properties of nature are inherent and obedient, not volitional; therefore, it is philosophically predicated that nature is without volition and innate perception. In this statement and principle we agree with the materialists. But the question which presents food for reflection is this: How is it that man, who is a part of the universal plan, is possessed of certain qualities whereof nature is devoid? Is it conceivable that a drop should be imbued with qualities of which the ocean is completely deprived? The drop is a part; the ocean is the whole. Could there be a phenomenon of combustion or illumination which the great luminary the sun itself did not manifest? Is it possible for a stone to possess inherent properties of

which the aggregate mineral kingdom is lacking? For example, could the fingernail which is a part of human anatomy be endowed with cellular properties of which the brain is deprived?[6]

In this context, the Bahá'í writings constantly assert that while the human being is an organic part of this Great Chain of creation, it is also the "fruit" of this hierarchical relationship, not merely another link among the myriad other links. And here we are not speaking of whether or not an individual has chosen to fulfill his or her latent capacity. We are simply appreciating that the potential for manifesting spiritual attributes is summarized or completed in the creation of the human being. So it is that Bahá'u'lláh writes,

> Having created the world and all that liveth and moveth therein, He, through the direct operation of His unconstrained and sovereign Will, chose to confer upon man the unique distinction and capacity to know Him and to love Him—a capacity that must needs be regarded as the generating impulse and the primary purpose underlying the whole of creation. . . . Upon the inmost reality of each and every created thing He hath shed the light of one of His names, and made it a recipient of the glory of one of His attributes. Upon the reality of man, however, He hath focused the radiance of all of His names and attributes, and made it a mirror of His own Self. Alone of all created things man hath been singled out for so great a favor, so enduring a bounty.[7]

In another place He writes,

> How resplendent the luminaries of knowledge that shine in an atom, and how vast the oceans of wisdom that surge within a drop! To a supreme degree is this true of man, who, among all created things, hath been invested with the robe of such gifts, and hath been singled out for the glory of such distinction. For in him are potentially revealed all the attributes and names of God to a degree that no

other created being hath excelled or surpassed. All these names and attributes are applicable to him. Even as He hath said: "Man is My mystery, and I am his mystery."[8]

THE MANIFESTATION IN RELATION TO THE CHAIN OF BEING

While all attributes are "potentially" revealed in the human being, the Manifestation, whom Bahá'u'lláh sometimes describes as the "perfect man," is another level of creation—ontologically another Being and a higher link in the chain. In the Manifestation all the attributes of God are not *potentially* manifested; they *are* manifested. What is more, they are manifested *perfectly* in a state of being that an "ordinary" human being is incapable of attaining, whether in this world or in the next. 'Abdu'l-Bahá makes the following statements on this point:

> For example, Peter cannot become Christ. All that he can do is, in the condition of servitude, to attain endless perfections; for every existing reality is capable of making progress.[9]

> Lastly the perfect man, the Prophet, is one who is transfigured, one who has the purity and clearness of a perfect mirror—one who reflects the Sun of Truth. Of such a one—of such a Prophet and Messenger—we can say that the Light of Divinity with the heavenly Perfections dwells in him.[10]

> To man is given the special gift of the intellect by which he is able to receive a larger share of the light Divine. The Perfect Man is as a polished mirror reflecting the Sun of Truth, manifesting the attributes of God.
> The Lord Christ said, "He that hath seen Me hath seen the Father"—God manifested in man.[11]

Bahá'u'lláh makes this concept emphatically clear in the Súriy-i-Haykal (Súrih of the Temple) with the following poetic elucidation of the station of the Prophet in relation to manifesting completely and perfectly the attributes of God: "Naught is seen in My temple but the Temple of God, and in My beauty but His Beauty, and in My being but His Being, and in My self but His Self, and in My movement but His Movement, and in My acquiescence but His Acquiescence, and in My pen but His Pen, the Mighty, the All-Praised. There hath not been in My soul but the Truth, and in Myself naught could be seen but God."[12]

Therefore, when Bahá'u'lláh states that the Manifestation is a "perfect man," or when we say that the Prophet is not an *ordinary* human being, we are not talking about a qualification within the category of human existence—*ordinary* as opposed to *extraordinary*. We are alluding to two distinct categories of existence: the ordinary human being (humankind) who is the "fruit" of creation or the "student" in the classroom that is the created world, and the "perfect human being" (the Manifestation) who is the Teacher of humankind and the Intermediary between the Creator and the created. The Manifestation exists in a different ontological category of existence on the Chain of Being.

THE CHAIN OF BEING AND THE ASCENT OF HUMANKIND

One of the most useful discussions of the Chain of Being in relation to the Bahá'í concept of creation is found in a well-known passage by 'Abdu'l-Bahá about the ascent of humankind. In this discussion—and in many similar discussions—'Abdu'l-Bahá alludes to the fact that any being contains the attributes of those beings that are ontologically its equal or ontologically beneath it. Therefore, by evolving through various physical stages, appearances, or degrees of existence, the human species (though ever ontologically human) gradually acquired all the attributes of those beings beneath it in creation:

In the world of existence man has traversed successive degrees until he has attained the human kingdom. In each degree of his progression he has developed capacity for advancement to the next station and condition. While in the kingdom of the mineral he was attaining the capacity for promotion into the degree of the vegetable. In the kingdom of the vegetable he underwent preparation for the world of the animal, and from thence he has come onward to the human degree, or kingdom. Throughout this journey of progression he has ever and always been potentially man.[13]

'Abdu'l-Bahá succinctly describes the Bahá'í view of human evolution as a process of gradual development and progress, but, as we noted in chapter 6, this transformation is not a mutation from one species to another. Evolution occurs solely within a species or state, even though these stages of transformation may be radically different in appearance.

ALL THINGS GREAT AND SMALL
INFORM OUR KNOWLEDGE OF REALITY

We now have a decent overview of what the Creator creates according to the logic implicit and explicit in the Bahá'í discussion of the concept of the Chain of Being. We have not yet touched upon how, within this hierarchical chain, there are vast possibilities derived from the additive properties of physical reality. That is, we know that the human being is the loftiest expression of creation insofar as complexity is concerned. It is a being capable of willful acquisition of knowledge of itself, and of the similitude between itself and its Creator, and of the common character-istics among all the diverse ingredients in the created universe. We have not yet explored how this same Chain of Being is also capable of being added together or reduced and divided so as to produce what have come to be thought of as entire worlds unto themselves: the reality of particles and the laws and relationships governing them, and the astronomical reality of the macrocosm in which particles added together in vast proportions become planets, solar systems, and galaxies.

Consequently, if we are to understand adequately how the bridge between spiritual and physical reality is accomplished, we need to investigate how a journey in either direction will eventually lead us to important information about the parallel nature between the spiritual and physical expressions of reality. For what we will discover as we probe in more detail the nature of what the Creator has created is that the further we proceed in either direction (towards the tiny world of particle physics or towards the vast world of astrophysics) the more physical reality begins to assume some of the fundamental properties of spiritual reality itself.

This is only as it should be if we take at face value the passage by 'Abdu'l-Bahá that states, the "spiritual world is like unto the phenomenal world. They are the exact counterpart of each other. Whatever objects appear in this world of existence are the outer pictures of the world of heaven."[14]

- 8 -

How Small Is That Quark?

Therefore, every primordial atom of these atoms, singly and indivisible, has had its coursings throughout all the sentient creation, going constantly into the aggregation of the various elements. Hence do you have the conservation of energy and the infinity of phenomena, the indestructibility of phenomena, changeless and immutable, because life cannot suffer annihilation but only change.

— 'Abdu'l-Bahá, *Foundations of World Unity*

Having established a foundational understanding of when, why, how, and what the Creator creates, we are now ready to approach the borders of physical reality to see if we can discover if there is a point at which the dual expressions of reality intersect, merge, or at least emulate each other more specifically than in an analogical or metaphorical way. For while we have already alluded to the Manifestations of God as divine Intermediaries between the two aspects of reality and as the essential means by which human civilization is guided and energized, we have yet to discuss in detail beyond the general concept of the Chain of Being how precisely this complex classroom that is physical reality corresponds to the spiritual realm which, according to Bahá'í thought, the physical world was created to express in concrete terms.

WHAT THE NATURE OF THE MICROCOSM TEACHES US

The word *latafah*, Arabic for "refinement," is employed frequently by Bahá'u'lláh in the Kitáb-i-Aqdas (Most Holy Book). While the word has

125

various connotations, it always retains the same essential application: It designates a process whereby something can become an ever more eloquent expression of divine attributes, whether this eloquence is manifest in a stone, a plant, an animal, a human being, a social structure, or the organization of the universe itself.

Bahá'u'lláh thus uses the term *refinement* in the Kitáb-i-Aqdas in reference to the personal process of paying constant attention to every aspect of our physical lives that we may thereby exemplify divine virtue ever more completely, whether in our speech, our comportment, or our relations with other human beings.

In this chapter, however, we are concerned with examining refinement as it pertains to ever more discrete expressions of physical reality so that we may determine if there is some final building block of reality. If there is, we might benefit from understanding what spiritual message that particle contains. If there is not, then possibly we can already guess at least one thought the world of smallness is telling us: that every aspect of our quest for knowledge of creation will remain an eternal and endless journey.

The basis for this part of our study is the observation with which we ended the previous chapter—that physical reality is the visible outer expression or counterpart of the unseen metaphysical or spiritual expression of reality. Therefore, if physical reality emulates spiritual reality in terms of refinement—that is, as a metaphorical expression of this spiritual attribute—then it would seem logical to conclude that there can be no final point at which physical reality is completely refined. For even as the Chain of Being is a metaphorical expression of the relationships among created beings, so physical refinement is essentially a metaphorical expression of various categories of spiritual refinement.

For example, we can speak of refinement as applied to wheat. To refine wheat, we separate the wheat from the chaff. We then grind the grains of wheat into flour. We can then further refine flour by sifting and resifting it. The result is a substance ever more aerated, delicate, ephemeral, and subtle. This process or concept of refinement as a literal physical action has further implications that help us appreciate how, at the borders of physical reality, the metaphorical classroom becomes so imitative of its metaphysical counterpart that we may be unable at present to discern important distinctions.

REFINEMENT IN THE MICROCOSM

We are aware of those material objects that are easily perceptible, but we are also aware that there is a world of refined particles quite beyond anything we can observe or presently study. 'Abdu'l-Bahá notes in the Lawḥ-i-Aflák (Tablet of the Universe) that the more refined matter becomes, the more closely it begins to resemble the properties of spiritual reality—a noncomposite reality.[1] Therefore let us review an outline of the history of particle physics, especially as it progressed during the last hundred and fifty years, because it has been during this time (perhaps not coincidental with the appearance of Bahá'u'lláh and the promulgation of His teachings and ideas) that the field has assumed vital importance regarding the relationship between physical and spiritual reality.

A BRIEF OUTLINE OF THE HISTORY OF PARTICLE PHYSICS

For about two thousand years before the emergence of "new physics," it was assumed that all material entities are composed of some form of atomic substance, some small, hard, primary building block. One of the first thinkers to conceive of an atomic theory was Leucippus of Miletus— though his student Democritus coined the term "atom"* around the middle of the fifth century B.C. Material change, according to Democritus, is simply a process of rearranging these particles.

Further discourses on atomic theory were put forth by Epicurus in the third century B.C. and by Lucretius in the first century B.C. But the Greek, Roman, and medieval scholars were not really much interested in studying particulate nature. Their primary concern took them in the opposite direction: How big is big? How is the universe structured? They were principally concerned with devising theories that could support various philosophical and religious views. Indeed the schism between science and religion that was confirmed around the fourteenth and fifteenth

---

* *Atomos* in Greek means "indivisible."

centuries derived largely from these early attempts to describe material reality, as opposed to Platonic thought, which, as some had come to interpret it, seemed to assert that material reality is but an illusion, a shadowy expression of the metaphysical realm of ideas and forms.

Consequently, it became the opinion of most Catholic theologians that materialist concepts such as Democritus' atomic theory were blasphemous because they implied material reality is autonomous and valuable in its own right, not an illusory shadow world or a reflection of spiritual reality. But with the advent of the nineteenth century, some progress began to be made with interest in and theories about the nature of matter.

English meteorologist and chemist John Dalton suggested that each chemical might have its own unique kind of atom. By the close of the nineteenth century, there were theoretical suggestions that atoms themselves might have constituent parts—or subatomic particles. In 1897 Cambridge physics professor J. J. Thomson discovered the electron, and by 1911 Ernest Rutherford accurately described the fundamental structure of an atom. He explained that most of the mass of an atom is in the center, which we now call the nucleus. He demonstrated that the nucleus is composed of a small dense portion of protons (which have a positive electrical charge) and of neutrons (which have no electrical charge).

Most important from a Bahá'í perspective, Rutherford postulated the theory that the structure of the atom parallels the structure of the solar system: The negatively charged electrons orbit the positively charged nucleus just as planets orbit our sun. This observation parallels an observation by 'Abdu'l-Bahá when he explains that the similitude between the structure and function of an atom and the solar system is not coincidental. He observes that the different levels of material reality are parallel in structure because all material reality is subject to the same laws and forces:

Nature is subjected to an absolute organization, to determined laws, to a complete order and a finished design, from which it will never depart—to such a degree, indeed, that if you look carefully and with keen sight, from the smallest invisible atom up to such large bodies of the world of existence as the globe of the sun or the other great stars and luminous spheres, whether you regard their arrangement, their composition, their form or their movement, you will find that all are in the highest degree of organization and are under one law from which they will never depart.[2]

The concept of quantum physics followed shortly after Rutherford's theory when in 1913 Danish physicist Niels Bohr incorporated the idea of *quanta,* or packets of energy (photons). This idea had been developed a few years earlier by the German theoretical physicist Max Planck.

This important theory helped explain a number of phenomena related to energy and subatomic particles. It also established the basis for much that was to follow in the study of subatomic particles and the attempt to discover what might be the most finite building block in material reality!

PLEASE PASS THE AETHER

The fact is that an atom consists mostly of space. The nucleus is one hundred-trillionth (1/100,000,000,000,000) the size of the atom itself, and yet the smallest nucleus is massive compared to the size of an electron. The lightest nucleus—that of the hydrogen atom—is 1,836 times larger than an electron. Consequently the electron is virtually weightless and massless. But the study of the microcosm hardly stops here!

The constituent parts of the nucleus (the protons and neutrons, collectively referred to as nucleons) we now know to be composite themselves. They consist of quarks, which themselves have now been divided into the quark, the anti-quark, and the gluon. In short, in the exponentially advancing field of particle physics, there is no need to try to keep track of what is presently considered to be the most discrete building block of matter, nor is it particularly important that we remember their innovative names, let alone attempt to understand more recent theories about the action and interaction of subatomic particles. Indeed, we will skip over hadrons, mesons, gluons, the colors of quarks, and quantum chromodynamics. Instead we will consider how such study has anything at all to do with refinement as a spiritual process. To accomplish this task, we will backtrack into an ancient theory that, Leon Lederman notes, is mentioned by Plato, affirmed by Descartes, alluded to by Newton, and reinvented by the Scottish physicist James Clerk Maxwell. It also happens to be mentioned repeatedly in the writings of 'Abdu'l-Bahá. It is the theory of the "aether."

Leon Lederman writes, "One of the most disturbing ramifications of Newton's theory is the problem of action at a distance. The earth pulls on an apple. It falls to the ground. The sun pulls on the planets; they orbit elliptically. How? How can two bodies, with nothing but space between them, transmit force to each other? One popular model of the time hypothesized an ether, some invisible and insubstantial medium pervading all space, through which object *A* could make contact with object *B*."[3]

As Lederman further observes, the theory of aether, long discarded as an arcane theory of classical physics, is now making a huge comeback: "As we shall see, the aether idea was seized upon by James Clerk Maxwell to carry his electromagnetic waves. However, Einstein offered an alternative hypothesis in 1905—that no support medium was necessary to explain electromagnetic phenomena (light). But like Pauline's, aether's perils come and go, and today we believe that some new version of aether (really the void of Democritus and Anaximander) is the hiding place of the God Particle."[4]

Lederman is suggesting we should consider that the atomic theory as discussed by Democritus required the existence of a void in order for atoms to move about so that material objects could assemble and disassemble. The French mathematician-scientist-philosopher René Descartes rejected the idea of a void and postulated that material reality, by definition, must be full of material. In other words, the totality of material reality must be composite. Likewise, he affirmed, there must be a medium through which all activity can be conveyed.

LET THERE BE A LITTLE LIGHT, PLEASE!

A *void* and a *vacuum* are not the same thing. A vacuum requires an area from which air has been removed, whereas the term *void* implies that absolutely every created or existent entity has been removed from some physical space. In view of this problem, the study that shed most light on the issue of aether, at least for the remainder of the nineteenth century, was, ironically, the study of light itself, particularly the study of light as waves propagated through electromagnetic fields.

For this study we are indebted to a series of pioneers: the Dutch mathematician, astronomer, and physicist Christiaan Huygens and his *Treatise on Light* (1690), which introduced the idea of aether as a medium through which light could be propagated; the English physicist and chemist Michael Faraday, who around 1832 studied Newton's law of action at a distance (magnetic attraction) and introduced the concept of a "field" through which this attraction could operate over time; and James Clerk Maxwell, who during the years 1860–65 transformed Faraday's theories into mathematical formulae. He also established that electromagnetic waves move through space at the same velocity as the speed of light.

Capping off such rapid advances in classical theory regarding what once had been a realm of mystery was the renowned Michelson-Morely light experiment. The experiment was created to determine the speed of the earth in relation to the luminiferous aether, the hypothetical substance or medium through which waves of light were thought to propagate. The presumption was that since the earth is spinning through this "substance," the speed of a beam of light would be affected (impeded or assisted) according to whether the beam was traveling with this aether flow or against it—just as the speed of a boat would be affected by the flow of a river in which the boat is traveling and the direction of the river's current. Thus, at its equator, the earth would be spinning through the aether about 25,000 miles per hour.

The experiment itself was ingeniously designed. It consisted of splitting a single beam of light into two beams traveling perpendicular to each other. This was done by aiming a beam of light from west to east at a half-transparent mirror, thus producing two beams. One beam then continued east, reflected off a mirror, returned to another centrally located mirror, whereupon it took a ninety-degree angle to the left (south) where it was received by a sensor. The second beam took a ninety-degree left turn (north), reflected off a fixed mirror, then proceeded due south until it also was received by the same sensor. In short, one beam went parallel with the rotation of the earth (going upstream and back downstream before heading "south" to the sensor), while the second beam went "north" across the aether flow, then back "south" across the aether flow to the sensor.

One point well worth noting is that the sensor itself was ingenious, the Michelson "interferometer." This instrument was capable of detecting which beam registered first and what the difference in time would be between the journeys through the aether. But to the disappointment of the observers, the experiment failed—or at least it *seemed* to fail. There was no difference in the speed at which the two beams traveled.

This result seemed to indicate one of two possible findings: Either the resistance encountered by the beam traversing the stream produced the exact same result as the initial resistance of the beam going first against the aether wind and then returning with its additive speed, or else the aether wind simply did not exist.

Thus, for some scientists the experiment was an incredible success. It proved, or seemed to them to prove, that (1) there is no such thing as background matter or an aether field and (2) the speed of light is constant regardless of the inertial frame of reference from which it is viewed— whether one is moving toward a light beam or away from it. So it was that in 1905 Einstein posited his "special theory of relativity"—that light travels at a constant speed regardless of the inertial frame of reference from which it is viewed.

Let There Be Aether after All!

While such inferences quickly advanced "new science" and quantum physics, at least one other conclusion regarding aether was clearly possible: The aether, like the photon and the neutrino, is so refined as to possess no "classically" measurable properties. Therefore, aether poses no resistance to photons of light. Furthermore, even though the experiment has since been repeated many times, always yielding the same result, no irreducible particle has been discovered.

Consequently, physicists such as James Rees have now reintroduced theories of aether or "background matter." Rees writes, "In loose analogy to how an invisible ocean of air covers the surface of the Earth, an invisible background ocean of massless matter was deduced to permeate the universe. The background ocean particles are invisible because they have no energy, neither rest-mass energy nor momentum energy." When Max Planck theorized in opposition to Maxwell's classical theory of wavelengths that radiation was emitted in discrete bundles, or *packets* of energy (*quanta*), new physics and quantum mechanics seemed to refute all that Sir Isaac Newton had established. But there still remained the enigma that light could be accurately described by, and performed in accordance with, both the quantum theory of the new physics and the wave theory of classical physics.[5]

The incredible advances in contemporary physics have proceeded from these beginnings. Lederman demonstrates the chain of causality leading us to where we stand today—still trying to discover that irreducible building block of creation, the "God particle," still trying to reconcile various aspects of quantum mechanics with those parts of classical physics that survive, and still trying to reconcile the parts of Einstein's theory of relativity that just do not seem to jibe with quantum mechanics.

Suffice it here to say that the theory of aether—or at least a theory very much like it—is once again alive and healthy. According to Lederman, the "Higgs boson particle" leads the way to understanding the absence of nothingness in the universe. He writes, "We can summarize the little we know: at least some of the particles that represent the Higgs aether must have zero spin, must be intimately and mysteriously connected to mass, and must manifest themselves at temperatures equivalent to the energy of less than 1 TeV."[6] In other words, it is conceivable that something so refined (literally) that it contains none of the detectable properties usually associated with matter could exist in a so-called vacuum. It is even conceivable that all space—because it is part of material reality—must be occupied by something because it is impossible for utter nothingness to exist in the realm of material reality.

Particle Physics and the Bahá'í Writings

These recent conclusions about the likelihood of the existence of an aether demonstrate that the views of Bahá'u'lláh and 'Abdu'l-Bahá about physics and science in general should not be discounted because of the historical context in which they lived and wrote. True, they were Persian prisoners living under strict confinement without access to scholars or scholarly texts, yet by whatever means, it is clear they were well aware of the latest scientific discoveries of the day. Furthermore, the more their observations about society, evolution, physics, or ethics are seen to be correct, the more difficult it will become for anyone casually to dismiss their ideas as arcane or misinformed simply because they had no access to Western scholarship. They may not have read about quantum mechanics and new physics, but, according to Bahá'í belief, both 'Abdu'l-Bahá and Bahá'u'lláh had direct access to knowledge about reality.

For example, the following statement about the existence of the aether was made by 'Abdu'l-Bahá around 1905—exactly the time Einstein was publishing his special theory of relativity based in part on his belief in the absence of aether. 'Abdu'l-Bahá stated, "If we wish to deny everything that is not sensible, then we must deny the realities which unquestionably exist. For example, ethereal matter is not sensible, though it has an undoubted existence. The power of attraction is not sensible, though it certainly exists. From what do we affirm these existences? From their signs. Thus this light is the vibration of that ethereal matter, and from this vibration we infer the existence of ether."[7] In 1921, in a tablet to the famous Swiss scholar Auguste Forel, 'Abdu'l-Bahá made the following observation regarding the inferential logic that must prove the existence of God, just as one infers in science the existence of an aether even though one may be incapable of detecting its properties:

Thus man cannot grasp the Essence of Divinity, but can, by his reasoning power, by observation, by his intuitive faculties and the revealing power of his faith, believe in God, discover the bounties of His Grace. He becometh certain that though the Divine Essence is unseen of the eye, and the existence of the Deity is intangible, yet conclusive spiritual proofs assert the existence of that unseen Reality. The Divine Essence as it is in itself is however beyond all description. For instance, the nature of ether is unknown, but that it existeth is certain by the effects it produceth, heat, light and electricity being the waves thereof. By these waves the existence of ether is thus proven.[8]

'Abdu'l-Bahá further notes that if every cause has to be greater than the effect it produces, then there must be a being greater than human beings to have produced the effect of the existence of such beings: "For instance, we observe that the existence of beings is conditioned upon the coming together of various elements and their non-existence upon the decomposition of their constituent elements. For decomposition causeth the dissociation of the various elements. Thus, as we observe the coming together of elements giveth rise to the existence of beings, and knowing that beings are infinite, they being the effect, how can the Cause be finite?"[9]

In 1923 J. E. Esslemont wrote in *Bahá'u'lláh and the New Era* that nature as an expression of divine reality will ever remain beyond the reach of any complete comprehension or description by science:

> In each drop of water are hidden oceans of meaning, and in each mote is concealed a whole universe of significances, reaching far beyond the ken of the most learned scientist. The chemist and physicist pursuing their researches into the nature of matter have passed from masses to molecules, from molecules to atoms, from atoms to electrons and ether, but at every step the difficulties of the research increase till the most profound intellect can penetrate no farther, and can but bow in silent awe before the unknown Infinite which remains ever shrouded in inscrutable mystery.[10]

One could argue that Esslemont was writing before 1972 when scientists assembled the particle accelerator at Fermilab.* But neither Fermilab nor any future developments will render Esslemont's observation any less valid if, indeed, material reality becomes so microcosmic that it descends infinitely into refinement.

---

* Fermi National Accelerator Physics Laboratory, a center for research in high-energy physics located in Batavia, Illinois.

The aether may not be a pervasive field of particles all the same size or a sea of matter one degree more refined than photons. Aether could be an array of endlessly refined divisions of materiality beyond what we can as yet perceive or describe. In the Lawḥ-i-Aflak (Tablet of the Universe), 'Abdu'l-Bahá makes a number of statements on the nature of material reality that help us appreciate the boundless future of the study of physics.

Regarding the question of a void, he observes that "these great orbits and circuits [of celestial bodies] fall within subtle, fluid, clear, liquid, undulating and vibrating bodies, and that the heavens are a restrained wave because a void is impossible and inconceivable." He goes on to note that whether we ascend to ever more encompassing macroscopic compositions or descend to ever more minuscule particles, we discover essentially the same laws and governing principles of composition at work: "All that may be said is that the material bodies of the ethereal regions differ in respect of some of the substances and elements from which they are constituted, the quantities and proportions of these that go into their composition, the peculiar characteristics causing the difference in the outward effects of these bodies, and the properties that emanate from them in rich abundance."[11]

'Abdu'l-Bahá affirms that particulate matter is ultimately reducible to a stage of refinement where it has no properties of weight or mass:

The celestial bodies that surround the material bodies also differ one from another in respect of subtlety, fluidity, and weight. It cannot be otherwise for a void is impossible.

The existence of a container implies the existence of something contained; what is contained can hardly be other than a body, but the bodies of the celestial spheres are in the utmost degree of subtlety, lightness and fluidity as bodies may be of diverse kinds: solid like rocks, malleable like metals and minerals, fluid like water and air. Lighter still they may be of a kind that ascends heavenwards, such as that which is used in dirigibles; and lighter than all of these are fire, electricity and lightening. All of these are bodies in reality, but some of them are weightless.[12]

In sum, there is no void in the material universe, and every created entity is composite and exists in a "sea" of materiality more refined than itself. Were it otherwise, chaos would ensue. If a photon had nonzero rest mass, then according to Einstein's theory of relativity (which says that mass and energy are interconvertible), its mass would approach infinity as the photon approached the speed of light, and it would thereby instantly destroy whatever it enlightened.

We thus conclude that as we approach infinity in refinement of particles, the microcosm increasingly emulates the properties of spiritual reality, a reality in which nothing is composite. And yet the gap between these expressions of reality remains: Materiality can become ever more refined without ever changing state and becoming spiritual, because within the state or condition of being material is the possibility of infinite refinement. By analogy, a human soul is capable of becoming ever more refined and spiritual in character without transforming into another essence, without ever transcending its nature as a human soul. Thus, because that which is material can mimic ever more accurately the properties of spirituality without ever becoming "metaphysical," our study of this law of composition in the microcosm will teach us ever more completely the nature of reality as a whole.

- 9 -

How Big Was That Bang?

The fact that philosophers and sages have posited limits and restrictions for such matters is to be explained by the limitations of people's minds and perceptions and the blindness of the followers of allusions, whose natures and intellects have been rendered dull and inanimate by the interposition of many veils.

—'Abdu'l-Bahá, *Tablet of the Universe*

If every physical entity "swims about" in a sea of materiality more refined than itself, then it follows that nothing in physical reality can exist in a final state of refinement. Conversely, it would seem to follow just as clearly that there is no point beyond which systems cannot be increasingly added together with other systems—unless we run out of "stuff" to add or unless the universe is finite.

Both of these conclusions seem to be a logical consequence of several axioms we have already established or asserted. For example, at the outset of our discussion we interpreted the tradition of the Hidden Treasure as affirming that producing human beings has always been the goal of the Creator in order that He might be known. It is only logical to conclude, therefore, that if the Creator is eternal, then the process of producing humans has always existed—unless this desire to be known was a sudden impulse. We have also noted that there is no point at which all the infinite attributes of the Hidden Treasure are comprehended, nor even a point where all the infinite levels of meaning of a single attribute are completely understood. Finally, given the nature of the Creator as portrayed by the

Manifestations, we cannot conceive of a point at which He would become stretched to the limits of His capacity to love, nor can we conceive of a point at which He would grow weary of creating human beings to know Him.

These conclusions, however, derive from the assumption that our observations about the tradition of the Hidden Treasure are reasonable, well-founded, and empirically grounded. But until we test this hypothesis against an equally rigorous study of the physical world, however minuscule or massive any given expression of physical reality might appear, our theory remains mostly unconfirmed. What happens as we venture out into the vastness of the macrocosm and the apparent limitlessness of space to lend support to our assertions thus far?

As we approach what are for us presently the borders of reality in the macrocosm—recent speculation that we have caught sight of the beginning of the "big bang"—we may be surprised to find that borders simply do not exist. Therefore let us explore the boundaries of reality as they are presently described by astronomers and cosmologists to see if we can discover how the Bahá'í writings respond to the assertion that the universe is a finite system. In doing so we are likely to discover—as with our journey in the previous chapter into worlds of smallness—that we increasingly approach the approximation of spiritual reality as we venture into the ever more encompassing systems of the universe.

THE IMPORTANCE OF STUDYING THE MACROCOSM

We have already noted that creation did not start with the inception of this particular planet. Furthermore, we should not be so naive as to assume that unity of this planet is the largest possible expression of social structure that could be devised. In creative works of science fiction, we commonly accept imagined social systems consisting of interplanetary, galactic, or even intergalactic federations as more encompassing forms of social unity.

Such visions of possible future advancement may help to explain why some might have trouble accepting the much-heralded theory of the big bang—a point of origin in time and space for our universe, and, implicitly, for a finite universe at that.

From the beginning of the twentieth century forward, there was a complete overhaul in the concept of the macrocosm—the study of the cosmos or "cosmology." Much of this advancement went hand in hand with similar advances we noted in our study of the microcosm and "new physics." As we review some of the discoveries that advanced the fields of cosmology and astrophysics, we will come to appreciate how these evolving sciences have radically altered our view of "refinement" in terms of an ever more complex universe, which, like the microcosm, is also capable of mimicking the properties of spiritual reality.

MODERN PROBLEMS WITH CLASSICAL PHYSICS

The big-bang theory of the evolution of the universe was conceived in the 1940s, became somewhat confirmed in the 1960s, and became more entrenched in the late 1980s and early 1990s. But it was sometime earlier that the classical Newtonian model of a mechanical universe began falling prey to new discoveries, new instruments, and new theories.

In 1864 James Clerk Maxwell (1831–79) theorized that light waves are actually electromagnetic waves that can be propagated in a vacuum, as opposed to waves of light propagated through aether as believed at the time. Maxwell also proved that electromagnetic waves proceed at the speed of light, some 186,282 miles per second. The Michelson-Morely experiment (1887) further vindicated this theory by demonstrating that the aether has no effect on the speed of light and, ostensibly, that the aether field does not exist.

Equally important was the emerging idea that the speed of light is constant for all observers. Einstein theorized the speed of light could be neither accelerated nor surpassed, regardless of the inertial frame of reference. The speed of light thus became for him the only reliable frame of reference from which to study the universe. Physicist David Bohm writes,

> Now, a basic feature of the classical order and measure of Galileo and Newton is that one can in principle catch up with and overtake any form of motion, as long as the speed is finite. However, as has been indicated here, it leads to absurdities to suppose that we can catch up with and overtake light. . . .

141

In Einstein's case, one sees that the speed of light is not a possible speed for an object. Rather, it is like a horizon that cannot be reached. Even though we seem to move toward the horizon, we never get any closer. As we move toward a light ray, we never get closer to its speed. Its speed always remains the same, *c*, relative to us.[1]

Einstein's Special Theory of Relativity, presented in his 1905 publication "On the Electrodynamics of Moving Bodies," followed both Maxwell's observations and the Michelson-Morely experiment and concluded that the speed of light is a constant in all frames of reference.

This theory meant that Newton's model of the universe would have to be modified because there could be no such thing as a "natural rest-frame" in the universe—an inherently stable or motionless (objective) perspective from which to study the universe. Unlike sound waves, which travel at increased or decreased speeds depending on the movement of the hearer relative to the sound source, the speed of light is always constant relative to the observer, regardless of whether the observer is moving toward or away from the light source.

This fact becomes extremely important when we start speaking of the cosmos in terms of "light years" (the distance that light could travel in the course of a year) because this measurement becomes a source of calculating both time and distance—each is relative to the other. This relationship also implies an important axiom about physical reality and our experience in it: No matter how quickly something is capable of transpiring in the physical universe, gradualness (time and timeliness) is still required for progress to take place. When we are striving for personal or collective transformation, this principle is essential to consider.

A CLOSED UNIVERSE

Perhaps the greatest blow to Newton's model of the universe was the theory proposed by Einstein of a closed universe, of space being curved back on itself such that it contains no boundaries but is not infinite. This model was achieved by postulating a four-dimensional universe (time being the fourth dimension) instead of Newton's Euclidean three-dimensional universe.

By this means Einstein replaced Newton's law of gravity as the organizing force in the universe with his general theory of relativity in 1916. Einstein had already demonstrated the relationship between energy, mass, and velocity ($E = MC^2$) in his Special Theory of Relativity in 1905. According to this latter theory, the mass of an entity increases as it approaches the speed of light. Thus where Newton's theory assumed that the gravitational attraction of the sun on its planets and the planets on their moons was instantaneous—a constant extant force—Einstein presumed that interactions among masses could not proceed faster than the speed of light.

According to the General Theory of Relativity, there is no such thing as instantaneous action at a distance (the mutual attraction of one mass to another—that is, gravity). Einstein proposed instead that the curvature of space creates the illusion that objects are attracted to each other. Of course, scientists can hardly pit one theory against the other within the context of our own solar system because of the relatively short distances between the sun and the planets. But this theory assumed tremendous value in particle physics and later in astrophysics.

The theory of a closed universe seemed to be confirmed for Einstein in 1919 when light coming from stars was photographed during a solar eclipse. The observation was made that the light "was bent as it passed through the curved space near the sun, making the stars appear to be in a different location in the sky." Where Newton's universe allowed for curved beams of light (since light was deemed to be waves passing through the aether and was thus subject to gravitational attraction), "Einstein declared that light beams are actually *straight* lines, and that space itself is curved." Therefore the "gridlines of Einstein's four-dimensional map [of the universe] are light beams," the one reliable constant in a system composed of otherwise fluctuating variables.[2]

AN EXPANDING UNIVERSE

Newton's three-dimensional infinite universe seemed to be eclipsed. His laws of gravity had been usurped by the general theory of relativity. The aether had vanished. Before the twentieth century was half over, quantum mechanics would soon proceed from theoretical mind experiments to the construction of particle accelerators and nuclear fission. But a good many surprises were in store for scholars in the evolving fields of astrophysics and cosmology, surprises that would call into question some of the certitude with which so many had accepted this revised (and presumed final) vision of the cosmos. To begin with, Newton assumed that the planetary system he observed was stable and changeless. Einstein believed that nothing in the universe was static. The theory thus emerged that the entire universe might be either expanding or contracting, composing or decomposing, if by definition it could not be stationary.

The confluence of a sequence of discoveries proved Einstein's theory correct. An important part of the sequence of this proof began earlier with a discovery by Austrian physicist Christian Doppler in 1842. Employing a spectroscope to examine spiral nebulae, Doppler discovered that the light emitted from these nebulae shifted towards the red end of the spectrum—the light assumed a lower frequency.

If these nebulae were at a constant distance, the spectral lines would remain constant. If the nebulae were approaching the observer, the light would shift towards the blue end of the spectrum—it would become higher in frequency. This "Doppler effect," which is most familiar to us as it applies to sound (the way the sound of an approaching or receding noise from a truck on the highway assumes different frequencies when it passes us by) became known as the "redshift" when applied to the nebulae.

Then in the early 1920s while working at the Mount Wilson Observatory in California, Edwin Hubble reached an astounding conclusion: He calculated that some of the "nebulae" that Doppler had examined were actually distant galaxies outside our own Milky Way Galaxy. This discovery totally revised and expanded existing cosmological theory, just as the Copernican theory had forced scientists in the sixteenth century to realize that the planets in our solar system do not revolve around our planet.

Similarly, scientists realized that the universe did not focus on our own Milky Way, that there are many galaxies. What was more important insofar as classical physics is concerned was Hubble's discovery in 1927 that the red shifts in the light from these galaxies indicated that they were receding rapidly from our own galaxy. These same findings indicated that the universe itself is expanding: The more distant the galaxy, the more rapidly it was speeding away from us.

But Hubble's observation about the relation of speed to distance, which became known as Hubble's constant, did not necessarily negate Newtonian laws of gravity in favor of Einstein's closed universe. After all, this same observation could be seen as confirming Newtonian physics, since the force of gravity is proportional to the mass of an object and its distance from that to which it is attracted. Therefore, as the galaxies achieved greater distance from each other, they would be released from the attraction or pull of those other galaxies in the same way that a space ship must acquire "escape velocity" to break free of the earth's gravitational pull before it can achieve great acceleration.

Of course, there is no inertial frame of reference from which we can assess this motion; therefore, we cannot become assured that these galaxies are only breaking free of attraction to the Milky Way Galaxy. They might be breaking free from attraction to a conglomerate of galaxies, or they may be attracted to something else, some other galaxies greater than our own which we cannot yet detect.

A GENESIS AFTER ALL

The impact on the Newtonian model of the universe was not the primary concern of astrophysicists and cosmologists. A question now presented itself as an obvious implication of the discovery of an expanding universe: If the universe is expanding so that everything is proceeding away from everything else, could a theoretical regression of this process determine the point in time at which this expansion began? In fact, if one could calculate accurately the rate of expansion, one could actually date the beginning of the universe—the beginning of time itself!

Certainly as we look into the heavens, we are now well aware that because of the time it takes the light from these distant planets and stars to reach us, we are actually observing the past—events that occurred on those distant celestial bodies hundreds or thousands or millions of years ago. It could well be that some of the celestial bodies we watch no longer exist. Therefore, this theory of a point at which the universe began from some immense explosion became popularly termed the "big bang."

According to this theory, the big bang took the form of a primeval fireball from which the universe began, then expanded with a velocity greater than the speed of light: "the universe is said to have expanded initially with a velocity much greater than that of light, and as a result, most galaxies are so far away that their light has not yet come within reach of our telescopes."[3] The theory postulated that if we could peer far enough into space, we could see the beginning of that point, the "edge" of the universe, a feat that astrophysicists speculated they had discovered within the past year with the improvements in the Hubble telescope.

This theory seemed to be somewhat corroborated when a haze of photons (microwave background radiation) was detected in 1965 with a radio receiver and was further confirmed in 1989 by a satellite that was launched to detect the temperature of this background haze. The temperature of the haze was determined to be approximately three degrees above absolute zero and equally distributed throughout space—a discovery that, according to popular science writer Timothy Ferris, seemed to confirm the validity of the hot big bang theory.*

From these observations, scientists concluded that the observable universe reaches about fifteen billion light years away from us in any direction. It would thus be some thirty billion light years across, but getting bigger by the nanosecond. Based on this calculation, contemporary astrophysicists are inclined to speculate that the universe is approximately fifteen billion years old.

Or is it?

RECONCILIATION AND RECIPROCITY

To name and to quantify are tools for attaining intellectual comfort, even, in some cases, for gaining a sense of superiority or control. Science virtually requires this if its adherents are to persevere in the face of what would otherwise seem unapproachable tasks in their continuous attempt to describe reality. This axiom is especially applicable when scientists

---

* In other words, instead of having a temperature of absolute zero, the haze still possessed some quantity of residual heat.

presume to study a cosmos so vast and mysterious that it becomes tantamount to a metaphysical realm. In fact, the one stark message we seem to encounter as we consider infinity in our search for some final encompassing model of macrocosmic order is that, however sophisticated we may in the future become in our capacity to study the cosmos, the universe as a whole will ever be beyond any final or complete comprehension.

While this assumption might be discouraging to some scientists and even to scientific thought itself, it is perfectly logical in the context of a physical creation whose very existence is to emulate in metaphorical form the preexistent ideas, forms, virtues, and verities whose noncomposite essences abide only in a metaphysical reality—the realm of the spirit. This realm or metaphysical aspect of reality is most certainly comprised of other dimensions transcending Einstein's four dimensions. But if our theory about a bridge between these expressions of reality exists, these dimensions would necessarily interact with the four dimensions of space-time.

Therefore, if we are able to learn about one reality from the other (each being the counterpart of the other), it might well be that, given the tenuous speculation about the nature and origin of the cosmos, we would do well to conclude this chapter by examining briefly some of the problems with contemporary theories of cosmology and by considering how they can be informed by, if not resolved by, guidance and verities set forth in the authoritative Bahá'í texts.

PROBLEMS WITH THE BANG

The most obvious problem with the big-bang theory from a Bahá'í perspective is that most versions of this theory hypothesize a single point of beginning, whereas the Bahá'í writings affirm repeatedly that material reality has no point of beginning either in time or in space. Material reality, from a Bahá'í point of view, has existed eternally in the past, regardless of how infinitely it has evolved or changed in form and relationship among its constituent members (maybe other universes).

One obvious reason given for this assertion by 'Abdu'l-Bahá is that existence cannot come from absolute nonexistence: "If it be said that such a thing came into existence from nonexistence, this does not refer to absolute nonexistence, but means that its former condition in relation to its actual condition was nothingness. For absolute nothingness cannot find existence, as it has not the capacity of existence."[4]

Another problem is encountered with the dating of the universe. If the universe is calculated to have begun roughly fifteen billion light years ago, how can certain stars be calculated to be at least sixteen billion light years old? Clearly something is amiss.

But a more mundane question also arises: What precipitated the big bang? If it was something physical, then something physical preceded that point in time. If it was metaphysical, then we suddenly introduce into science the existence and influence of a metaphysical dimension of reality and the necessity of a bridge from that reality to the physical aspects of reality, something that would cause us to rethink totally the concept of scientific laws—laws dealing exclusively with physical entities and relationships—as being a sufficient or complete description of physical reality.

What is more, if we accept that such a big bang occurred once, what is to prevent it from happening again, or three times, or constantly, or infinitely? And if it can occur again, who can posit with any certainty that what we are observing is the *first* occurrence of such a creative event?

And there are other problems. If the big bang occurred, where did it occur? If we presume that the explosion went outward, then there should be some point in space from which it proceeded and which is static, thus contradicting Einstein's theory that there is no static inertial frame of reference. And if the universe expanded, in what did it expand? If it expanded in space, then space preexisted the big bang.

According to Ferris, space itself was created and grew or "stretched" with this first event, but in what environment did it stretch? And if space is something capable of "stretching," then it could not possibly be a void, and if it is not a void, then have we not recreated the aether, or something more ephemeral—"space"?

Even more bothersome is another question. Could there not have been a "bang" before this one that, after incalculable time, collapsed back on itself until it reached a point of critical mass and exploded again? And if this is possible, we could be witnessing big bang number 27, or number 227, or one in an infinite series of such explosions. As such, if viewed from a timeless reality or with a time-lapse lens, the universe might appear as a vast heart pulsing in the matrix of . . . what?

If the universe is infinite in space as well as in time, which no one has yet disproved, then everything we witness would be confined to the assemblage of galaxies we are presently capable of viewing. Certainly no one thinks we have taken our final or most exacting view of the universe, not even with our renovated Hubble telescope.

THE "GLUMP" THEORY OF THE UNIVERSE

To facilitate a mind experiment of our own, let us designate the portion of the universe we can presently view with contemporary instruments as a "glump"—a glump of galaxies. Furthermore, let us posit the theory that if there is one glump, there doubtless could be other glumps. Furthermore, if some glumps are a sufficiently vast distance from our own glump, perhaps they are not expanding but contracting, preparing to coalesce and explode again to offset the energy expended by our own expanding glump.

In this mind experiment, we might think of the universe as a vast engine in which the gas in one cylinder explodes and pushes the piston down even as another piston ascends to expel the carbon monoxide in preparation for another explosion. Or perhaps a better and more useful analogy would be to think of the universe as a vast body in which each glump is like a cell. Some cells are just coming into being to nourish and be nourished by the universal body, while others are at the end of their usefulness and are in decline. But the endless universal body is essentially always the same, always in a state of health, or else always expanding. After all, if it is infinite, what's to stop it?

There is also the possibility that the big-bang theory has had its fifteen minutes of fame since Stephen Hawking published *A Brief History of Time: From the Big Bang to Black Holes* in 1988. We now have a "cold big-bang theory" to explain how all this particulate matter that expanded in the first second or so formed into solar systems and galaxies. We also have the "inflationary theory" to explain how an expanding universe creates space, instead of having space already there in which matter can expand. We have great interest in "superstring theory"—that the most discrete expressions of physical reality are vibrating string-like forms of energy with an infinite variety of forms. After all, string theory adds a complex of many other dimensions to Einstein's meager four dimensions (Euclidian three-dimensional space plus the fourth dimension of time).

What is more, the long abandoned aether theory has reemerged. This time around it is not a sea of matter *per se,* but a sea of energy: "This plenum is, however, no longer to be conceived through the idea of a simple material medium, such as an ether, which would be regarded as existing and moving only in three-dimensional space. Rather, one is to begin with the holomovement, in which there is the immense 'sea' of energy. . . ."[5] Consequently, whether we are referring to CMB (cosmic microwave background) or other expressions of existence, it is clear that we need not become discouraged when 'Abdu'l-Bahá refers to a theory that many contemporary scientists might view as an archaic remnant from the now dated "classical" physics of the Newtonian model.

WORLD WITHOUT END

The idea of a finite universe or "closed system" has never been universally accepted, and it is presumptuous to assume it is proven. To presume that the universe is limited on the basis of what we can presently observe or what theories we can derive from our present information would be totally arbitrary and needless

Certainly the Bahá'í writings affirm that such is not the case, asserting that solar systems are infinite in number:

Just as particulars are infinite in number, so also universals, on the material plane, and the great realities of the universe are without number and beyond computation. The Dawning Places of Unity, the Daysprings of Singleness and the Suns of Holiness are also sanctified beyond the bounds of number, and the luminous spiritual worlds are exalted above limits and restrictions. In like manner the worlds of bodily existence the mind of no man can reckon nor the understanding of the learned comprehend. Consider the following

150

well-known tradition and examine its meanings indicative of the vastness of the cosmos and its awesome limitless expanse: "God, exalted be He, fashioned one hundred thousand, thousand lamps and suspended the Throne, the earth, the heavens and whatsoever is between them, even Heaven and Hell—all of these in a single lamp. And only God knows what is in the rest of the lamps." The fact that philosophers and sages have posited limits and restrictions for such matters is to be explained by the limitations of people's minds and perceptions and the blindness of the followers of allusions, whose natures and intellects have been rendered dull and inanimate by the interposition of many veils.[6]

If, then, the physical "worlds" are beyond comprehension or limit, as are the "Dawning Places of Unity, the Daysprings of Singleness and the Suns of Holiness" (the Manifestations of God), why should we bother attempting to comprehend anything much about the macrocosm?

Here the answer is the same as the reason why we should study the microcosm. If the physical world in all its properties is an outward image, sign, or metaphor of the unseen world, then the fundamental principle by which we can obtain knowledge of the unseen reality begins with a single premise: To understand the operation of a particular part of the Chain of Being or a particular ingredient in universal composition is to gain useful insight into all the other levels of reality. 'Abdu'l-Bahá writes,

Know then that those mathematical questions which have stood the test of scrutiny and about the soundness of which there is no doubt are those that are supported by incontrovertible and logically binding proofs and by the rules of geometry as applied to astronomy, that are based on observations of the stars and careful astronomical research, and are in conformity with the principles of the universal themes expounded in the divine sciences. For it is by applying the outward world to the inner, the high to the low, the small to the large, the general to the particular that, with abundant clearness, it becometh apparent that the new rules arrived at by the science of astronomy are in closer accord with the universal divine principles

151

than the other erroneous theories and propositions, as we have explained and illustrated.[7]

To summarize, then, we see in this concept of refinement, whether we descend into the realm of particle physics or ascend into the realm of vast celestial "glumps," that the Creator has fashioned an infinitely complex classroom for our training, a classroom whose lessons will never become tedious because they will never be completely or finally understood. As we approach the borders of material reality, the gap between these two expressions of reality becomes so infinitesimal as to be beyond any distinction we could calculate.

Therefore, while physical creation is clearly the product of and subordinate in station to the unseen reality it manifests, we grievously err if we value it solely as a breeding ground where our souls begin, take on an identity, and receive rudimentary or foundational education to prepare us for the next stage of infinite growth in the dimension of the spirit. In fact, in its capacity to manifest even the most refined expressions of metaphysical reality, the physical world is indeed a counterpart of the spiritual world and coexists with it as an infinite, integrated, and organic enterprise.

- 10 -

The Fruit of Creation:
The Genesis of "Self"

True loss is for him whose days have been spent in utter ignorance of his self.

—Bahá'u'lláh, *Words of Wisdom*

Now we have arrived at a point where we can harvest the rewards of the vast analogy we have constructed between the macrocosm and the microcosm. As we have noted, 'Abdu'l-Bahá asserts that smaller systems parallel larger systems in structure and in function. He writes, "For particulars in relation to what is below them are universals, and what are great universals in the sight of those whose eyes are veiled are in fact particulars in relation to the realities and beings which are superior to them. Universal and particular are in reality incidental and relative considerations. The mercy of thy Lord, verily, encompasseth all things!" Elsewhere 'Abdu'l-Bahá has made a similar observation by stating, "Universal beings resemble and can be compared to particular beings, for both are subjected to one natural system, one universal law and divine organization. So you will find the smallest atoms in the universal system are similar to the greatest beings of the universe. It is clear that they come into existence from one laboratory of might under one natural system and one universal law; therefore, they may be compared to one another."[1]

With these assurances in mind, we can now apply our observations about how the Creator fashions and runs the universe in our attempt to understand how the soul runs the body. Such an analogical approach should help us acquire some new understanding about how the gap is bridged between the two categories of our human reality—between our soul (our metaphysical self) and our body (the physical or composite self). If our analogy is valid, we should discover that our metaphorical self (our body) is the outward expression of our metaphysical self (our soul) in much the same way that the physical universe is, poetically speaking, like the outward expression or body of God—it is an "outward" or visible expression of His invisible and otherwise essentially unknowable essence.

THE BEGINNING OF "HUMAN" LIFE

We have already discussed the various concepts of "beginning" regarding human reality. We have established that this planet and the human beings who occupy it had a beginning in time. Also, we have seen that material creation as a whole is a timeless counterpart of metaphysical reality and thus has no beginning. We have also established that because human beings represent the fruit of creation—the manifest fulfillment of the Hidden Treasure—it logically follows that there always have been and will always be human beings somewhere in the created universe.

Furthermore, it also logically follows that there is no necessary limit to the size of the universe or to the plenitude with which the Creator creates. At any given moment there may be an infinite number of planetary systems containing human life and, necessarily, an infinite number of Manifestations ministering to each planetary system that contains human life.

THE RELATIVITY OF "BEGINNINGS"

We have concluded that all concepts of "beginning" are necessarily relative. At some point in the future we may be able to date the age of our galaxy, of our solar system, or of this planet with exactitude. We may also be able to calculate precisely the period of time it took for human life on this planet to evolve to its present physical appearance. We may also discover a method of dating when various milestones occurred in the evolution of human social and intellectual development—the use of fire, or the invention of the wheel, or—my personal favorite—the post-hole digger.

But however knowledgeable we may become about our history and our origins, we will always remain aware that we are speaking of periods of beginning relative to this planet alone, not to creation as a whole nor to any of the other countless planets where a parallel process has occurred, is occurring, or will occur. As we have also noted, this same concept of relativity regarding time applies only to the origins of the part of the universe that we can presently study and observe—our "glump." There may have been some point at which our glump began, but we can be sure that before that beginning, there were other beginnings.

THE WOMB ANALOGY

So far in our discussion we have repeatedly compared the evolution of the macrocosm to the development of the child in the womb. Indeed, this analogy has been usefully applied to our considerations of philosophy and science. Because the earth is the source of our nourishment, it is understandable that ancient tribal philosophies arising among peoples whose daily lives were intimately attuned to the laws of nature in places as remote from one another as China, Europe, or the Americas came to think of the earth in female terms, as the mother of humankind.

Naturally there has also existed in these philosophies and religious views a father image or symbol: Life on earth is produced by the sun's interaction with fertile soil, even as the sperm penetrates the egg. The conjoining of complementary forces produces a new being. So it is that in Taoist thought, for example, the earth is considered female, dark, passive, and receptive (the Yin), while the sun is considered male, active, light, and penetrating (the Yang).

DOES *ONTOGENY* RECAPITULATE *PHYLOGENY*?

Ernst Haekel's largely abandoned "recapitulation theory" of 1866 provides a useful analogy as we consider how, in the words of 'Abdu'l-Bahá, "Universal beings resemble and can be compared to particular beings."[2] That is, *ontogeny* (the evolution of an individual organism) recapitulates *phylogeny* (the evolution of a species) to the extent that the development of the human embryo traces the evolutionary development of the species.

EVOLVING SOCIAL SYSTEMS
AND THE SENSE OF THE COLLECTIVE "SELF"

As we noted in our discussion of evolution, the human embryo is utterly helpless and bears little resemblance in its beginning to the relatively autonomous and extraordinary being it is destined to become—just as humankind, in the early stages of its development, no doubt bore little resemblance to the fully evolved human being. 'Abdu'l-Bahá states,

> Let us return to our subject that man, in the beginning of his existence and in the womb of the earth, like the embryo in the womb of the mother, gradually grew and developed, and passed from one form to another, from one shape to another, until he appeared with this beauty and perfection, this force and this power. It is certain that in the beginning he had not this loveliness and grace and elegance, and that he only by degrees attained this shape, this form, this beauty and this grace. There is no doubt that the human embryo did not at once appear in this form; neither did it then become the manifestation of the words "Blessed, therefore, be God, the most excellent of Makers."* Gradually it passed through various conditions and different shapes, until it attained this form and beauty, this perfection, grace and loveliness. Thus it is evident and confirmed that the development and growth of man on this earth, until he reached his present perfection, resembled the growth and development of the embryo in the womb of the mother: by degrees it passed from condition to condition, from form to form, from one shape to another, for this is according to the requirement of the universal system and Divine Law.[3]

---

* Koran 23:14.

There is an even further parallel. There comes a point in human evolution when the physical being is mature, when it achieves more or less its finished and perfected condition of evolutionary growth. Yet during the time prior to that stage of existence—which we can be certain was not a single moment, or even a brief period of a few days or years—other types of development were also occurring.

For example, collective human knowledge of reality was evolving and developing. Archeological evidence of these stages of progress can be seen in the gradually more sophisticated types of tools used in the various ages of human development—the Old Stone Age, the New Stone Age, the Bronze Age. The archeological evidence also suggests that these advances in technology paralleled advances in the expansion of social awareness and the development of increasingly complex, cooperative social systems.

These increasingly inclusive and complex social systems demonstrate that the individual's sense of self was expanding. In earlier stages, the individual may have assumed a vision of self that encompassed little more than self-interest as related to the well-being of one's immediate family. But very early in the evolutionary process, when human beings were in a state similar to that of evolving primates, well-being and sense of self became inextricably bound up in familial well-being as related to community or tribal interests.

Now that this sense of self has today expanded to encompass the planet as a whole so that all humanity are commonly considered the members of one integrated family, we might conclude that humanity has achieved the beginning stages of collective or social maturity. Bahá'í scripture affirms that we have reached a state where we are ready for and in need of a social system that describes the newly emerged reality of interdependence among all peoples in our planetary community.

Clearly, as these intellectual capacities and self-concepts evolve in the collective human organism, individual capacities and concepts of the self also change. For example, we can compare the embryonic stage of individual growth during which development is fundamentally unconscious and nonparticipatory to the early physical stages of human evolution on this planet. In such a condition, there is external assistance in the form of nutrition and love.

THE EVOLVING ROLE OF THE MANIFESTATIONS

As we observed earlier, humankind is watched over by Manifestations of God who may or may not be among them, depending on the stage of development of the human species. As previously discussed, the Manifestations may be in an as yet unincarnated condition, which 'Abdu'l-Bahá terms Their "preexistent condition," and may be instigating and shaping creation from the realm of the spirit in Their capacity as Vice-regents of God operating in the third of Their three stations: "Know that the Holy Manifestations, though They have the degrees of endless perfections, yet, speaking generally, have only three stations. The first station is the physical; the second station is the human, which is that of the rational soul; the third is that of the divine appearance and the heavenly splendor."[4]

THE IMPORTANCE OF THE "THIRD" STATION

'Abdu'l-Bahá states that in this "third" station of divine appearance and heavenly splendor, the Manifestations are effectively synonymous with the "Holy Spirit" and the "Word of God." In this exalted condition, which Bahá'u'lláh terms the station of "Essential Unity," there is no distinction among Them. Neither do They have a beginning nor end:

> The third station is that of the divine appearance and heavenly splendor: it is the Word of God, the Eternal Bounty, the Holy Spirit. It has neither beginning nor end, for these things are related to the world of contingencies and not to the divine world. For God the end is the same thing as the beginning. So the reckoning of days, weeks, months and years, of yesterday and today, is connected with the terrestrial globe; but in the sun there is no such thing— there is neither yesterday, today nor tomorrow, neither months nor years: all are equal. In the same way the Word of God is purified from all these conditions and is exempt from the boundaries, the laws and the limits of the world of contingency. Therefore, the

reality of prophethood, which is the Word of God and the perfect state of manifestation, did not have any beginning and will not have any end; its rising is different from all others and is like that of the sun.[5]

What is more, the individual Manifestations have no beginning in terms of Their preexistent station of unity. 'Abdu'l-Bahá states, "Briefly, the Holy Manifestations have ever been, and ever will be, Luminous Realities; no change or variation takes place in Their essence. Before declaring Their manifestation, They are silent and quiet like a sleeper, and after Their manifestation, They speak and are illuminated, like one who is awake."[6]

For this reason, when Shoghi Effendi speaks of Bahá'u'lláh's ascension, he speaks not of the departure of Bahá'u'lláh's influence and power, but rather of His release from the constraints of the earthly persona He chose for a time to assume (the second, or human, condition). Although the Manifestation of God may no longer walk among human beings, He still exerts a powerful influence on the world of humanity. Shoghi Effendi writes, "The dissolution of the tabernacle wherein the soul of the Manifestation of God had chosen temporarily to abide signalized its release from the restrictions which an earthly life had, of necessity, imposed upon it. Its influence no longer circumscribed by any physical limitations, its radiance no longer beclouded by its human temple, that soul could henceforth energize the whole world to a degree unapproached at any stage in the course of its existence on this planet."[7]

Returning to our analogy of the complementary forces required to create a new entity, we observe that the Manifestation is endowed by God with a dual responsibility. Inasmuch as the Manifestation facilitates the instigation of human genesis, He functions as "father" of the planet. To the extent that He is also empowered by God to nurture and guide humankind throughout its embryonic evolution, He might also be said to function as "mother" of the planet.

THE SACRIFICIAL ACT OF THE "HUMAN" CONDITION

When the physical human being evolves to a condition where it is capable of being taught in an overt—or as Shoghi Effendi puts it, "normal"—manner, the Manifestation demonstrates the ultimate sacrificial expression of parental love. Of His own free will, He accedes to the First Will of the Creator and takes on human properties of the first and second stations—a human soul associating with a human body. This He does so that He might appear among us to teach us to become sufficiently self-aware, autonomous, and spiritually mature that we may recognize our essential dependence on divine nourishment and guidance.

In this incarnate condition, the Manifestation has a beginning—when His soul associates with a human body at conception. However, throughout His life, the Prophet is well aware of His unique spiritual station and knows what His mission and fate will be. 'Abdu'l-Bahá states, "Verily, from the beginning that Holy Reality is conscious of the secret of existence, and from the age of childhood signs of greatness appear and are visible in Him. Therefore, how can it be that with all these bounties and perfections He should have no consciousness?" In fact, Shoghi Effendi notes that while the Manifestation is in this condition, His full powers are purposefully withheld; however He is still "omniscient at will."[8]

Therefore, while we may in Taoist fashion bestow the appellations of father and mother or male and female on the material aspects of our planet (for example, the material earth and the material sun), the Manifestation is genderless in the world of the spirit and assumes both male and female roles in functioning as the parental source for human creation by being God's Vice-regent:

Whomsoever He ordaineth as a Prophet, he, verily, hath been a Prophet from the beginning that hath no beginning, and will thus remain until the end that hath no end, inasmuch as this is an act of God. And whosoever is made a Viceregent by Him, shall be a Viceregent in all the worlds, for this is an act of God. For the will of God can in no wise be revealed except through His will, nor His wish be manifested save through His wish. He, verily, is the All-Conquering, the All-Powerful, the All Highest.[9]

In Taoism, the Yin and the Yang, while forming a complementary whole in the physical world, proceed from the metaphysical *T'ai Chi*, the ultimate or supreme reality. In other words, the male and female aspects of the earth and sun, working in concert to bring about human life, derive from and are guided by the ultimate expression of God, the Supreme Manifestation of God, "the Hidden Mystery, the Treasured Symbol, through whom the letters B and E (Be) have been joined and knit together."[10]

SOME INTERESTING PARALLELS

It may seem we have wandered far afield of our quest to discover the origin of the individual, but we have not. We have established that we can observe a parallel process at work in the macrocosmic and microcosmic genesis of self.

THE CHILD IN THE WOMB

Regarding the origin of humankind, we observe ourselves emerging from the womb of the planet in a gradual evolutionary process of physical, intellectual, social, and spiritual growth. We have ascertained that, while a materialist explanation might seem to justify the generation of human life on the planet as the result of the random chance of such a thing occurring, we noted earlier that such randomness defies scientific laws. Furthermore, we have noted that at every stage of development, some external source of guidance and intervention must be present if human evolution in all its myriad forms is to occur. As we have also observed, the Bahá'í explanation for this intervention is that the Manifestation works on God's behalf by educating and guiding humanity during this evolutionary journey.

Naturally we know the same thing applies to individual conception and growth as well—the parents must conjoin forces to create a new being. Likewise, while the child proceeds through embryonic stages of development, the parents—who are effectively outside the child's reality—exert influence physically, through the umbilicus, and spiritually, through prayers and other positive stimuli that can have long-term effects on the child's development.

When the child is born and gradually develops the ability to communicate and learn, the parents assume the role of teachers. Like the more advanced Manifestations, the parents must constantly evaluate their own educational methodologies and guidance to be sure that the educational process always accords with the child's advancing state of knowledge and capacity. Finally, we can assume that after the parents have ascended to the spiritual realm, they continue to exercise a benign influence on their progeny through their prayers, just as children are assured in the Bahá'í writings that their own prayers exert a beneficial effect on the spiritual progress of their deceased parents, who exist in the realm of the spirit. This spiritual assistance parallels the influence and assistance that Shoghi Effendi assures us we receive from the Manifestation after His ascent.

Another worthwhile analogy between genesis of self in the macrocosm and the genesis of self with regard to individual development concerns the expanding sense of self. Even as the advancement of the human body politic is portrayed in terms of an "ever-advancing civilization," so the advancement of the individual can be portrayed in terms of an ever more inclusive or expansive definition of "self." The stages of human development—from infancy, to childhood, to adolescence, to maturity—are readily acknowledged and understood to be an expanding sense of one's relationships with and obligations to others, even eventually to the whole of humankind.

This parallel regarding inclusivity is especially relevant to our previous observations about this period in history representing the maturation of humankind. Bahá'í scripture specifically designates the appearance of the Báb (the "Primal Point") as the point of humankind's transition to the stage of maturation because His appearance marked the confluence of the end of the preparatory Prophetic (or Adamic) Cycle with the beginning of the Era of Fulfillment, the "Bahá'í Era." Shoghi Effendi explicitly articulates this concept when he discusses the execution of the Báb: "Thus ended a life which posterity will recognize as standing at the confluence of two universal prophetic cycles, the Adamic Cycle stretching back as far as the first dawnings of the world's recorded religious history and the Bahá'í Cycle destined to propel itself across the unborn reaches of time for a period of no less than five thousand centuries."[11]

THE CONCEPT OF MATURITY

But if all points of beginning are relative, what does "maturation" mean with regard to humankind, and how does it relate to our understanding of our own maturation? Shoghi Effendi states in *The World Order of Bahá'u'lláh,* "Humanity is now experiencing the commotions invariably associated with the most turbulent stage of its evolution, the stage of adolescence, when the impetuosity of youth and its vehemence reach their climax, and must gradually be superseded by the calmness, the wisdom, and the maturity that characterize the stage of manhood. Then will the human race reach that stature of ripeness which will enable it to acquire all the powers and capacities upon which its ultimate development must depend."[12]

It is not difficult to see in the events of the past century patterns that parallel the vehement climax of adolescence. Events that have occurred since World War II amply demonstrate that humankind is rapidly arriving at an awareness of the planet as a global community. The dawning realization that the earth is one community and that it is, therefore, in desperate need of global systems and just global governance to manage its affairs surely betokens the dawning of the maturation of the human race.

Thus, while all points of beginning are relative regarding creation as a whole, this transition to maturity is not a cyclical event in terms of a single organism. Any given organism achieves maturity only once in its evolutionary development. It is for precisely this reason that the Bahá'í writings extol the importance and critical nature of this juncture in the history of human social and spiritual evolution. The time of achieving a shared perspective about who we are, what we are, and where we are in our collective progress as a body politic has been foretold and eagerly awaited from time immemorial. Indeed, such a period has been alluded to with various terms in all the world's religious scriptures and oral traditions.

In terms of personal development, the period of adolescence is a time during which authority shifts from parental guidance to individual responsibilities, rights, and freedoms. Similarly, one result of the maturation of human society will be the shift in governmental authority from patriarchal forms to representative bodies exercising authority under the umbrella of the structure and laws provided by the Manifestations.

This change does not mean that society will no longer need constant mentoring from the world of the spirit or that there will be no further periodic appearances of Manifestations of God. This newly emerged stage in the history of humankind on planet Earth simply requires that the kind of guidance we will receive will be markedly different from the guidance of earlier Manifestations.

For this reason, Bahá'u'lláh's Kitáb-i-Aqdas (Most Holy Book)—the primary repository of His laws and ordinances—contains relatively few laws and instead confers tremendous responsibility for decision making on the individual and on administrative institutions wherein elected consultative bodies render judgments and make decisions for the community.

Of particular importance in regard to this concept of maturity is the fact that we find relatively little explicit guidance about exactly how one should express spiritual understanding in human action. Instead, Bahá'u'lláh emphasizes that all action undertaken with spiritual motive in the service of humankind is an act of worship.

Always Human?

Another point bears repeating: If human evolution is continuous from the beginning, whether collectively on the universal level or particularly on the individual level, then there is no point of transformation in the continuum of development at which we become a human being. We are human from the beginning and will remain human: We will always remain a human soul, regardless of our physical appearance or the meagerness of our abilities, and regardless of whether we associate with reality through the intermediary of a physical body or dwell in a metaphysical environment.

This axiom has bearing on both the macrocosmic and microcosmic levels. As we noted in our discussion of evolution, this verity implies that the concept of evolution as a process wherein the human species derives from a lower species is patently erroneous. Regardless of what likeness may have existed between the evolving human form and other species, we were always destined to evolve into our present form, because at every stage of progression we were distinct from other species that did not evolve into human beings and did not, consequently, possess latent human faculties and capacities.

Applied to individual reality, this realization has immediate major legal consequences. If the human being is essentially human from the beginning, even at the moment of conception, a new human creation has been set in motion. One might correctly assert that this new creation is only *potentially* a human being, but it would be incorrect to assert it is *not* a human life. That is, while it is true that this new creation has within it all the potentialities of human life as dictated by the paired chromosomes, all human life at every stage is in a state of potentiality: Our progress never reaches some final point of attainment.

Therefore, to state that a diploid zygote is only *potentially* human would be equivalent to asserting that a teenager is only "potentially human." This observation has no real bearing on the indisputable fact of a being's humanness because a human being at any stage of development is always in a state of becoming. Even the so-called state or age of "maturity" signals not the end of development but the true beginning of our capacity to accomplish that for which we have been created.

Likewise, if we use what has become the amorphous concept of "viability" (some ability to survive outside the womb) as a gauge of humanness, then it could be argued that such a stage is attained only when one has achieved the capacity to hold down a decent job, and even then one requires a social infrastructure to create that job and to provide the other essentials of life such as water, electricity, and so forth.

Furthermore, viability outside the womb is determined by an ever-advancing technology. The criterion of "viability" in this sense—as an index to humanness—cannot thus be determined as a fixed point of natural or organic development. Consequently, the legal definition of a human being with appropriate human rights has become subject to almost daily advances in medical technology, together with the struggle of various legal systems to reflect those advancements.

Clearly, then, the criteria as to when we become human will never be a fixed point, except with the obvious and undeniable fact that as soon as "love sets us going," we are created. Until society reconciles itself to this fact, we are faced with paradoxical and contradictory legal and moral standards whereby the exact same act at one point in time is legal and a few days later is considered infanticide, one of the most inhumane crimes one can commit.

The motive force at the heart of all questions about individual human genesis is the same concern that arises when similar questions emerge about the termination of life. Any discourse about abortion is almost inextricably linked to a similar discourse about euthanasia. The reason for this relationship is obvious—a physical being only seems "human" to us when it can manifest human faculties and powers.

But there exists an immense gray area between the categories of "human" and "not human." We might even have trouble ascribing the term "human" to a good number of individuals among us who commit the grossest sorts of crimes or abuses against others. Yet these beings we usually categorize as "inhuman" or "miscreants" rather than "nonhuman." They are human beings, but they have so debased their station by making wretched choices that we describe them in terms of violating what should be the norms of any being classified as human. For however perverted or distorted or wretched such individuals may become, they still possess a conscious mind, are capable of rational thought, can make moral distinctions, and have the capacity to behave differently than they do.

This consideration, then, brings us to the point at which we must consider the essential means by which we derive and exercise our humanness—the mind, the soul, the "ghost in the machine," as the metaphysical self is sometimes called. For however much we may debate when that physical temple before us is capable or not capable of being classified as human, what we are really discussing is whether or not the spark of conscious awareness of self is visible. That sign may be no more than a grin, the squeeze of a finger, a look in the eyes that manifests the glimmer of that light. But what we are trying to discern in our quest to describe what makes us distinctly human is something other than "viability" of an infant or the self-sustaining body of an elder. We are trying to ascertain if "self" is there or capable of being there, something we are not sure a machine can determine for us.

The Ghost in the Machine:
Some Proofs of the Soul

The rational soul—that is to say, the human spirit—has neither entered this body nor existed through it; so after the disintegration of the composition of the body, how should it be in need of a substance through which it may exist? On the contrary, the rational soul is the substance through which the body exists.

—'Abdu'l-Bahá, *Some Answered Questions*

In the epigraph of the previous chapter, Bahá'u'lláh states succinctly, "True loss is for him whose days have been spent in utter ignorance of his self."[1] The careful reader may be tempted to think that this passage contains a grammatical error—that "his self" should be "himself or herself." But this translation renders into English Bahá'u'lláh's observation that the critical and essential objective of existence for each one of us is to attain knowledge of the nature of the "self," that metaphysical essence to which we allude with terms such as *soul, conscious mind,* or *spirit.*

In other words, while it is important to know what we are like in traditional terms of personality traits and capacities, Bahá'u'lláh is stating that it is a more central task of our physical existence to gain understanding of the essence that gives meaning to all of our characteristics. For in addition to helping us focus on our true objective for this life—preparation of the soul for further progress—this process also helps us fulfill another essential objective of our earthly existence—to attain the knowledge of God, though in truth, the knowledge of one facilitates knowledge of the other.

Bahá'u'lláh confirms this methodology in a passage we have already cited and will cite yet again because it is so crucial to understanding the Bahá'í concept of the essential nature of our own reality:

> How resplendent the luminaries of knowledge that shine in an atom, and how vast the oceans of wisdom that surge within a drop! To a supreme degree is this true of man, who, among all created things, hath been invested with the robe of such gifts, and hath been singled out for the glory of such distinction. For in him are potentially revealed all the attributes and names of God to a degree that no other created being hath excelled or surpassed. All these names and attributes are applicable to him. Even as He hath said: "Man is My mystery, and I am his mystery."[2]

PROGRAMMED OBSOLESCENCE

The *ubi sunt* theme in literature cautions us about the transitory nature of our physical lives and the illusory nature of physical power and status. While concern about the fleeting nature of our earthly experience offers no proof of the existence of the metaphysical self, the realization of the transitory nature of physical existence should instigate in us a desire to attain something beyond acquisitions, social status, and power. At worst, these same realizations might incite in us a lust to become so powerful, to acquire so much status and material wealth that our name may live on in the collective memory of history—whether as a corporate magnate, as a sports hero, or as a serial killer. Hence being aware of the brevity of life does not necessarily urge us to become better people unless we are simultaneously aware of some alternative means of enduring.

ETERNALITY AND MOTIVE

Material power and glory are goals because they are thought to be a means by which some degree of ease or felicity can be achieved. These dreams are persistent, unrelenting, and perilous because they are the addictive urgings of the ego, which 'Abdu'l-Bahá terms the "insistent self." The Bahá'í writings also make clear that this desire for acquisition and self-aggrandizement is the very force that is described in the scriptures of so many religions as the symbolic figure of Satan, which the Bahá'í scriptures allude to as "satanic" fancy and "vain imaginings": "Alas! Alas! O Lovers of Worldly Desire! Even as the swiftness of lightning ye have passed by the Beloved One, and have set your hearts on satanic fancies. Ye bow the knee before your vain imagining, and call it truth. Ye turn your eyes towards the thorn, and name it a flower."[3]

Ego, together with envy—one of ego's many offspring—is what causes us to seek relief by glancing at the covers of grocery store periodicals to discover the dark side of the lives of the rich, the famous, and the beautiful. The message we want to derive from these tabloid exposés is that we who are not rich or famous or beautiful have as much chance at happiness and well-being as they, or, conversely, that none of what they have acquired or have attained assures them of felicity or safeguards them from the perils of us ordinary folk.

What we really need if we are to counter the caveat implicit in the *ubi sunt* perspective is a vision of self that confirms in us the certitude that we will endure beyond the illusory rewards of social status or the trials and suffering that are, in Shakespeare's words, the "whips and scorns of time, / The oppressor's wrong, the proud man's contumely."[4]

But such a belief, if based on blind faith alone, is entirely feeble and liable to doubt. Therefore let us attempt to discover proofs that the inner self has an existence apart from or independent of the physical body. Otherwise, we have no adequate response to those who assert that the sense of self is naught but an illusory construction fashioned by the circuitry of the brain in a desperate quest for survival.

Knowledge of an Essential Reality

Offhand, this problem seems unresolvable. How can we as human souls prove our own existence if we have to rely solely on our own faculties and subjective observations to substantiate the proof? As we noted earlier, if we are referring to our "essential" reality—the soul itself—our efforts may indeed be doomed to failure. Not only are we veiled from comprehending the essential nature of the soul, we are withheld from comprehending the "essence" of anything. We can know *about* things, but we cannot know the *essence* or inner reality of anything because the essential reality of *everything* is metaphysical. 'Abdu'l-Bahá states,

> When we consider the world of existence, we find that the essential reality underlying any given phenomenon is unknown. Phenomenal, or created, things are known to us only by their attributes. Man discerns only manifestations, or attributes, of objects, while the identity, or reality, of them remains hidden. For example, we call this object a flower. What do we understand by this name and title? We understand that the qualities appertaining to this organism are perceptible to us, but the intrinsic elemental reality, or identity, of it remains unknown. Its external appearance and manifest attributes are knowable; but the inner being, the underlying reality or intrinsic identity, is still beyond the ken and perception of our human powers. Inasmuch as the realities of material phenomena are impenetrable and unknowable and are only apprehended through their properties or qualities, how much more this is true concerning the reality of Divinity, that holy essential reality which transcends the plane and grasp of mind and man?[5]

Let us ponder for a moment the implications of this passage. If we see a tree that we have never seen before, we do not question whether or not it is a tree. We recognize immediately that it partakes of the attributes of "treeness" because the essence of the tree is an idea, an abstract notion of "tree."

But where is "treeness"? Where does it exist? Certainly it is in our mind, in the repository of our memory of trees we have encountered in the past. But this is something a computer could do—compare visual images and sort out those that have the attributes of appearance common to trees. So let us consider an abstract attribute of "treeness"—its beauty, for example. If we live in a northern clime, we might immediately identify the "beauty" of a tree as being the majesty of an oak or elm, or the colors of a maple tree in the fall. If we live in a tropical clime, we might think of the beauty of "treeness" as containing the attributes of a King Sago palm, a Queen Anne palm, or a crape myrtle. In short, the concept of "beauty" is not definable in common terms or purely physical attributes.

If we cannot define precisely what constitutes beauty in a tree, how much less can we define human attributes, which are characterized by both inner and outer qualities? These concepts, these "ideas" or "forms," are only as abstract or illusive as the people employing them. If someone is limited in his or her perception of human beauty to a certain physical configuration, then our computer might be a better judge. Thus, when we say we cannot know the "essence" of anything, we are assuming that we agree on a shared definition of "essence" as relating to the capacity of something to reflect inner, concealed, or divine attributes.

The point is that regardless of how sophisticated or "deep" our concept of "essence" may be, the concept itself is ultimately an idea *about* the essence, *not* the essence itself. The computer may recognize a tree if we program the physical attributes into the computer and then program it to classify all objects complying with these criteria as belonging to the category of "tree." But the computer cannot by itself devise abstract notions of being, define criteria for itself, and determine to sort the data accordingly. We must program it to do these things or else create a program that can create a program to do these things. Even with something relatively simple such as a tree, our computer is just as likely to reject the palm if its criteria are based on a northern bias. Or if the criteria include the sparse foliage of a palm, the computer might identify a green cell phone tower as a majestic palm or pine.

But it matters not whether we have adequately proven our point about the inability of a binary machine to think abstractly, because the human brain is not a binary machine. For us to assert that our consciousness (our true self) exists independent of the physical organ that is the brain or that the brain is something other than a hunk of flesh with a complex system of nerve cells capable of generating "thought," we need some other sort of proof.

THE THEORY OF "SELF" AS PRODUCT OF THE BRAIN

In his book *Theories of the Mind,* philosopher Stephen Priest rejects the idea of the soul—self-consciousness as a metaphysical entity—but he also rejects a strict materialist theory of consciousness because he seems to feel that mental activity by definition is metaphysical activity, inasmuch as it is capable of considering abstract concepts and ideas.

Priest theorizes that metaphysical thoughts are the product of the physical brain because thinking is precisely what this intricate organ is designed to do. Therefore, while Priest rejects materialist views *per se,* he also rejects the idea of what he calls an "interface problem"—the very subject of this volume. That is, he does not accept any notion that there must be a "bridge" between the physical self and the metaphysical product of the brain (ideas) because he does not accept Cartesian dualism as an accurate portrayal of human reality. He writes, "The relationship between thinking and the brain is this: thinking is the mental activity of the brain. Crucially, there is no interface problem between things and their activities. There is no ontological or metaphysical problem about what the relationship is between something and what it does." He gives an example of this principle at work to dispel what he calls the "metaphysical illusion" that the self is something other than a product of brain activity: "A light-bulb increases and diminishes in brightness, but there is no 'light-bulb-brightness' problem." He then cites the "grin without a cat" from *Alice in Wonderland* (that is, there can be no effect without a sufficient cause) to show the impossibility of the metaphysical activity of the brain existing without the brain itself existing.[6]

There are a number of useful, logical, and scientifically based responses to Priest's opposition to the idea that there is some metaphysical source of "self" or consciousness independent of the metaphysical activity of the brain. The most obvious response is that it matters little whether or not Priest sees an explicit *need* for the existence of a metaphysical self existing independent of the brain; it matters only whether or not a metaphysical "self" does, in fact, exist independent of the brain. Second, while a light bulb as a physical mechanism produces light (physical energy), he states the brain (a physical entity) produces metaphysical effects (ideas). Therefore, the "interface" problem does exist because two entirely different realities are breached or bridged.

Another response is that if the brain is capable of "producing" or "conceiving" a metaphysical reality, then the brain must be deluded if no such reality exists. Hence the brain must not be creating metaphysical entities (ideas, thoughts, and theories), but only experiencing the sensation or illusion of creating them.

The simplest response is that if metaphysical reality exists, it exists independent of whether or not the brain perceives it. But if the brain really is participating in a metaphysical activity—for example, creating theories and ideas—then a metaphysical reality must necessarily exist. Furthermore, if the brain is part of the human reality from the beginning of conception, though evolving in its various capacities, we must again note that there is no single point at which the brain achieves a capacity that is distinctly human.

Priest might argue that an "illusion" is itself metaphysical, but the problem with his thesis is clear. If the brain is capable of transmitting metaphysical information (as his light bulb is capable of creating light), this sequence of causality does not necessarily imply that the brain is the ultimate source of such activity, just as the light bulb is not the source of light—the electricity that travels across the filament produces the light. Similarly, the brain might still be part of a sequence of causality, the ultimate cause of which is a metaphysical source, a "conscious self" operating through the instrumentality of the brain.

But these responses, though valid, are not particularly convincing or emotionally fulfilling because they hinge primarily on strictly logical and semantic distinctions. A meaningful response to materialist assertions about the illusion of a metaphysical self requires phenomenal evidence to be convincing for the ordinary human being. So let us turn to proofs that seem to indicate a source and a process that supercede the power of analogies and rely instead on actual evidence of metaphysical activity from metaphysical sources.

Some Quasi-Scientific Proofs of a Metaphysical Self

In recent decades some extremely important studies demonstrating with scientific evidence the lack of a locality for the conscious self have been published. A quick look at a few of these will demonstrate both the kinds of proofs that have emerged and the kind of "self" that this evidence seems to reveal.

NEAR-DEATH EXPERIENCES

The first category of evidence is actually not new, but it has survived some severe scrutiny and skepticism to become increasingly difficult for materialists to dismiss. It is the near-death experience (NDE) and the accompanying out-of-body experience (OBE). Much of the recent evidence has come from physicians who have accepted the existence of a metaphysical essence as the true "self" (a soul) based on their firsthand observation of patients experiencing NDEs. The patients who had the subjective evidence of the NDE did not need to be convinced.

Some of the most remarkable and persuasive accounts of NDEs come from oncologists, who must consult daily with those who are approaching death incrementally and inexorably. On a number of occasions as disease brings patients ever closer to the point where the body can no longer struggle against the invasive growth of cancer, the subtle transition from this life to whatever lies beyond occurs by degrees in such a way that an attending physician can become acutely aware of the patient's gradual release from attachment to physical reality and the comforting assurance the patient seems to acquire of a continuity of existence beyond physical experience.

Other equally convincing reports come from neurosurgeons who operate on those who have sustained various forms of traumatic brain injury and from physicians who rehabilitate patients who have experienced brain trauma, often as the result of automobile accidents.* One of the better-known collections of NDE accounts comes from a pediatric physician who took the accounts of children seriously because they were too young to acquire a strongly held belief system about what to expect at death.

---

* These reports were made in the course of numerous personal telephone conversations with Hamid Moayyed, M.D., John Amin, Ph.D., and George Saab, M.D., in 2004 and 2005—JSH.

While the accounts are not uniform in what they demonstrate about the "self," the consistent conclusion drawn by many physicians is that these events, albeit subjectively experienced by patients, are convincing proof that there exists a metaphysical "self," a "soul." The experiences seem uniformly to indicate to those who accept them at face value the existence of an afterlife, the continuity of "self" beyond physical existence, and a sense of expanded understanding and continuity of learning in the afterlife. Such experiences seem to imply that there is no end to the individual consciousness or "self" at death, but a transition or birth of the self into a more expansive, more comprehensive, and more advanced learning experience unencumbered by the veiling effects of physicality.

Any decent theorist will point out, however, that every case is necessarily reported by someone who ultimately did not die. This fact alone has called into question for many the reliability of NDEs as proof of a metaphysical reality. However real and authentic the experiences may seem to the individual involved, how do we know that they are not some sort of dream reality stimulated by the biochemical processes in the brain trying to comfort the "self" (or the brain itself) as death and nonexistence approach? As an ostensible vindication of this denial of NDE experiences as based on reality, Swiss researcher Olaf Blanke observed that the stimulation of the right temporal lobe by electrodes implanted to help a woman patient deal with seizures created a sensation (the woman later reported) that she was watching herself from above the bed while floating near the ceiling.[7]

Of course, the woman was not dying. Moreover, her experience did not parallel most of the established paradigms described by those who have undergone a NDE.

Other materialist explanations attribute the NDE and other forms of OBE to hallucinations caused by oxygen deprivation or by the release of endorphins resulting from brain trauma. Most physicians question whether there is necessarily a single explanation for all such experiences, even if some NDEs may have some physiological basis.

And yet the mounting numbers of such experiences that have been recorded (literally millions) contain such detail and such consistency that many experts find it difficult to attribute them solely to a physiological reaction. Certainly any of the initial concerns that these experiences were the result of expectations on the part of patients who had certain cultural or religious orientations toward death have long since been dispelled by the wide variety of cultural and religious backgrounds of those who have had these experiences.

In some cases there does seem to be a fulfillment of expectation. The dying patient may encounter a dead relative or some figure relevant to their belief system (Jesus, for example). If such experiences are not illusory, then quite possibly each person enters the next stage of reality experiencing an existence individually fashioned to make them understand what has happened to them. Certainly if such an experience is conceived by a cognitive and loving Creator or Manifestation, then it would make sense that this Being would want to make them feel welcomed or comforted, unless, of course, their choices in physical reality have been such as to bring about the need for some contrary experience.

Some of the most convincing proofs about metaphysical reality derived from these experiences are those instances in which the patient is able afterwards to recount events or conversations that occurred when the patient was "clinically dead" and was not in actual physical proximity to the place where the recollected events or conversations took place. Had the body not been clinically dead, the patient would not have been able to see or hear these events. Furthermore, in some of these cases the patient had no opportunity after being revived to learn about these events or conversations from others.

Such experiences, when accurately recorded, serve as fairly decent proofs of the non-locality of human consciousness. They suggest that the real "self," the conscious self, is not resident in the body, nor is it merely a product of the brain. Such evidence would indicate, instead, some sort of associative relationship between the body and human consciousness by means of the brain. Nevertheless, except for those who have had a NDE or who have observed those who have had them, such anecdotal evidence of a metaphysical "self" will always remain somewhat suspect since it is only by sheer accident that something close to laboratory conditions allows for verification of the fact that a human consciousness has experienced something at a distance from the brain as the result of a NDE.

SOME SCIENTIFIC PROOFS OF A "METAPHYSICAL SELF"

Aside from NDEs and OBEs, there are an increasing number of other more exacting scientific proofs of the existence of a metaphysical "self," proofs that avoid the necessarily anecdotal nature of NDE evidence. These proofs are discussed in detail by such pioneers in the field as Elizabeth Kübler-Ross (*On Death and Dying,* 1969) and Raymond A. Moody, Jr. (*Life After Life,* 1973). We should also note that *Transformed by the Light* (1992), by Dr. Melvin Morse, gives some valuable scientific observations to which we will refer in the next chapter. Especially interesting is Morse's observation of the relationship between the NDE and changes in a person's electromagnetic field, together with his evidence that these experiences are not hallucinations.

Recent studies, however, demonstrate the metaphysical powers of the conscious mind and discuss the logical possibility of a physical and metaphysical reality existing simultaneously and being interrelated without violating natural law.

DOSSEY'S WORK WITH PRAYER

Worth noting is the work of Larry Dossey, M.D., who is well known for his accounts of the effects of prayer in healing and the effects of prayer on physical reality in general. While his best-known work is *Healing Words* (1993), he has also written *Recovering the Soul* (1989), the work in which he first introduced case studies demonstrating that conscious will produced physiological changes in patients. Many years earlier in 1970, writer Norman Cousins wrote *Anatomy of an Illness as Perceived by the Patient,* in which he described how he successfully used humor as a means of fighting cancer.

Humor and other attitudinal or affective methodologies are now widely recognized as efficacious in the treatment of cancer. We need not invoke a belief in the supernatural to appreciate the effectiveness of a patient's attitude in treating physical illness. Physicians now uniformly recognize the importance of emotional affect in healing and recovery. Furthermore, the case of Cousins as well as cases cited by Dossey in *Recovering the Soul* result from willfully focusing the consciousness (a metaphysical reality or else the illusion of a metaphysical reality) on the disease and on images of health and healing.

One case cited by Dossey involves a thirty-nine-year-old woman who had followed the Eastern religious practice of meditation for some nine years. In 1985 a team of investigators led by Dr. G. Richard Smith at the University of Arkansas reported that the woman focused her attention on her own healing: "This experiment and many others like it bring the power of science into the task of showing that the mind can extend its influence far beyond the brain. . . . No longer in the category of mere folk wisdom or superstition, the body-mind connection is now a matter that has been demonstrated by careful scientific inquiry." Of particular relevance is the fact that the woman began her meditation by dedicating "her intention concerning the study for universal good instead of self-advancement."[8]

Before we mention other observations Dossey made, we should note that it is not incidental that the woman had studied Eastern religious practices. In a 1995 television series called *Healing and the Mind,* host Bill Moyers devoted the first program to "The Mystery of Chi," a presentation which alludes to the power of the mind to channel universal energy so that, once mastered and properly employed, this practice can be used for the purpose of healing. In one scene a Chinese physician who is a practicing surgeon trained in Western medicine manipulates the energy flows that presumably surround the patient's body. The effect on the patient, who is critically ill with a brain tumor, is quite visible: The patient breaks out in a sweat and is soon relieved from discomfort.

One of Dossey's most profound observations occurs in a section titled "Where Is Love?" in which he notes that abstractions such as "love" or "patriotism" can be some of the most powerful human forces, yet they do not exist in time or space. Dossey writes, "In his important book, *God and the New Physics,* physicist Paul Davies discusses the error of regarding certain concepts as things requiring allocation and made of some sort of stuff. 'What stuff is the soul made of?' he asks. 'The question is as meaningless as asking what stuff citizenship or Wednesdays are made of. The soul is a holistic concept.'" This essential concept of "mind," or "self," or "soul," or "consciousness" as nonlocal and nonmaterial—though capable of interacting with physical reality—is critical to our discussion. To consider that the consciousness and its powers (will, memory, rational thought) can function through a transceiver (the brain) without being localized is at the heart of the Bahá'í concept of an "associative" or "counterpart" relationship between the physical self (especially the brain) and the metaphysical self (the soul). Dossey states the concept succinctly: "the fact that the mind may be nonlocal does not mean that it could not act *through* the brain."[9]

METAPHYSICAL ACTION ON PHYSICAL REALITY

Besides dealing with proofs concerning the "nonlocal," metaphysical nature of mind and consciousness, Dossey also brings to the fore a second sort of study that is much more scientific because it does not require belief nor does it require that a person be affected by the process. Dossey presents evidence that he believes demonstrates simultaneous action at a distance.

One of Einstein's foremost problems with the classical, or Newtonian, physics was its inability to account for a universe organized by an extant simultaneous force without apparent physical cause—some intermediary conductor of the force. Dossey's work seems to demonstrate not only the existence of a metaphysical self but also that this metaphysical self can produce observable physical effects at a distance and without regard to time.

This is not a new idea. Any belief system that affirms the soul is the essential reality of the "self" and that this metaphysical essence can operate through an associative relationship with the physical body is affirming this same idea—that all human activity results from a constant interaction, or discourse, between the metaphysical self and the physical self. Whether we are speaking of a simple action (handing someone a glass of water) or a complex action (designing an engine), we would, from this perspective, be alluding to this same interplay between a metaphysical realm of forms and ideas and the metaphorical world of specific names and things.

Such considerations threaten materialist thinking about the "self" and about everything else because these theories allow for the possibility that metaphysical reality exists, and, even more confounding, that it might be at least one of the possible causes for every single physical event. And if there is a metaphysical cause capable of affecting physical events, how can its influence possibility be accurately detected or measured, except, perhaps by the effects that cannot be accounted for by physical causes?

In *Recovering the Soul,* Dossey himself speaks of a study designed to do just that—to investigate scientifically the effects of prayer on 393 patients admitted to a coronary care unit at San Francisco General Hospital. The well-known test, conducted by cardiologist Randolph Byrd, was designed so that the patients were arbitrarily and unknowingly divided by a computer program into two groups: one that was prayed for by "home prayer groups" and another that "was not remembered in prayer." The study was "designed according to the most rigid criteria that can be used in clinical studies in medicine." Dossey writes, "It was a randomized, perspective, double blind experiment in which neither the patients, nurses, nor doctors knew which group the patients where in. . . . The prayer groups were given the names of their patients, something of their condition, and were asked to pray each day but were given no instructions on how to pray. 'Each person prayed for many different patients, but each patient in the experiment had between five and seven people praying for him or her.'" The results were that the "prayed-for" patients were five times less likely to need antibiotics; they were three times less likely to "develop pulmonary edema"; and none of them needed intubation (an artificial airway), as opposed to twelve in the "not prayed-for group" who required intubation.[10]

As Dossey notes, had a drug or a surgical procedure produced the same results, it would have been hailed universally as a medical breakthrough. Dossey concludes the results demonstrate that "something about the mind allows it to intervene in the course of *distant* happenings," which would seem to suggest "that there is no 'energy' involved in prayer as we understand this term in modern science" because the intensity of the cause (the prayer) does not diminish with distance. From a Bahá'í perspective, we could conclude that there *is* energy involved, but it is spiritual rather than physical in nature. Furthermore, if this "gap" can be bridged bidirectionally, one form of energy can affect the condition of a being extant in the other reality.

One of the more poignant and relevant observations Dossey makes alludes to the concept of the "mind" or "self" in relation to quantum physics:

> Although heretical when viewed against the backdrop of modern biological materialism, Margenau's views [Margenau posits a view of quantum "fields" that are not material in nature, yet have an effect] on the mind's nonmaterial nature would find sympathy with some of this century's greatest physicists. Niels Bohr stated, "We can admittedly find nothing in physics or chemistry that has even a remote bearing on consciousness." And his contemporary, Werner Heisenberg, the originator of the Uncertainty Principle in modern physics, also put the matter bluntly. "There can be no doubt," he said, "that 'consciousness' does not occur in physics and chemistry, and I cannot see how it could possibly result from quantum mechanics.[11]

WHAT IS THE MEDIUM OR "BRIDGE" FOR THIS INTERACTION?

Dossey's most popular work, *The Healing Words: The Power of Prayer and the Practice of Medicine,* is a bit more rigorous than *Recovering the Soul,* and it is more satisfying to skeptics because it introduces intricate problems of understanding how prayer works rather than simply marveling that it has a demonstrable effect. For our purposes, the most interesting question it raises is whether or not there must be a God for prayer to work.

Comparing the modern model of prayer with the traditional Western model, Dossey notes that, according to the modern view there is no need for God as an intermediary since prayer is internal, whereas in the traditional model God is crucial as "a necessary intermediary."[12] But the study has a much broader interest and application, examining as it does different types of prayers, different modalities of praying, and various personalities among the suppliants. He also broaches the broader issue of the effect of love on healing, since, in the final analysis, it is the *concern for others* expressed through the prayer that induces a healing process, not a set form of meditation. In other words, prayer is the medium, but *love* or *concern* for another is the message, energy, or power conveyed through it.

Here again our analogy of electronic intermediaries comes to mind. We could use a phone to convey to someone our affection and concern. The expression of this affection would possibly have a remedial influence on the listener. Yet we would not say that the person was assisted by a telephone but rather by the emotion that was expressed in words that the electronic medium or intermediary conveyed.

Our purpose here is not to give some final assessment of Dossey's work. Instead, we cite his work as an example of ever more rigorously conducted scientific studies demonstrating that the conscious self can produce action at a distance, most obviously on other conscious selves. Whether we view this action as taking place primarily on the metaphysical level of reality (soul to soul), or as an interpenetration of dual aspects of reality (the soul influencing the body of another individual, or the soul influencing the soul of another individual, which, in turn, has a positive effect on the healing of the body), the evidence is still critical to our definition of the conscious "self" as being metaphysical and capable of producing physical effects. The gap is bridged via an intermediary.

Two Other Studies

Two other studies about the reality of the conscious "self" are helpful in considering the essentially metaphysical nature of consciousness. They are Lothar Schäfer's *In Search of Divine Reality: Science as a Source of Inspiration* (1997) and David J. Chalmers's *The Conscious Mind: In Search of a Fundamental Theory* (1996).

In Search of Divine Reality

After giving excellent presentations on the dual theories of light (quanta of particles versus waves of energy) and other questions we have already discussed in earlier chapters, Schäfer concludes that "the background of reality has mind-like qualities." He explains, "This view is also suggested by the fact that the order of the universe is determined by *probability fields and symmetry principles* which are closer by nature to elements of the mind than of the material world. They are mental concepts, mathematical, not necessarily bound to objects of mass-energy." He concludes,

> Whether mind exists separately from my brain or not, I do not know. Strangely enough, I have a feeling of all kinds of parts of my body—my feet, my hands, my stomach—but no feeling of my brain. Whether my mind is the offspring of blind chance or teleonomic guidance, I do not know. However it is quite clear that I do have a mind and, above all, I *am* it, and it is of exceeding personal importance that this mind exists before a background that is itself mind-like. The web of probability fields extending through all of space, the flow of non-local, thought-like influences from unknown sources, molecules in superpositions of states: *That the background of reality is mind-like, in all likelihood means that it communicates with other minds.*[13]

Stated in terms of the Bahá'í cosmological view, this "mind-like" or metaphysical quality of reality means that the mind is susceptible to guidance by metaphysical influence—for example, by the creative power of the Manifestations as God's Vice-regents.

Schäfer argues that there is "a level of the brain and another of mind":

> A new quality arises in the latter that in vain one would search for in the former. In that sense, even if not separate from the brain, the self-conscious mind is the *independent* self-conscious mind.
>
> *Thus, the metaphysical foundations of science are the principles of the independent self-conscious mind.* It is this mind that makes scientific knowledge possible, not by inventing it, but by being part of a level of reality that, by its principles, is higher in hierarchy than the visible part of the world alone affords true knowledge. In this sense *ultimate reality resides in ideas,* as Plato said. In this sense, *the laws of nature are made by the mind,* as Kant said—(not

185

fabricated by mind, but derived from its connection to a higher reality).[14]

Schäfer discusses many other related issues such as his proposition that the self-conscious mind is the basis for ethics and his discussion of the mindlike order of the universe. He concludes, "It is now possible to believe that the mind is the realization of universal potential, a manifestation of the essence of the universe, whatever name we give to that essence. Therefore, *the good life is in harmony with the nature of physical reality.*"[15]

Our Conscious Minds

David Chalmers's *The Conscious Mind* is a bit wider in scope than Schäfer's study, but it approaches the same critical issue: Is consciousness merely the product of brain function, as the materialists suggest, or is consciousness a metaphysical faculty that employs the brain as intermediary?

For our purposes, one of the more potent sections of Chalmers's discussion appears at the end of the chapter titled "The Irreducibility of Consciousness." Discussing the rejection of dualism as a necessary approach to perceiving consciousness as metaphysical, Chalmers observes, "On the view I advocate, consciousness is governed by natural law, and there may eventually be a reasonable scientific theory of it. There is no *a priori* principle that says that all natural laws will be physical laws; to deny materialism is not to deny naturalism. A naturalistic dualism expands our view of the world, but it does not invoke the forces of darkness." The "forces of darkness" to which Chalmers alludes are, he says, the "various spiritualistic, religious, supernatural, and other anti-scientific overtones of the view." He objects, it would seem, more to the illogical and alogical dogmatism that has passed for true religion than to the concept of the "supernatural" in the purest sense of a metaphysical reality, which includes spiritual realities and forms that he labels "naturalistic."[16]

Chalmers admits that his view is a sort of consciously chosen middle ground between the materialist view of consciousness as a physical activity and the dualist view of consciousness as deriving from (and abiding in) a metaphysical reality: "Ideally, it is a view that takes the best of both worlds and the worst of neither."[17]

Though Chalmers ostensibly denies a metaphysical reality derived from a cognitive essence (God), he broadens his definition of reality from things "physical" to things "natural." According to Chalmers, reality can well include a guiding force such as a Creator. As he puts it, "nature" includes all activity, including "psycho physical laws in a theory of consciousness."[18]

THE ORIGIN OF THE METAPHYSICAL SELF

We have thus far given little attention to the number of works that offer elaborate and well-argued expositions on the feasibility of consciousness being the product of brain activity rather than the brain functioning as the executor of a conscious will. We will discuss these theories more amply in the next chapter as we examine the various functions of the self, and, in particular, how the abstract world of ideas is processed into physical action.

But before we can leave our survey of concepts of the self, we need to deal with two final issues, both of which we will treat more fully later, but each of which is essential to any fit definition of "self."

THE ORIGIN OF CONSCIOUSNESS.

The first concern has to do with consciousness and human evolution. That is, if we compare our individual evolutionary development to that of humankind on this planet (as we have already done several times), we are urged to question at what stage the human species reaches a point of self-consciousness or self-awareness that is distinct from or superior to that of animal species.

For example, we might cite toolmaking as such a sign, and yet numerous animals fashion and employ tools to dig for roots, to slay other animals, or to perform a myriad other functions. Perhaps we could consider language as the key, because language is a constructed symbolic system of communication, and yet many animals use a variety of sounds to symbolize or express a wide variety of emotions—fear, affection, domination, anger. Perhaps we might think of cave art as a sign of the emergence of conscious thought, for even if we presume that this art was believed to have some pragmatic or totemic function, such as enhancing the prospects for the hunt, it still represents a noninstinctive behavior that is far beyond anything an animal could accomplish. For while many animals have hunting or mating rituals, these activities are not innovative but instinctive, even if we view them as aesthetically beautiful or artful.

In this case, the comparison of what happens in the macrocosm does not help us much. We know that the process of human evolution is gradual and that it consists of quantum leaps forward at certain times. From the Bahá'í perspective, we might well conclude that such periods of rapid advancement are directly related to the appearances of Manifestations. But for the present, we are left with only crass speculation about the process that brings about self-consciousness on a collective level. Certainly we might conclude that there is no fixed point when this essential awareness of self, this self-conscious power, suddenly emerges, no single point of awakening, but rather that there is an awareness that grows gradually over time.

Our own recollected awareness of self would seem to corroborate such an inference. When we attempt to recall our earliest awareness of "self," we probably remember isolated images, powerful but disconnected recollections of sensory perceptions associated with some palpable emotion, most probably an experience when we were two or three at the youngest.

As we observe our own children in a state of infancy, we are immediately aware of their distinct personalities. We also are acutely aware of their varying emotional responses to experiences and stimuli. We know when the infant is pleased, has learned a specific skill, or instigates its own pleasure by playing with a toy.

And yet why is it that when this same infant is grown, it will probably not recall these earliest events? Is it that the events are repetitive and, like our own workdays, so much alike as to be indistinguishable from one another? Or is this simply so early a stage in the awakening of the conscious mind that the child experiences these events without conceiving their meaning—having no mental context in which to do so—and thus cannot store these images in the repository of memory?

Jaynes's Theory of the Origin of the Conscious Mind

Psychologist Julian Jaynes presents a fascinating theory about the evolution of human consciousness that might be understood to apply both to the macrocosmic and to the microcosmic evolution of human consciousness. In his 1976 work titled *The Origin of Consciousness in the Breakdown of the Bicameral Mind,** Jaynes proposes that there is a discernible period in the evolution of human society when the human species ceases to function in an instinctive mode and begins thinking volitionally (consciously).

Jaynes presents a most interesting analysis of societies functioning within what he terms the "bicameral mode." In such societies the individual receives commands (for example, from literal or imagined voices of authority) and obeys. Society functions "successfully" this way, if by successfully we mean in ways that are efficient, orderly, and highly structured—as opposed to contemporary standards of judgment that would necessarily evaluate the justice and human rights operant within the society.

After discussing the characteristics of human consciousness as we commonly employ the term (meaning creative and volitional activity that is capable of producing art and invention) Jaynes discusses the origin of civilization. Considering the origins of complex human faculties, Jaynes rejects theories that language "is such an inherent part of the human constitution that it must go back somehow through the tribal ancestry of man to the very origin of the genus *Homo*, that is, for almost two million years. . . . But with this view, I wish to totally and emphatically disagree. If early man, through these two million years, had even a primordial speech, why is there so little evidence of even simple culture or technology? For there is precious little archaeologically up to 40,000 B.C., other than the crudest of stone tools." Jaynes traces evidence of the progress of primitive language from "intentional calls" and "commands," to an age

---

* The term *bicameral* as employed by Jaynes refers to a state in which human beings function according to commands or expectations such that there is no need to have conscious awareness of, or analysis of, our response or actions.

of "modifiers" (around 40,000 B.C.), to the age of a complete sentence (a noun with a predicate modifier) between 25,000 and 15,000 B.C.[19]

Jaynes notes that these are not "arbitrary speculations." He explains how the evolving structure of the social unity and the evolving complexity of tasks would produce a logical sequence in the emerging languages by which the tasks could be carried out. He thus suggests that it may have been as late as the Mesolithic era (between 10,000 and 8,000 B.C.) before names first occurred: "This is the period of man's adaptation to the warmer post glacial environment. The vast sheet of ice has retreated to the latitude of Copenhagen, and man keys in to specific environmental situations, to grassland hunting, to life in the forest, to shellfish collection, or to the exploitation of marine resources combined with terrestrial hunting."[20] Jaynes catalogs the progress of society through the advent of agriculture and the emergence of the concept of the town, as evidenced by the Natufian settlement at Eynan (discovered in 1959), which existed around 9000 B.C.

But Jaynes proposes that the Natufians "were not conscious," at least not to the extent that they had a sense of self beyond the existential response to each minute, "to cues in a stimulus-response manner, and controlled by those cues."[21] They were, in other words, operating almost entirely in a "bicameral" fashion. They received the command of the king, and they did what they were told. And when the king died and was buried, the burial place of the king, who had been the source of authority and command, became the house of God, the source of command—the voice that had come from His authority still echoing in their minds.

THE BREAKDOWN OF THE JAYNES THEORY

Now what does the central effect of this emphasis on a form of worship have to do with Jaynes's theory of the breakdown of functioning in a bicameral fashion and the emergence of the conscious mind?

Such a theory of evolutionary change might seem to corroborate the Bahá'í theory of history, which proposes that all human progress derives ultimately from the advent of Manifestations of God. Even at such an early period of development, the evidence of forms of worship as playing a central role in the evolving sense of self and the reflective or contemplative aspect of human thought might well indicate an increasing awareness of the mystical or metaphysical aspect of the self and of reality as a whole. Indeed, totemic religious objects would seem to imply some sort of personal reflection about metaphysical reality.

But this is not Jaynes's point. According to his concept of the breakdown of the bicameral (unconscious) processing of commands, the very complexity of society caused a cumulative stress on the ability of the human beings to function "unconsciously" or in a "bicameral" fashion. The "voices" or "commands" (the sense of external expectations) seemed contradictory and confusing. Consequently, to survive, people were impelled to develop conscious thought to determine how best to respond to the exigencies of life. This process, Jaynes theorizes, occurred around 1000 B.C.

The obvious problems with such a theory are implicit from the beginning. If the "nonconscious" people followed the commands and presumably the inventive designs of a king or leader for creating social order and social dictums, how did that king come to possess a type of consciousness his "drones" did not have? According to Jaynes, ancient writings like the Homeric epics and the early books of the Old Testament were composed by "nonconscious minds" as part of a mnemonic or ingrained practice. In fact Jaynes traces evidence of people responding to "imagined voices," or "hallucinations," showing in an examination of Greek philosophy and poetry the traces of this same sense of inspiration.

Jaynes concludes by examining this same "quest for authorization" in the Judeo-Christian religious tradition. He describes these commands, these voices, the bicameral response to authority, as comparable to the natural phenomenon of an animal in an advanced but understandable stage of evolution. Clearly, as a materialist theorist, Jaynes never considers that perhaps the chain of causality derives from actual voices, even if sensed rather than described in sophisticated recorded discourse.

In short, the process or sequence of social change that Jaynes has hypothesized is real and well presented. He traces a sequence of social structures evolving to the point where a less mechanical or more creative response is required of the individual, or at least of the general populace. But individual invention and genius is acknowledged by Jaynes long before the three thousand-year-old breakdown in the "nonconscious" processing of commands and information.

No doubt what Jaynes describes as taking place beginning in Mesopotamia is an accurate description of how a more complex society requires people themselves to become more complex. Certainly today each individual has to ponder the pros and cons of a hundred different critical issues regarding personal morals, social issues, and family finances much more completely than did our predecessors precisely because of the disappearance in contemporary society of any shared norms or perspectives.

The problem with Jaynes's theory is that if a human being is simply another animal—as Jaynes posits—then why have not other animals also become conscious when stress invaded their social milieu, particularly now, when their entire environment and the survival of so many species are being systematically threatened and destroyed? Furthermore, while the exigencies of progress (or complexification) obviously required a higher level of response and therefore a more "thoughtful" mode of processing information, one cannot invent a capacity that is not latent, at least not something as distinct as the human capacity for reason, reflection, invention, and imagination.

To press the issue further, we need only pose simple questions: Who designed the artistic patterns on the pots, tools, and weapons? Was this art essential or necessary? Even if it was ordained by a leader, was it not still inventive and fulfilling on the part of the artisan? Even if the decoration came from the imagined voices, what was the source of the imagined voice?

But rather than rehash the totality of Jaynes's work and attempt to demonstrate what is misleading versus what is informative and helpful to our examination of the sense of self, let us take from this study its most useful premise: that human conscious thought—especially autonomous reflection and imagination—develops gradually, whether in the individual or in the society as a whole. Additionally, this capacity for creative thought and its application in providing practical solutions to an increasingly complex life is the last stage in the evolution of the human being, other than the progressive application of spiritual principles to our recently emerged global community. It is precisely in this context that the Bahá'í writings speak of the present age as the advent of the maturation of humankind as we become universally aware that we are essentially metaphysical beings operating through our physical counterpart of self—the body and its intricate mechanisms that serve as an intermediary between the conscious self and physical reality.

Finally, and most importantly, we see in Jaynes's paradigm of the evolution of human consciousness the crucial part played by the concept of authority, especially authority derived from some metaphysical source, whether it be from the tomb of the deceased king or from the house gods that were symbolized by totemic objects. For surely the desire to be in touch with the "voices" or the spirit from which authority and command seemed to emanate did not occur spontaneously. Someone or some force superior to the aggregate of the human body politic had to introduce this idea.

To think that this occurred all of a sudden and from necessity is as archaic and invalid as the now largely abandoned theory of "folk art"—the notion of the spontaneous emergence in a culture of works of art, songs, stories, and dances. We now know that for every work of art there is an artist. And we can similarly assume that for every advancement in human understanding and social organization there is a designer, a planner, a teacher.

From the Bahá'í perspective on history, we can confidently assume that the ultimate source of these advancements is a Manifestation, or else someone who has become inspired by the insights imparted or exemplified by a Prophet.

The answer to the initial question Jaynes poses, then, is simple and unavoidable. Consciousness is an inherent capacity of the human being that develops incrementally in the course of human history even as it does in our individual development and in the development of the individual's relationship to society. There is no precise point at which such an awareness of self begins. Consciousness of self is always in a relative state of becoming, a verity that is applicable to us even now, whether as individuals searching for personal meaning or as a society trying to figure out how to discover a just and effective way to minister to the needs of a planet suddenly contracted into one thoroughly inter-dependent community.

Sometimes we proceed through our daily routine in a mindless or mechanical manner. If we are not careful, we can let others define what that routine will be. At other times we are forced into a state of focused reflection about ourselves, our relationships, our goals, or our progress towards those goals. Most often these occasions occur as a result of stress or the breakdown of our routine because of death, disease, or other difficulties. Only at such points do we become consciously aware of willfully employing the powers of thought, logic, prayer, memory, and imagination to respond to our changed routine, unless we have established as a part of our daily routine a period of time when such reflection is practiced systematically. Doubtless the rich benefits of systematic reflection and self-assessment account for why the Bahá'í writings describe periods of suffering and difficulty as opportunities for growth and ordain the daily practice of prayer and reflection.

The Bahá'í View of the Conscious Mind

The Bahá'í writings state that the individual human soul emanates from the spiritual realm at the conception of the physical self: "The soul or spirit of the individual comes into being with the conception of his physical body." Moreover, 'Abdu'l-Bahá notes that the essential characteristics of personality and individuality result from the fact that each individual is a unique creation: "The personality of the rational soul is from its beginning; it is not due to the instrumentality of the body. . . ."[22]

Nevertheless, these observations about inherent distinction in no way lessen the degree to which the conscious soul with its unique capacities depends for development on assistance: "Personality is obtained through the conscious effort of man by training and education. A fruitless tree under the influence of a wise gardener becomes fruitful; a slab of marble under the hand of a sculptor becomes a beautiful statue." Thus the parental responsibility to help the child develop and prosper is one of the foremost obligations a human being can assume. A letter written on behalf of the

Universal House of Justice states, "The great importance attached to the mother's role derives from the fact that she is the *first* educator of the child. Her attitude, her prayers, even what she eats and her physical condition have a great influence on the child when it is still in womb."[23] 'Abdu'l-Bahá also confirms what any parent witnessing the birth of a child readily observes—that the distinct character and personality of the individual child, however much it may be changed by future experience, exists from the beginning. He states,

> The rational soul—that is to say, the human spirit—has neither entered this body nor existed through it; so after the disintegration of the composition of the body, how should it be in need of a substance through which it may exist? On the contrary, the rational soul is the substance through which the body exists. The personality of the rational soul is from its beginning; it is not due to the instrumentality of the body, but the state and the personality of the rational soul may be strengthened in this world; it will make progress and will attain to the degrees of perfection, or it will remain in the lowest abyss of ignorance, veiled and deprived from beholding the signs of God.[24]

This same passage brings to the fore what may be the most critical observation we can make about the associative coexistence of the soul with the body: The soul is not a product of conception, nor is it simply coincidental with conception. When a human temple becomes a fit vehicle for the soul, there emanates simultaneously from the Creator (from the metaphysical realm) an individualized spiritual essence that is the soul, the essential reality of every human being.

Furthermore, this connection does not terminate once the created being has emanated from its divine source. This point more than any other should interest someone who finds Jaynes's discussion worthwhile. Our connection to the source of our emanation produces in us an inherent need, desire, or longing to discover or have a reunion with that source from which we originated. This is an inescapable destiny in every human being, no matter how inadequately understood or how distorted, confused, or perverted that internal longing and attraction may become. 'Abdu'l-Bahá states,

> The spirits of men, with reference to God, have dependence through emanation, just as the discourse proceeds from the speaker and the writing from the writer—that is to say, the speaker himself does not become the discourse, nor does the writer himself become the writing; no, rather they have the proceeding of emanation. . . . Therefore, the proceeding of the human spirits from God is through emanation. When it is said in the Bible that God breathed His spirit into man, this spirit is that which, like the discourse, emanates from the Real Speaker, taking effect in the reality of man.[25]

The Bahá'í writings also confirm that the process whereby the consciousness evolves as a function of the soul from the point of conception is, like the evolution of the human species, a gradual process. A letter written on behalf of Shoghi Effendi states, "You have asked as to what point in man's evolution he becomes conscious of self. This consciousness of self in man is a gradual process, and does not start at a definite point. It grows in him in this world and continues to do so in the future spiritual world."[26]

Now while it may go without saying at this point in our discourse, let us reiterate here that, according to Bahá'í belief, human consciousness, together with all other powers that materialists attribute to the brain, are actually powers of the soul operating through or in association with the brain. 'Abdu'l-Bahá explains, "Man has also spiritual powers: imagination, which conceives things; thought, which reflects upon realities; comprehension, which comprehends realities; memory, which retains whatever man imagines, thinks and comprehends."[27]

Another power that we will discuss more fully in the next chapter is that of will. For while we have implicitly discussed the operation and power of will as an expression of the metaphysical dimension of human existence (for example, Dossey's evidence of the conscious self and "action at a distance"), we would do well to discuss the matter in light of several other contemporary studies on the subject.* Let us conclude this part of our attempt to define the essence of self with a final but, for many, most weighty proposition—the concept of preexistence.

THE ISSUE OF PREEXISTENCE

Plato seems to have believed in preexistence. Hindus, Theosophists, Mormons and many others believe in preexistence. For those who believe in reincarnation, the concept of preexistence is essential, both theologically and ontologically. Some adherents of various religious and philosophical traditions believe the soul is destined to experience successive incarnations until it achieves a state of purity and worthiness such that it requires no further refinement in the physical classroom—a condition in which it is worthy of a purely spiritual existence. This ancient belief is especially appealing to a contemporary audience that finds it difficult to justify the existence of a divine Creator in light of the blatant suffering and injustice that so many people in the world must endure. Reincarnation would seem to give those who suffer another chance.

The Bahá'í teachings explicitly deny the validity of reincarnation, and the Bahá'í writings offer a variety of arguments to uphold this rejection of both preexistence and reincarnation. While we will examine these concepts in more detail later, the following statements written on behalf of Shoghi Effendi leave no room for quibbling on this important issue:

Regarding your question concerning the passage in "Seven Valleys" referring to pre-existence. This in no way presupposes the existence of the individual soul before conception.[28]

It is clear from the teachings of Bahá'u'lláh about the nature of the soul and of life after death as published in *Gleanings from the Writings of Bahá'u'lláh*, that the Bahá'í position on this subject is wholly incompatible with the theory of reincarnation.[29]

---

* For example, Brenda J. Dunne and Robert G. Jahn, *Margins of Reality: The Role of Consciousness in the Physical World* (Harcourt Brace, 1987), and Daniel M. Wegner, *The Illusion of Conscious Will* (MIT Press, 2002).

We know from His Teachings that Reincarnation does not exist. We come on to this planet once only. Our life here is like the baby in the womb of its mother, which develops in that state what is necessary for its entire life after it is born. The same is true of us. Spiritually we must develop here what we will require for the life after death. In that future life, God, through His mercy, can help us to evolve characteristics which we neglected to develop while we were on this earthly plane. It is not necessary for us to come back and be born into another body in order to advance spiritually and grow closer to God.[30]

According to Bahá'í belief, then, the individual soul begins at the conception of the physical body, continues infinitely its endless journey towards enlightenment and spiritual advancement, but has only one experience in the physical aspect of reality because, according to the Bahá'í writings, that is all we need, regardless of how successfully or poorly others may think we have fared and regardless of how lengthy or brief that experience may be.

THE PROBLEM OF THE INEQUALITY OF PHYSICAL EXPERIENCE

If we reject the possibility of preexistence and reincarnation, how can we account for the injustice that the lack of an equal chance at common experience seems to imply? If a soul passes on to the spiritual realm without any significant experience of this reality, how can it become prepared for what is to follow? How can we consider the Creator just if all people do not have an equal opportunity to benefit from their experience in the physical world?

Of course, the same objection could be raised about those who live many years, but who lack the opportunity for education (both spiritual and intellectual) or who must live in dire circumstances. How can such a process be just when not all souls have the same opportunity at happiness, success, or at expressing their free will? And even if we can figure out some explanation for the apparent lack of equanimity and justice that the concept of reincarnation might seem to redress, we are still left with another issue.

Logically we know that something cannot come from nothing. 'Abdu'l-Bahá states, "Every cause is followed by an effect and vice versa; there could be no effect without a cause preceding it."[31] Hence the concept of the soul as an emanation from the realm of the spirit must be foremost in our consideration of this topic. From a Bahá'í theological perspective, the desire, wish, or will of God to cause spiritual emanations is sufficient cause in and of itself for the soul to emanate. But the seeming lack of justice among life experiences does not produce a material process to resolve this apparent flaw in the divine process. Indeed, the origins of reincarnation doctrine stem from literalist interpretations of figurative images in religious scripture. Such images of the progress of souls in the "worlds" of God in the afterlife, as well as the interpretation of physical experiences of "heaven" and "hell," occur in the Judaic, Christian, and Islamic scriptural traditions.

There is a statement in the Bahá'í writings that might seem to give credence to a belief in a degree of preexistence, however amorphous such an existence might be:

In the human world, soul signifies the "rational being" or mind. This has a potential existence before its appearance in human life. It is like unto the existence of a tree within the seed. The existence of the tree within the seed is potential; but when the seed is sown and watered, the signs thereof, its roots and branches, and all of its different qualities, appear. Likewise the "rational soul" has a potential existence before its appearance in the human body, and through the mixture of elements and a wonderful combination, according to the natural order, law, conception and birth, it appears with its identity.[32]

The implications of this passage regarding individuality or identity are clear. The "ingredients," if you will, for the creation of the soul may exist in potential form in the world of the spirit, but the soul as an individual creation assumes its reality only once, and that occurs when and only when conception takes place; "potential" existence is not actual existence, and all doctrines of reincarnation assume a preexisting identity or soul.

Clearly this does not mean that conception is the cause of the soul's existence. As we have stated, the cause of the soul's creation is the will of God from which the spirit emanates. The conception of a physical temple to provide an associative relationship through which the soul can express itself and communicate with material reality is *incidental* to the soul's development but not *coincidental*.

As we will later discuss, the soul can develop with or without physical experience, but given an opportunity to participate willfully in this indirect metaphorical or physical learning experience, we as individual and conscious souls are obliged to take advantage of the physical stage of our existence to develop our souls and to fulfill our spiritual potential.

But how does this exercise take place, this constant traffic of information between the soul as spiritual essence and the brain, which channels ideas into action? Or put another way, we consider the "process" of thinking as a cerebral activity, a series of actions taking place in the physical circuitry of the brain. Therefore, while the reflecting soul may will the mind to think and decide upon a course of action, at what point does the brain take charge of the task and marshal the forces at its command? Is there any meaningful distinction between the soul's wish and the mind's administration of that intent?

– 12 –

Some Distinctions between Mind and Soul

Having recognized thy powerlessness to attain to an adequate understanding of that Reality which abideth within thee, thou wilt readily admit the futility of such efforts as may be attempted by thee, or by any of the created things, to fathom the mystery of the Living God, the Day Star of unfading glory, the Ancient of everlasting days. This confession of helplessness which mature contemplation must eventually impel every mind to make is in itself the acme of human understanding, and marketh the culmination of man's development.

—Bahá'u'lláh, *Gleanings*

As mentioned in chapter 11, from the Bahá'í perspective, human consciousness derives from the metaphysical essence that is the soul. In fact, from this essential reality emanates all that we are in terms of human capacity. We also noted earlier that because the soul is a spiritual essence, it is, like the essence of God Himself, essentially unknowable. Bahá'u'lláh explicates this concept when He writes,

Thou hast asked Me concerning the nature of the soul. Know, verily, that the soul is a sign of God, a heavenly gem whose reality the most learned of men hath failed to grasp, and whose mystery no mind, however acute, can ever hope to unravel. It is the first among all created things to declare the excellence of its Creator, the first to recognize His glory, to cleave to His truth, and to bow down in adoration before Him. If it be faithful to God, it will reflect His light, and will, eventually, return unto Him. If it fail, however, in its allegiance to its Creator, it will become a victim to self and passion, and will, in the end, sink in their depths.[1]

Even as we can attain knowledge of God by discerning the attributes of God manifest in physical reality, so we can by the same method come to know something about the qualities of our own soul. Furthermore, since our primary mandate as human beings is to know and to worship God, this process is accomplished partly by fulfilling the mandate that we come to know ourselves, inasmuch as we are fashioned in His image. Bahá'u'lláh writes, "in him [the human being] are potentially revealed all the attributes and names of God."[2]

What we are unable to comprehend with any exactitude is "that Reality which abideth within" us, the spiritual essence that is the soul itself.[3] Neither can we comprehend the spirit that vivifies or animates that essence, even though the human soul is neither uncaused nor perfected. As we have repeatedly acknowledged, the human soul is ever in motion, always progressing or regressing. For unlike the essence of God, which is eternal in the past, the essential human reality has a beginning, and while the Essence of God is self-sufficient, the human soul requires constant nourishment to survive and prosper. It is alive and progressing only as long as the Holy Spirit endows it with capacity and life. Furthermore, as we have also noted, while all the divine attributes are "potentially revealed" in us, they are perfectly revealed in the Manifestations.

CAN WE FOSTER OUR OWN SPIRITUAL PROGRESS?

As we discussed earlier in our study, receiving spiritual nourishment requires a sequence of actions on our part. We must first recognize the need for divine assistance, recognize the reality of God through His Manifestations as the source of that assistance, and become obedient to Their guidance. This reciprocity between our search for guidance and our subsequent responsibility to implement that guidance in action means that we can actively participate in advancing our own spiritual condition.

In this sense, the soul is the source of our being and the starting point for any sequence of causality governing our physical actions. At the same time, the individual soul is not a static reality. Like all other organic life, the soul is in a state of ceaseless change. During its period of association with the human temple, that change can be progressive or regressive, depending on our freely chosen path of response to the challenges we face in discovering the spiritual meaning concealed in the "Kingdom of Names."*

Some passages in the Bahá'í writings can be understood to imply that progression is assured in the afterlife, that regression is not possible in the realm of the spirit, that all truth will be apparent and we will no longer be required to exert effort or free will to discover reality. But let us compare two statements of 'Abdu'l-Bahá contrasting these realities insofar as spiritual progression and regression are concerned.

'Abdu'l-Bahá states, "In this material world time has cycles; places change through alternating seasons, and for souls there are progress, retrogression and education." In another statement dealing with the continuity of the soul, 'Abdu'l-Bahá says, "But with the human soul, there is no decline. Its only movement is towards perfection; growth and progress alone constitute the motion of the soul." If we interpret this statement to mean that no effort or will is required in the continuation of life beyond physical reality, we need to turn to yet another statement on this same issue in which 'Abdu'l-Bahá makes it clear that all is not so simple. As the soul continues in the afterlife, the law of change remains operant; furthermore, to cease to progress is tantamount to regression: "Now, as the spirit continues to exist after death, it necessarily progresses or declines; and in the other world to cease to progress is the same as to decline; but it never leaves its own condition, in which it continues to develop."4

BEGINNING WHERE WE LEAVE OFF HERE

The result of these considerations is the verity that our "second birth" begins where we leave off here. Therefore we would do well to pay

---

* An appellation in Bahá'í scripture that alludes to physical reality.

careful attention to the daily task at hand, to make willful progress here and now. Whatever principles for progress may be operant in the afterlife, we have arrived at one stark and unremitting truth in our quest to understand the spiritual purpose of physical reality: The more we understand and engage in the spiritual process devised for our progress in this life, the easier will be our birth pangs as we enter the next stage of our existence and the better equipped we will be to understand and navigate that reality.

THE INHERENT LOVE OF KNOWLEDGE

As we read these words and consider these ideas, we can be said to exist in the world of physical reality. However, if our conscious self and powers of ideation and rational thought derive from the soul, then, unwittingly, the true "self" is currently abiding in the realm of the spirit. We are, if this is true, bridging the gap between these dual aspects of reality at this very moment.

For this period of time while we endure or experience this relatively transparent associative relationship, we have the subtle and challenging task of refining our spiritual essence through physical exercises—a sort of allegorical or symbolic dramatization of what we wish to become as spiritual beings. We might compare this arrangement to those pictures we have seen of lab technicians tediously working with robotic arms and hands to manipulate dangerous materials at a distance. Unlike the technicians, however, we have the distinct sensation that this physical device—our body—is actually our real self, at least until we age sufficiently that we become ever more acutely aware that our vibrant and vital ideas must be expressed through an ever more ineffectual machine.

But, as a mighty and unrelenting incentive to discover the truth about this relationship, the Creator has implanted in us an inherent love of knowledge that can be accurately depicted as an overwhelming desire to understand reality. Consequently, if we respond correctly to this desire and work well with the tools at our disposal, we can in time solve the fundamental mysteries about our own existence. In this context 'Abdu'l-Bahá states, "Science is the first emanation from God toward man. All created beings embody the potentiality of material perfection, but the power of intellectual investigation and scientific acquisition is a higher virtue specialized to man alone. Other beings and organisms are deprived of this potentiality and attainment. God has created or deposited this love of reality in man."⁵

"Science" in this passage clearly indicates not a specific field of study, but all forms of investigating reality—the general love of knowledge. It is also worth noting in the context of this same discussion by 'Abdu'l-Bahá that he says this desire is not only the most primal instinct or fundamental faculty bestowed on humankind, woven by the Creator into the very fabric of our being, it is also an eternal power or faculty, a permanent part of our being, whether we exist in the "Kingdom of Names" or in the realm of the spirit:

All blessings are divine in origin, but none can be compared with this power of intellectual investigation and research, which is an eternal gift producing fruits of unending delight. Man is ever partaking of these fruits. All other blessings are temporary; this is an everlasting possession. Even sovereignty has its limitations and overthrow; this ["the power of intellectual investigation and research"] is a kingship and dominion which none may usurp or destroy. Briefly, it is an eternal blessing and divine bestowal, the supreme gift of God to man. Therefore, you should put forward your most earnest efforts toward the acquisition of science and arts. The greater your attainment, the higher your standard in the divine purpose.⁶

SOUL VERSUS SPIRIT

Since the desire for knowledge is the first emanation of God to man, it might seem logical to discuss the mind and its function before we discuss anything else. But while the mind is an integral part of our being, it cannot respond to this thirst for knowledge until the soul becomes aware of a potential source of knowledge. Therefore, as we discuss the path of causality in the microcosm of our individual existence, let us begin at the beginning—with the created soul and its connection to the body.

'ABDU'L-BAHÁ'S TERMINOLOGY

'Abdu'l-Bahá's native language was Persian, and all of his writings and discourses were conducted in that language. The English terms employed to translate his discussions about the soul and its relationship to the other components and powers of the human being, particularly those referring to the spirit and the mind, may sometimes be confusing because various translators have used different terms to render the concepts into English. Shoghi Effendi acknowledges this problem:

> When studying at present, in English, the available Bahá'í writings on the subject of body, soul and spirit, one is handicapped by a certain lack of clarity because not all were translated by the same person, and also there are, as you know, still many Bahá'í writings untranslated. But there is no doubt that spirit and soul seem to have been interchanged in meaning sometimes; soul and mind have, likewise, been interchanged in meaning, no doubt due to difficulties arising from different translations. What the Bahá'ís do believe though is that we have three aspects of our humanness, so to speak, a body, a mind and an immortal identity—soul or spirit. We believe the mind forms a link between the soul and the body, and the two interact on each other.[7]

Examples of what Shoghi Effendi refers to are most clearly discovered in those passages where 'Abdu'l-Bahá makes reference to the human soul, but the English translation employs the term "rational soul." This term might make us think 'Abdu'l-Bahá is designating the mind or the rational faculty as opposed to the spiritual essence that is the soul itself.

The reason for the translator's use of the term "rational soul" is that in many of his discussions of the soul 'Abdu'l-Bahá employs the term *nafs-i-náṭiqih,* a Persian translation of an Aristotelian term that means "talking soul." This choice of terms is important because it alludes to one of the most obvious distinctions in capacity between humankind and the animal kingdom—the capacity for abstract thought as evidenced in the ability to articulate concepts into symbolic expressions through language. Another noteworthy observation is that 'Abdu'l-Bahá sometimes employs the term *spirit* to allude to the human soul, while at other times he may use the same term to refer to the power that animates the soul and emanates from it.

THE SOUL AS INTERMEDIARY FOR THE SPIRIT

The primary conclusion we derive from these variations and apparent inconsistencies in 'Abdu'l-Bahá's discussions about the soul, the mind, and the spirit is that the more we read his discussions and the more carefully we compare his comments, the clearer his analyses of these components and their relationships become. In particular, 'Abdu'l-Bahá makes clear distinctions about the path of causality regarding the soul, the spirit, and the mind, especially as these components interact. Indeed, it is in this context that Shoghi Effendi in the previous passage speaks of the manner in which "the mind forms a link between the soul and the body, and the two interact on each other."

In effect, Shoghi Effendi is alluding to the "link" between the metaphysical powers and the physical edifice of the human temple, the very heart of our quest in this volume. For as we have noted, the soul is the essence or fundamental reality of an individual from which emanate all our powers and faculties—cognitive thought or reason, imagination, contemplation, memory, will, and so forth. Likewise, the soul is the intermediary through which the powers from the realm of the spirit become expressed in physical action.

While the conscious mind associates with the brain—a condition that endures so long as the body remains a fit vehicle for the soul—we are largely unaware of any distinction between ourselves as spiritual beings and ourselves as sensate, contemplative, but physical beings. This ingenious and, until recently, almost impenetrable illusion has baffled all who have attempted to determine the source of our humanness, the realm of consciousness, the cause of our sense of "self."

The reason for this problem is the grand illusion created by our periscopic relationship to reality through our conscious mind. Since all insights and information are conveyed to the human consciousness, we are unable to assess the extent to which our conscious thoughts are being shaped and affected by the health and capacity of the brain.

Once we understand that the soul as a divine emanation is our essential reality (the spiritual "organism" comparable to the "Hidden Treasure" that is God in the macrocosm) then perhaps the next step in our examination of how the soul runs the body is to consider how the spirit animates the soul and thence emanates from it in the form of thoughts, ideas, or wishes.

'ABDU'L-BAHÁ'S TREE ANALOGY

'Abdu'l-Bahá distinguishes between the soul and the spirit in an analogy that alludes to the intermediary process as the means by which something is accomplished:

> You perceive how the soul is the intermediary between the body and the spirit. In like manner is this tree the intermediary between the seed and the fruit. When the fruit of the tree appears and becomes ripe, then we know that the tree is perfect; if the tree bore no fruit it would be merely a useless growth, serving no purpose!
>
> When a soul has in it the life of the spirit, then does it bring forth good fruit and become a Divine tree. I wish you to try to understand this example.[8]

'Abdu'l-Bahá discusses the spirit as the *élan vital,* the life-giving sustenance emanating from God through the Holy Spirit as rays of energy emanate from the sun, creating, empowering, nurturing, and sustaining the soul. We are, as it were, like branches growing on a tree that remain sustained so long as they remain connected to the tree.

This description is precisely parallel to the language that is used to describe the process by which the Manifestation of God emanates from God, becomes filled with the Holy Spirit, and, as a perfect intermediary, becomes effectively synonymous with the Holy Spirit because the Holy Spirit is reflected to us flawlessly via the intermediary of the Manifestation.

At times, then, 'Abdu'l-Bahá implies the spirit is an essential property of the soul, but not identical with the soul. For example, in discussing the two main faculties of the soul, 'Abdu'l-Bahá states,

The spirit in the soul is the very essence of life. . . . The second faculty of the soul expresses itself in the world of vision, where the soul inhabited by the spirit has its being, and functions without the help of the material bodily senses. There, in the realm of vision, the soul sees without the help of the physical eye, hears without the aid of the physical ear, and travels without dependence upon physical motion. It is, therefore, clear that the spirit in the soul of man can function through the physical body by using the organs of the ordinary senses, and that it is able also to live and act without their aid in the world of vision.[9]

We will discuss this relationship in more detail later, but it is crucial to observe here that 'Abdu'l-Bahá notes how the soul functions while associating with the body "through the physical body by using the organs of the ordinary senses," but when the soul dissociates from the body at death, it functions "in the realm of vision" and "without the help of the material bodily senses." We might add that the soul functions in the realm of the spirit unencumbered by the bodily senses, which, over the course of our earthly lives, inevitably become increasingly unreliable.

'Abdu'l-Bahá notes that we can no more distinguish the soul from its essential power than we can distinguish the sun from its rays. We might well ponder, therefore, whether or not it is futile and unimportant to make any distinction between these two realities.

For our purposes, this distinction will assume more importance as we elaborate the two methodologies by which the spirit operates as the conduit for information channeled to the conscious soul. Hence the distinction between the soul and the spirit is relevant to our study.

The spirit emanates from the soul and sustains and empowers the soul. Yet even as the Manifestation is effectively synonymous with the Holy Spirit or the Word of God, so our own spirit is, for us, effectively indistinguishable from that spiritual essence which is animated by this force. Returning to 'Abdu'l-Bahá's simple yet profoundly useful analogy of the tree, we can, by comparing the soul to the tree, understand that the soul is the intermediary in the sense that it is the mechanism, or organism, by which the spirit (like the life force animating the tree) can cause the tree to bring forth fruit (in our case, good works).

THE HOLY SPIRIT ANIMATES ALL SOULS ALIKE

In this sense, the spirit exists prior to the soul, and each individual soul is a means (or intermediary) by which the spirit can make itself manifest in physical reality. This profound fact does not imply that all sense of our individuality, our distinct essence, is erroneous or illusory, but it does imply that we all emanate from the same source, are nourished by the same spirit, and are all exhorted to bring forth the same fruit: recognition of the Beloved and obedience to His loving guidance for us.

Therefore when Bahá'u'lláh says, "Of one tree are all ye the fruit, and of one bough the leaves," He is not merely asserting a poetic image about world unity, but stating a critical fact about our essential reality.[10] The selfsame spirit animates the souls of all humankind. It takes on an individualized expression as our distinct personalities channel this life-giving force into individual lives. In this way we may willfully bring forth fruit to assist in this collective enterprise and, in so doing, simultaneously instigate our own refinement. Perhaps the most important conclusion we take from this analogy is the understanding that we have no more individual existence apart from the spirit, this source of our existence, than would a branch severed from the tree.

CONCEPTS OF "OVERSOUL" OR PANTHEISM

While we are all nourished from the same fountain, we are not merely increments of a vast Oversoul, as Emerson and other Transcendentalists thought. Neither does this concept admit a sort of Pantheism where all creation is a *part* of God, or, conversely, where "God" signifies the sum total of the spiritual power of all beings and all souls. The Bahá'í writings state that the spirit, like the rays of the sun, illumines all creation, but each part of creation reflects that light according to its capacity. 'Abdu'l-Bahá explains that all beings themselves are thus recipients and mirrors of light, not sources of light in the strictest sense: "The first emanation from God is the bounty of the Kingdom, which emanates and is reflected in the reality of the creatures, like the light which emanates from the sun and is resplendent in creatures; and this bounty, which is the light, is reflected in infinite forms in the reality of all things, and specifies and individualizes itself according to the capacity, the worthiness and the intrinsic value of things."[11]

THE CONSCIOUS MIND OR "RATIONAL FACULTY"

Naturally the analogy of the tree bringing forth fruit is a simplified version of the path of causality by which the soul brings about a spiritually progressing human being as manifest in refined character and meaningful social action. As we have noted, this process is reciprocal so that the act of willfully responding to our inherent desire to know reality and of expressing this acquired knowledge in creative action fosters the soul's advancement and refinement.

THE AWARENESS OF THOUGHT

How exactly does the spirit, working through the intermediary of the soul, cause the body to function? We have mentioned that the love of knowledge is inherent in us. But how does this desire become expressed as a process?

The first part of this process we are aware of is our conscious decision to behave in a certain manner, either because we think a course of action is fulfilling or because we accede to someone else's urging. Possibly our actions are the result of an emotional need rather than a carefully considered path chosen willfully after reflection. But at some point we become aware that we have a degree of control over what sort of person we will become or what sort of "fruit" we will empower the tree of our being to bring forth. We have decisions to make.

Most of the time this awareness of "self" is effectively our awareness of our own mind, the cognitive faculty of the soul. While we exist in an associative relationship with our human temple, the link between the faculty of the mind and the soul itself is through the intermediary of the brain, though most of the time we are not aware of any important distinction between our mind as a rational power of the soul and the soul itself.

THE RATIONAL FACULTY

As we have noted, according to Bahá'í belief, the conscious mind as a power or function of the soul endures beyond our existence in the physical world. But we have also observed that our ability to utilize this primary faculty of the soul can be affected by the condition of the brain during our physical existence, our indirect or "periscopic" relationship with reality.

We have already cited some statements about the inherent nature of the rational faculty and its eternal existence. A few pertinent passages from the Bahá'í writings will explain more exactly how to define and understand this rational power, especially as it is distinct from other powers of the soul. For example, in one passage 'Abdu'l-Bahá states that even though the mind associates with the brain during our physical existence, it is not resident there: "The mind which is in man, the existence of which is recognized—where is it in him? If you examine the body with the eye, the ear or the other senses, you will not find it; nevertheless, it exists. Therefore, the mind has no place, but it is connected with the brain."[12]

'Abdu'l-Bahá makes this point in more detail in his letter to Auguste Forel, which speaks explicitly of the mental faculties as "properties of the soul": "Now concerning mental faculties, they are in truth of the inherent properties of the soul, even as the radiation of light is the essential property of the sun." While the mind—this unique capacity of human beings to investigate and discover reality and the laws that govern creation—is an essential capacity of the soul, it is not synonymous with the soul. The soul is an existent being, and thought or meditation is an inalienable faculty or power of that reality.[13]

Thus while the mind is not the only faculty or power of the soul, it is the crucial power of rational thought that is the most essential means by which we can function as a human being. For this reason it is the power of the mind that we find most emphasized in the Bahá'í writings. Bahá'u'lláh praises the mental or rational faculty as the principal means by which the human being is enabled to utilize his experience in the physical world: "Consider the rational faculty with which God hath endowed the essence of man. Examine thine own self, and behold how thy motion and stillness, thy will and purpose, thy sight and hearing, thy sense of smell and power of speech, and whatever else is related to, or transcendeth, thy physical senses or spiritual perceptions, all proceed from, and owe their existence to, this same faculty."[14]

Bahá'u'lláh also notes that the mind as a metaphysical reality is distinct from the physical senses, which are at its disposal to investigate physical reality: "It is indubitably clear and evident that each of these afore-mentioned instruments [the senses and the power of speech] has depended, and will ever continue to depend, for its proper functioning on this rational faculty, which should be regarded as a sign of the revelation of Him Who is the sovereign Lord of all." Shoghi Effendi likewise affirms in a letter written on his behalf that the "rational faculty is a manifestation of the power of the soul." And yet, as the passage from Bahá'u'lláh makes clear, the mind has at its disposal a number of subsidiary tools through which it fulfills its essential function of enabling the human being to become somewhat autonomous in attaining an understanding of reality and in willfully determining to comply with the laws of reality.[15]

THE MIND IN RELATION TO THE BRAIN

If the mind is the most critical link between the soul and the body, then we need to understand how that link is fashioned. If it associates with the brain, to what extent does spiritual development depend on a well-functioning or well-developed brain? For example, is mental acuity an index of spiritual achievement? What function does the brain play in spiritual development if it is the "seat" of the rational faculty (the conscious mind)? Is the brain merely an elaborate transceiver for two-way communication between the mind and the physical world?

'Abdu'l-Bahá notes that for the mind to become manifest in the physical world the body must be sufficiently healthy so that the brain can conduct its function as transceiver for the mind: "Consider how the human intellect develops and weakens, and may at times come to naught, whereas the soul changeth not. For the mind to manifest itself, the human body must be whole; and a sound mind cannot be but in a sound body, whereas the soul dependeth not upon the body. It is through the power of the soul that the mind comprehendeth, imagineth and exerteth its influence, whilst the soul is a power that is free."[16]

213

The distinction between mind and soul becomes clearer still. The mind as a cognitive faculty in association with the brain can become encumbered or even nullified by injury to the brain. Therefore someone who has a brain injury, a severe neuromuscular disorder, a mental illness, or some form of retardation may appear to observers in the physical world as someone whose soul is maimed, whose "self" is degenerate or nonexistent.

However, the true "self" or the "personality" of the individual are aspects of the soul and are not dependent on the physical edifice with which the soul associates. The soul and its powers—for example, the rational faculty—are not adversely affected by the incapacity or dysfunction of the brain. The soul and its powers are also not defeated by the temporary inability of the mind to function associatively with the brain or to communicate effectively with the physical world.

No interference with the two-way communication between the soul and physical reality can affect our essential reality—our soul, our "self," or the powers deriving therefrom. Bahá'u'lláh writes,

> Know thou that the soul of man is exalted above, and is independent of all infirmities of body or mind. That a sick person showeth signs of weakness is due to the hindrances that interpose themselves between his soul and his body, for the soul itself remaineth unaffected by any bodily ailments. Consider the light of the lamp. Though an external object may interfere with its radiance, the light itself continueth to shine with undiminished power. In like manner, every malady afflicting the body of man is an impediment that preventeth the soul from manifesting its inherent might and power.[17]

What Bahá'u'lláh seems to imply here is that *any* "malady afflicting the body" prevents the soul from "manifesting its inherent might and power" to the physical world and to those who occupy it, or even, in some cases, to the conscious "self," so long as this condition endures. But such a malady does not affect the essential health or progress of the soul itself.

'Abdu'l-Bahá makes the same observation while further distinguishing between the soul and the mind. He states that while the soul is ever active and strong, the mind may be temporarily bereft of power when the senses do not function, when the individual is in an embryonic state of existence, or when the individual is in early infancy: "The mind, moreover, understandeth not whilst the senses have ceased to function, and in the embryonic stage and in early infancy the reasoning power is totally absent, whereas the soul is ever endowed with full strength. In short, the proofs are many that go to show that despite the loss of reason, the power of the soul would still continue to exist."[18]

Once freed from the associative relationship with the body, the soul evinces its true condition and powers because it is no longer constrained by the periscopic relationship with physical reality. We thus cannot assume that once we have ceased to function indirectly with reality by means of the body and its powers we no longer have awareness of our relationship with physical reality.

The Bahá'í writings indicate clearly that those who have "ascended"—who are no longer constrained by the physical temple—labor to assist those in this world who are promulgating the Cause of God.

TWO METHODS

Another distinction 'Abdu'l-Bahá makes between the mind and the soul concerns two methods of acquiring knowledge about reality. First, the mind can learn about abstract concepts by examining their particular expressions in the physical world. The mind infers or induces the general from the particular and the unknown from the known. This is what we commonly allude to as the scientific method.

However, the soul also has at its disposal methods for acquiring information about reality directly from the spiritual realm—through prayer and reflection, meditation, dreams, intuition, inspiration, and so forth. 'Abdu'l-Bahá writes, "The mind comprehendeth the abstract by the aid of the concrete, but the soul hath limitless manifestations of its own. The mind is circumscribed, the soul limitless. It is by the aid of such senses as those of sight, hearing, taste, smell and touch that the mind comprehendeth, whereas the soul is free from all agencies. The soul as thou observest, whether it be in sleep or waking, is in motion and ever active. Possibly it may, whilst in a dream, unravel an intricate problem, incapable of solution in the waking state."[19]

THE REPOSITORY OF THE CONSCIOUS MIND

But regardless from what source information derives, it ends up in the same "place" so long as we exist in the periscopic relationship with reality—it ends up in our conscious mind. The soul can partake of the knowledge derived by the rational faculty (the indirect, inferential, or scientific method), and the rational mind can partake of information derived directly from the spiritual world via inspiration, prayer, meditation, or reflection. The fact is that all information we receive ultimately ends up in the same repository of our conscious thoughts so long as we are bound by the constraints of physical existence.

Once ideas or bits of information arrive in our consciousness, we must then determine what to do with them. We must willfully evaluate the information we have received, reflect on its authenticity, its importance, and its relevance to our present circumstance. Then we must decide what should be our appropriate response to this knowledge. When we have decided on a course of action, we must next employ our will both to instigate the action and to see it through to completion.

This process of acquiring information, reflecting on it, determining a course of action, and then willfully following it through to completion is essentially the same procedure indicated by 'Abdu'l-Bahá in one of his most familiar axioms on the subject. He observes, in *The Promulgation of Universal Peace,* that the "attainment of any object is conditioned upon knowledge, volition and action."[20] What we now need to discover is exactly how this procedure takes place. Therefore in the next chapter we will compare the process that occurs at the macrocosmic level when the Manifestation appears as teacher with the parallel process that occurs in our individual consciousness.

- 13 -

Mind and Will

If the human spirit will rejoice and be attracted to the Kingdom of God, if the inner sight becomes opened, and the spiritual hearing strengthened, and the spiritual feelings predominant, he will see the immortality of the spirit as clearly as he sees the sun, and the glad tidings and signs of God will encompass him.

—'Abdu'l-Bahá, *Some Answered Questions*

Moving from the fundamental distinctions and definitions we made in the previous chapter regarding the concepts of mind, spirit, and soul, let us now pursue in more detail how the soul runs the body. To accomplish this, let us return to our analogy between the macrocosm and the microcosm. By so doing, we will be able to compare how the Creator fosters the progress of humankind through the intermediary of the Manifestation to the means by which the soul instigates the progress of the individual through the intermediary of the rational faculty.

SOME PARALLELS

We have observed that the source of creation is the Creator. This axiom holds true for creation as a whole as well as for the individual, since all created reality emanates from the Creator. But a parallel between the creation and evolution of a macrocosmic system, such as our planet, and a microcosmic system, such as ourselves, can be seen in the intermediary process by which each system is nurtured and assisted.

217

On the macrocosmic level, the First Will emanates from the Creator, "fills" (empowers or animates) the Manifestations with the "Holy Spirit," which the Manifestations in turn convey flawlessly to humanity in forms of guidance, example, knowledge, and patterns of action. In a comparable fashion on the microcosmic level, the will emanates from the soul in the form of the spirit of the individual, empowers the mind or rational faculty, which in turn conveys information to the physical temple in the form of conscious knowledge and patterns of behavior or action.

The main distinction between the two parts of this analogy is that we are describing the Holy Spirit as the power that is the intermediary between the First Mind and the Manifestation, whereas we are describing the "spirit" of the individual as the intermediary between the soul and the mind. The intermediary between the world of God and the world of creation is the Holy Spirit, which traverses all realities but which employs the Manifestation as the medium (perfect mirror or transceiver) to fashion the world of creation into an outer expression of the "unseen kingdom of Thy oneness."[1] Between the human soul and the human temple is the intermediary of the human spirit, which employs the medium (imperfect mirror or transceiver) of the rational faculty or the mind to bring about patterns of action that enable the daily life of the individual to demonstrate an ever more refined spiritual or "inner" life.

We have observed that at a certain point in the evolution of humankind, the Manifestation temporarily assumes an associative relationship with a human temple in order to assist the transformation and progress of the world of creation—to help human society emulate by degrees the nature of spiritual reality. A parallel process occurs in the transformation of the individual human being when the conscious mind or rational faculty as intermediary for the soul assumes its temporary associative relationship with the human temple (that is, with the brain).

Without the intermediary of the Manifestations to convey the Holy Spirit to the world of creation, 'Abdu'l-Bahá states, "the world of souls and thoughts would be opaque darkness."[2] Likewise, without the intermediary of the rational faculty to convey the powers of the human spirit to the human temple, physical human faculties would instantly cease to function. Bahá'u'lláh writes,

So closely are they [human powers] related unto it [the rational faculty], that if in less than the twinkling of an eye its relationship to the human body be severed, each and every one of these senses will cease immediately to exercise its function, and will be deprived of the power to manifest the evidences of its activity. It is indubitably clear and evident that each of these afore-mentioned instruments has depended, and will ever continue to depend, for its proper functioning on this rational faculty, which should be regarded as a sign of the revelation of Him Who is the sovereign Lord of all. Through its manifestation all these names and attributes have been revealed, and by the suspension of its action they are all destroyed and perish.[3]

SPIRIT AND KNOWLEDGE

One of the most amazing parallels between the macrocosm and the microcosm lies in the manner in which knowledge is acquired. As we have already mentioned, the Bahá'í writings describe two fundamental methods by which we acquire information about reality—the indirect method, which involves the senses (the scientific method), and the direct method, which does not involve the senses (inspiration, prayers, dreams, intuition, and so on). However, there is also a type of knowledge of reality that 'Abdu'l-Bahá states is simply extant, "an absolute gift."[4]

On the macrocosmic level, such knowledge is given to the Manifestations in Their "human" condition. Shoghi Effendi observes that the Manifestations are "omniscient at will." 'Abdu'l-Bahá indicates that the Manifestations have a direct knowledge of reality because Their spirit "surrounds" reality: "Since the Sanctified Realities, the supreme Manifestations of God, surround the essence and qualities of the creatures, transcend and contain existing realities and understand all things, therefore, Their knowledge is divine knowledge, and not acquired—that is to say, it is a holy bounty; it is a divine revelation."[5]

We can acquire a better understanding of the knowledge the Manifestations possess about reality by comparing it to the knowledge we possess about ourselves. That is, the microcosmic parallel to this divine knowledge of reality concerns our sense of our own condition. Here we are alluding not to the "self" that is the spiritual essence from which we derive all of our powers, but rather to the awareness of ourselves to which Descartes and Schäfer refer. It is the subjective sense of our own existence and of our bodies as somehow part of that existence because the spirit emanating from our soul "surrounds" the body in the same way that the spirit of the Manifestation "surrounds" reality as whole. 'Abdu'l-Bahá explains, "For example, the mind and the spirit of man are cognizant of the conditions and states of the members and component parts of the body, and are aware of all the physical sensations; in the same way, they are aware of their power, of their feelings, and of their spiritual conditions. This is the knowledge of being which man realizes and perceives, for the spirit surrounds the body and is aware of its sensations and powers. This knowledge is not the outcome of effort and study. It is an existing thing; it is an absolute gift."[6] Besides providing a profound and useful insight into the distinction between our own knowledge of reality and that which the Manifestation possesses, this analogy also provides additional confirmation of the fact that the Manifestation is ontologically distinct from ordinary human beings.

CAN SPIRIT "SURROUND" ANYTHING?

Does this statement about the spirit "surrounding" the body in the microcosm mean that the spirit emanates from the soul and *literally* surrounds the body in some physical sense? Is this the key to the "close connection" we are discussing?

It would seem ludicrous to ascribe physical properties and conditions to a nonphysical reality or force. Perhaps proponents of Kirlian photography would suggest that the condition of the spirit is precisely what is being captured in the various colors radiating around the body in the form of auras. Likewise, one who advocates the manipulation of auras or acupuncture meridians (as energy fields) might find this concept appealing as literal fact.

But while we might find it impossible to accept that a metaphysical power can have physical properties, we have already asserted that a metaphysical power can have a physical effect. What else are we talking about when we posit the theory that the Manifestation is responsible for human progress or that the human soul is the source of human conduct? Therefore, while we cannot ascribe physical *properties* to an essentially metaphysical reality, we can presume its powers are indeed capable of producing detectable physical effects.

This knowledge of the self, described as an "inherent gift," is not the only knowledge that comes to us in a direct manner. 'Abdu'l-Bahá also alludes to "subjective" knowledge as that information which is obtained directly from the realm of vision, from the spiritual world. It includes insights such as those derived from dreams, inspiration, intuition, prayer, and meditation.

THE OBJECTIVE METHODOLOGY AND THE "COMMON FACULTY"

The second means of acquiring knowledge about reality is the indirect method, by which sensual data about reality is transformed into a mental image. 'Abdu'l-Bahá refers to this method as the "objective" mode, which enables us to obtain "knowledge derived from perception." He explains, "For instance, sight is one of the outer powers; it sees and perceives this flower, and conveys this perception to the inner power—the common faculty—which transmits this perception to the power of imagination, which in its turn conceives and forms this image and transmits it to the power of thought. . . ."[7]

It is very important for us here to reflect on two considerations. The first is whether or not there exists for the Manifestation a parallel deductive process that the Prophet also must employ during His earthly appearance. All descriptions by the Manifestations about Their having immediate access to whatever They need to know would seem to indicate that, while aware of deductive processes by which a verity can be proved, the Manifestations are not like the rest of us—They are not dependent on this indirect methodology for acquiring information about reality. For example, Bahá'u'lláh states in the Tablet of Wisdom (Lawḥ-i-Ḥikmat) that even though He has never "perused" books of learning, whenever He desires "to quote the sayings of the learned and of the wise, presently there will appear before the face of thy Lord in the form of a tablet all that which hath appeared in the world and is revealed in the Holy Books and Scriptures."[8]

But besides having access to this metaphysical and divinely empowered "search engine," the Manifestations also know intuitively and directly what may take scientists centuries to discover or prove. Decades before advances in travel and communication caused visionaries to discuss the concept of a global community, Bahá'u'lláh sent, beginning in the mid-1860s, explicit letters to political and religious leaders announcing that the world had already become a single community. In these same epistles He exhorted world leaders to reduce armaments and usher in this new reality by constructing a world commonwealth of nations. Among many other admonitions, He urged them to establish a global economy with an international currency, a universal system of weights and measures, a universal auxiliary language, and a system of collective justice.

But the Manifestations not only possess a direct, intuitive view of reality regarding the social and economic needs of humankind. They also possess direct knowledge of the physical laws of the universe. Bahá'u'lláh clearly alludes to atomic energy in a number of passages. For example, in the Kitáb-i-Íqán (Book of Certitude) He observes that "within every atom traces of the sun hath been made manifest." Similarly, in the seventh century when students of the heavens still upheld the Ptolemaic theory of a geocentric universe, Muḥammad asserted the origin of the earth to have occurred when it broke off from the sun and assumed its proper orbit around the sun: "Do not the unbelievers see that the heavens and the earth were joined together (as one unit of Creation), before we clove them asunder?"; "It is He Who created the night and the Day, and the sun and the moon: all (the celestial bodies) swim along, each in its rounded course [proper orbit]."[9]

This "common faculty," then, possibly has no parallel in the processing of information on the part of the Manifestation. Yet, in the causal pathway employed by ordinary human beings, this bridge between the two expressions of reality would seem to be a critical juncture. For example, 'Abdu'l-Bahá describes "the common faculty" as the power to transmit information from the "outer" powers to the "inner powers." He explains, "The intermediary between the five outward powers and the inward powers is the sense which they possess in common—that is to say, the sense which acts between the outer and inner powers, conveys to the inward powers whatever the outer powers discern. It is termed the common faculty, because it communicates between the outward and inward powers and thus is common to the outward and inward powers."[10] In chapters 14 and 15 we will consider more carefully whether or not this "common faculty" could be the *bridge* between the two aspects of our reality.

CONSCIOUS KNOWLEDGE, WILL, AND OUR PERISCOPIC VIEW OF REALITY

Upon reflection, we might conclude that the Manifestation, as God's Vice-regent, would need to employ little effort or will to accomplish His goals. Various passages from Bahá'í scripture indicate that He has but to will something and it is: "He Who hath been manifested is the Hidden Mystery, the Treasured Symbol, through Whom the letters B and E (Be) have been joined and knit together."[11] Yet in our discussion of the Manifestation in chapter 4, we noted several passages which demonstrate conclusively that the Manifestation does employ will to accomplish tasks and that He is not impervious to pain or to the strains His mission imposes upon His human condition.

If the Manifestation Himself must employ will, how much more will must we employ, given our general lack of awareness of the reality in which we dwell? Within this context 'Abdu'l-Bahá affirms that our own advancement, however much it may be assisted from forces outside ourselves, must be instigated and sustained by our own will. Therefore, having traced the causal pathway through which information about reality arrives in our conscious minds, let us now determine what is the source of action from this point forward.

THE NATURE OF WILL

We could spend volumes discussing the nuances of *will*, but for our purposes here, we need only acknowledge that one essential faculty of any human endeavor is the endeavor itself, a process that ultimately depends on our willful examination of ideas followed by conscious action.

In short, "will" is a part of all meaningful knowledge that we acquire and of all subsequent actions we perform as a result of that knowledge. 'Abdu'l-Bahá makes this point clear when he states, "Mere knowledge of principles is not sufficient. We all know and admit that justice is good, but there is need of volition and action to carry out and manifest it."[12]

Nowhere is the power of will more apparent than in our ability to shape our own destiny for good or ill in terms of our spiritual development. For while we may have little or no control over the path our life will take or what tests and calamities will befall us, we do have control over how we will respond to all circumstances. Bahá'u'lláh writes, "All that which ye potentially possess can, however, be manifested only as a result of your own volition. Your own acts testify to this truth."[13]

THE CONTEMPORARY DEBATE

While such observations about conscious will may seem unsophisticated and obvious, the concept of volition or will is, in fact, hotly contested, especially by some materialist thinkers who, in denying the existence of a metaphysical aspect of "self," seem to be forced logically to deny as well the concept of "will" inasmuch as it too is necessarily metaphysical in origin and nature.

For if conscious will exists, it must derive from the "self," and if the "self" is not a metaphysical reality but an illusion created by the biochemical circuitry of the brain, then will itself would necessarily also be illusory. How could a nonexistent entity cause something physical to occur? And if our will is illusory, then in what sense are we responsible for acts attributed to us—either great accomplishments or great crimes?

The unavoidable conclusion we would derive from accepting such thinking is that we as a society should cease celebrating our heroes and punishing our criminals—a position that has been argued with some degree of success in many American courtrooms in attempt to attribute a criminal's guilt to pernicious forces and addictive influences beyond conscious control—for example, video games, bad nutrition, or excessive peer pressure. The general background against which this issue of consciousness and will is debated we have already discussed in great detail—to admit metaphysical reality into existence flies in the face of materialist thought. To affirm that such a reality exists and is related to, or integrated with, physical reality is even more threatening, because then all theories about physical laws would have to take into account the possible interaction between unseen (and, at this point, totally immeasurable and unquantifiable) metaphysical laws and the physical universe.

One response to the more simplistic materialist observations is Jeffrey Satinover's *The Quantum Brain*. He observes that most modern neuroscientists say, "'One day we will understand *how* the organization of the brain gives rises to consciousness,' meaning how such and such an organization of matter *necessarily must be conscious.*" He also discusses the modern materialist view—that consciousness is an illusion, or else, *if* mind exists, "it can have no influence whatever on matter, because materialism requires no nonmaterial influences."[14]

Satinover humbly but logically concludes that he has no idea what consciousness is or what causes it. He writes,

> the mysteriousness of consciousness, it seems to me, is self-evidently of a different order from other puzzles. Unlike lightning, say, consciousness cannot even be shown to exist. . . .
>
> . . . The arguments that consciousness doesn't exist are vastly superior in their consistency and logic to any argument that it does, let alone that it necessarily arises from the interactions of matter or has evolved while yet having no reality of effect. Belief in consciousness is just that: a belief. And beliefs are themselves products of minds. So if there's no mind, there are no beliefs and no illusions that there are minds with beliefs.[15]

The obviousness of the non sequitur articulated here calls to mind how we might respond to the beliefs espoused in the writings of Mary Baker Eddy (founder of Christian Science). She argues that God is perfect, and as a perfect Creator, God could not create imperfection. She concludes that because physical reality is imperfect by virtue of its physicality, physical reality must be an illusion projected by our conscious minds. The problem with such an argument is that if God created us and if we subsequently create illusions of imperfection, then God is responsible for creating beings who create imperfect illusions and are, consequently, imperfect creations.

In short, while our concern here is with the concept of will or volition, we are aware that we have to be conscious to impose that will. And while we need not back into an assertion that *will* exists because it must for our belief system to work or for people to be held accountable for their actions so that we might have a stable society, we can see in Satinover's discussion that whatever consciousness is, it associates with the brain, is capable of thought, and is the only evidence we have (à la Descartes) that we ourselves exist. Furthermore, the only way the existence of consciousness or will can be disproved is by someone's consciously employing a willful argument and thereby imploding their own discourse.

Of course, to a large extent we have demonstrated that consciousness has the capacity to affect physical reality. Dossey's work seems to demonstrate this fact with what he broadly categorizes as the application of conscious prayer. And what he categorizes as prayer would certainly take into account forms of intentionality or the projection of desire other than more restrictive or formal definitions of prayer wherein one specifically implores assistance from the metaphysical realm, from God, or from other beings in the metaphysical realm.

A materialist could argue that since detectable electronic waves emanate from the brain, somehow these emissions stimulate the recipient. However, the distance over which such physical waves would have to travel and the power they would have to possess in order to transmit these barely detectible waves over long distances surely calls into question a physical explanation for such an effect.

A work by Daniel M. Wegner, *The Illusion of Conscious Will*, sets forth the theory that will, like consciousness, is also an illusion, even when it is applied to the most fundamental physical actions. Wegner explores "how the mechanisms of the human mind create the experience of will. . . . Rather than a ghost in the machine, the experience of conscious will is a feeling that helps us to appreciate and remember our authorship of the things our minds and bodies do."[16]

While his statement may seem convoluted, Wegner goes on to explain that will is merely a "feeling." From this point of view, the sense of having willed something is an emotional perspective that does not comply with reality: ". . . the will is not some cause or force or motor in a person but rather is personal conscious feeling of such causing, forcing, or motoring." He observes, "The research to date on the anatomy of conscious will, taken as a whole, suggests that there are multiple sources of this feeling. It appears that a person can derive the feeling of doing from conscious thoughts about what will be done, from feedback from muscles that have carried out the action, and even from visual perception of the action in the absence of such thoughts or feedback." Wegner concludes that will is a "kind of authorship emotion" that results from "an interpretive system, a course-sensing mechanism that examines the relationships between our thoughts and actions and responds with 'I willed this' when the two correspond appropriately."[17]

Wegner and others seem to propose the concept of a human being as an advanced machine made of flesh and blood (and powered by electrical impulses), a machine incapable of consciousness, will, or incapable of existence apart from the illusory construct of consciousness that is caused by biochemical phenomena in the brain. As mentioned in chapter 11, materialists offer this same explanation for the phenomena of near-death experiences and out-of-body experiences.

Of course, the simplest response to such arguments is that if these hypotheses are fashioned by the author's own illusory faculties, then the hypotheses themselves may be illusory or baseless. In effect, any hypothesis to the contrary has quite as much weight if all suppositions about reality are purely subjective and self-constructed.

In fact, if Wegner's thesis is correct, it would be totally improper for him to accept royalties for his book since he could not possibly have willfully created it. He possesses only the "emotion" of authorship. Anyone else having this same sensation about Wegner's book could reasonably approach the publisher to request a share of the royalties.

SCIENTIFIC PROOF OF CONSCIOUS WILL

A more effective response to the materialist or postmodern view of human consciousness and human will (together with the objective existence of reality) is not entirely a ludicrous battle of wits predicated on the power of rhetorical panache. Neither is anecdotal subjective experience effective—however corroborated it might be according to the standards of science—the most efficacious and convincing response. Ultimately the most important proof regarding these questions will derive from investigations in a variety of scientific fields, studies dedicated to discovering the ultimate nature and source of human consciousness. This "scientific" research alone will ultimately vindicate for most the assertion that human will, albeit a metaphysical faculty, can have phenomenal effects.

Margins of Reality

While we might think we would have to await some innovative experiments in the distant future to investigate the existence of will and its effects on physical reality (the bridge between spiritual and physical reality), convincing scientific study has already been carried out. Among the most rigorously devised experiments in this regard are those discussed in *Margins of Reality: The Role of Consciousness in the Physical World*, by Robert Jahn and Brenda Dunne (1987). The scholarship depicted in this work—a "paragon of scientific methodology"—documents experiments demonstrating evidence of cause-and-effect relationships between human will and physical reality.

For our purposes, the most meaningful experiment described in this work is presented in the second section of the study. In this experiment, a room was constructed in which observers could be seated comfortably for the purpose of observing a wall on which was placed a pachinko-like device ten feet high and six feet wide, which was framed in glass. Inside this glass frame were columns of equi-spaced pegs. As in a pachinko game, an aperture at the center of the frame's top allowed balls to descend in an RMC (Random Mechanical Cascade), bounce from peg to peg, and finally settle at the bottom into one of the array of columns formed by the pegs.

This device, called "Galton's desk" in scientific terminology, is used to show that the balls will inevitably become distributed at the bottom in a bell-shaped curve according to the laws of probability. The largest concentration will be in the middle, and the balls will be distributed in ever decreasing numbers from column to column going away from the center to the right and to the left.

But unlike a pachinko game or a "Galton's desk" in which metal shot is used, extremely light polystyrene Ping-Pong balls were released. Though the descent of balls was slow, the end result would be the same—a bell-shaped curve of distribution at the bottom. But according to exacting and repeatable protocol, the participants seated in the chairs before this large glass-encased device were asked to focus their collective consciousness on willing the balls to fall more to one side or the other. Amazingly, the documented results revealed an interplay between the conscious will of the participants and the distribution of the balls. When they "willed" the balls to go to the left, there was a nonrandom or improbable shift of the curve to the left. The same result (a shift in distribution) also occurred if the participants willed the balls to shift to the right.

It is well worth reading the book and noting the care that was taken to exclude any other influence in this "violation" of probable distribution—other than the influence of the conscious will of the participants. No less impressive are some of the other equally well-documented experiments in the book demonstrating the ability of "metaphysical" conscious will to have an effect on physical events.

In short, this seminal study seems to demonstrate quite clearly that the gap between spiritual or metaphysical and physical reality can be bridged, unless the influence on the descending balls was indeed the result of the physical properties of brain waves (quanta of energy). But even if brain waves did play a part in the outcome, we would still be left with the question as to *how* the participants could "will" their brain waves to emit this energy. After all, our determination to employ our will is still a metaphysical event.

THE FEAR OF METAPHYSICS?

Interestingly, Jahn and Dunne do not conclude their impressive report on their experiments by advocating belief in some sort of metaphysical reality or even by asserting that a metaphysical power is the best explanation for these scientific demonstrations of the individual's ability to produce action at a distance through conscious will. Instead, they attempt to explain these abilities in terms of brain waves, quantum mechanics, and other materialist explanations: "Whichever of these wave-mechanical options are applied, the model and the experiments agree that under certain circumstances human consciousness can interact with physical systems to broaden their observable behavior beyond chance expectation."[18]

Nevertheless, because they have offered substantial evidence that there can be an interaction between the conscious will and the outer or physical world, they conclude that observations about the mechanistic and deterministic model of the material world must necessarily include interaction with powers derived from the conscious will: "Clearly, much more extensive experimentation and much more comprehensive and quantitative theory will be needed to support or discredit such potentialities. Nonetheless, the possibility that certain man/machine interactions may require generalization of traditional mechanistic models to include consciousness as an active, synergistic component of the overall system has legitimately been raised."[19]

WHAT THE FUTURE HOLDS

If we are correct and metaphysical reality—or a metaphysical aspect of reality as a whole—exists, the end result of scientific attempts to render material explanations for that which is metaphysical in nature, or for powers that are metaphysical in origin, will necessarily achieve the opposite of their intended result. Even as the simplest explanation for reality ultimately caused scientists to accept the Copernican description of the solar system, so in time will sciences be compelled to accept the simplest and most reliable explanation for the interplay between "metaphysical" and physical events: that a metaphysical reality exists, and that there is a demonstrable interplay between the metaphysical and physical expressions of reality, and that these bidirectional influences are predictable in character. No doubt the acceptance of the existence of metaphysical reality and of its role in the operation of physical reality will occur not with a single event, but with the accumulation of evidence over time.

Nevertheless, it seems clear from all we have thus far discussed that our will is an inextricable part of every single spiritual exercise we undertake. It also seems clear that we can personally arrive at a convincing proof of this capacity and employ it to shape our lives long before such knowledge and practice is commonly accepted in the academic community. For example, when individuals empowered by the spirit of faith and conviction employ the causal pathways of prayer to accomplish altruistic objectives, the results may well prove to be infinitely more impressive and productive than having a random group of subjects trying to maneuver a bunch of Ping-Pong balls.

From the perspective of the Bahá'í teachings, the reason for a substantial increase in effect is easy to explain. The metaphysical pathway of prayer is specifically designed and designated to channel the power of will into action. We might compare this distinction to the difference between the power of static electricity to make our hair stand on end, and the power of this same electricity to communicate ideas and information when it is conducted through a wire with a telephone on either end.

- 14 -

The Daily Miracle

Build thee more stately mansions, O my soul,
As the swift seasons roll!
Leave thy low-vaulted past!
Let each new temple, nobler than the last,
Shut thee from heaven with a dome more vast,
Till thou at length art free,
Leaving thine outgrown shell by life's unresting sea!
—Oliver Wendell Holmes,
"The Chambered Nautilus"

Once knowledge about reality is obtained and resides in the repository of the conscious mind, a process of conscious reflection or meditation takes place so that the self can decide on an appropriate sequence of responses to this new knowledge. The self then applies will to the brain to set the body in motion and carry out the mind's intent. The brain as transceiver and executor of the mind's ideas stands ready to coordinate the appropriate functions of the body by manipulating the five senses, stimulating the autonomic nervous system, and doing whatever else is required to translate abstract objectives into a concrete course of action.

THE DAILY MIRACLE

If all systems are healthy, this operation will be seamless. No division will be experienced or observed among the powers, faculties, and capacities, nor will there appear any distinction between the true "self" (the soul) and the metaphorical "self" (the human temple). The intricate physical system operated by the brain, the single most complex entity in creation, will replicate in physical systems an exacting image of the metaphysical "self." 'Abdu'l-Bahá states, "This perfected body can be compared to a mirror, and the human spirit to the sun."[1]

We thus might think of this small miracle as similar to the large one that occurs when the Manifestation appears and becomes the perfect mirror in which humankind can perceive an image of the Creator, even as Christ affirmed, "He who has seen me has seen the Father" and as Bahá'u'lláh announced in reference to Himself, "Fix your gaze upon Him Who is the Temple of God amongst men."[2]

In both cases the Manifestation states that His physical appearance among humankind represents the "outer" or phenomenal appearance of the unseen attributes of God. We might think of this relationship as a poetic image of God, even as we might consider our own physical temple to be the outer expression of the inner or unseen attributes of our soul. As long as this reciprocal relationship endures and the body is in a condition of health, the performance of our physical temple may function as a fairly accurate gauge of the condition of our metaphysical state of being. Indeed, by such means we can assess our spiritual progress in terms of our daily performance in a physical environment—we can determine how well we are doing according to the guidance and standards set forth in the authoritative Bahá'í texts.

When both the metaphysical self (the soul and its powers) and the metaphorical self (the body and its powers) are in a state of health, they will coexist seamlessly and harmoniously in such a fashion that an observer, even an astute scientist, would find it difficult to discover any distinction between the holographic self, which is constructed by physical systems, and the metaphysical self, which is noncomposite. This effect is successful because the consciousness instigates and carries out the supreme illusion that the body is the source and cause of "self."

The process by which the conscious mind sends guidance to the senses and limbs through the brain draws upon memory (both conscious and unconscious) to recall past patterns of action. Then present performance is compared with long-term goals and objectives to evaluate the progress of the self. This internal assessment requires a constant, unremitting communication back and forth between the two selves. Therefore, if Bahá'í assertions about the existence of the soul are indeed correct, causal pathways between the metaphysical and physical expressions of the self must exist.

THE COMMON FACULTY

How does this holographic miracle occur, and what exactly does 'Abdu'l-Bahá mean when he speaks of the "common faculty" as the intermediary between these two realities, these two expressions of "self"?

As we have observed, 'Abdu'l-Bahá refers to the "common faculty" as the critical connection between the inner and outer powers in connection with the "objective" method of learning, the scientific method we discussed in the previous chapter. 'Abdu'l-Bahá states, "The intermediary between the five outward powers and the inward powers is the sense which they possess in common—that is to say, the sense which acts between the outer and inner powers, conveys to the inward powers whatever the outer powers discern. It is termed the common faculty, because it communicates between the outward and inward powers and thus is common to the outward and inward powers."[3]

'ABDU'L-BAHA'S REFERENCE TO THE SYMPATHETIC NERVE

'Abdu'l-Bahá does not further explain the nature of the "common faculty," nor does he ever allude to it again. In another instance he does allude to what has been translated as the "sympathetic nerve," which he portrays in similar fashion: "The powers of the sympathetic nerve are neither entirely physical nor spiritual, but are between the two (systems). The nerve is connected with both. Its phenomena shall be perfect when its spiritual and physical relations are normal." 'Abdu'l-Bahá also speaks of a synchronistic and reciprocal relationship between the inner spiritual self and the outer physical self, implying that coordination and harmony between the two realities is a remedy for both personal affliction and universal health: "When the material world and the divine world are well co-related, when the hearts become heavenly and the aspirations grow pure and divine, perfect connection shall take place. Then shall this power produce a perfect manifestation. Physical and spiritual diseases will then receive absolute healing."[4]

Unfortunately, the original Persian text from which this passage was translated is no longer extant. According to a note in the text, 'Abdu'l-Bahá was responding to a question put to him by a physician regarding the nature of the "sympathetic nervous system," but because we lack the original manuscript, we do not know whether or not his discussion of the "sympathetic nerve" bears any relationship to his similar discussion of the "common faculty."

It may well be that 'Abdu'l-Bahá was discussing the function of the autonomic nervous system, which is responsible for involuntary actions such as regulating visceral processes and a variety of other bodily functions. This system has a large role to play in the response to and expression of the powerful emotions of stress, fear, and sexual excitement. It also functions in regulating the sleep cycle and maintaining homeostasis. Therefore 'Abdu'l-Bahá might indeed have been referring to an overall reflection in bodily function of what is occurring internally (metaphysically) within the true "self."

Stated another way, if he were referring to the autonomic nervous system as an involuntary response that affects the homeostasis of the entire body because of what is occurring in the central nervous system (for example, decisions, indecision, conflict, fear, guilt, and so on), then the harmony and synchronicity of the outer expression of the inner self would indeed be a crucial "link" or bridge to our internal metaphysical condition.

Scientists in various fields are coming to appreciate more and more the reciprocal nature of this relationship, as we noted in our discussion of the relationship between prayer and healing. We can ease mental or emotional tension by massaging the feet or the back. Conversely, we can relax the muscles by meditating. In sum, we are beginning to understand more and more about the complete integration of the physical, mental, and spiritual expressions of "self," an integration that abides so long as our "self" is in this intricate, comprehensive, associative relationship with the human temple.

It is perhaps in this vein that 'Abdu'l-Bahá makes an enigmatic comment at the end of this statement about the sympathetic nerve when he exhorts us to ponder his meaning so that we might understand its most expansive implications: "The exposition is brief. Ponder and thou shalt understand the meaning. Although, on account of lack of time, the answer is short, by close reflection it shall be made long."[5]

'ABDU'L-BAHÁ'S COMPARISON OF THE INDIVIDUAL TO THE BODY POLITIC

It is further encouraging that in discussing this integrative "faculty" or "nerve," 'Abdu'l-Bahá also employs the analogy of the function of the body politic to the individual, precisely as we have done throughout this discourse as we attempt to discover how the soul runs the body. In this vein, 'Abdu'l-Bahá draws an analogy between the relationship of the parts of a body to the whole and the relationship of a single individual to the whole of humanity:

> Regarding reciprocity and cooperation: each member of the body politic should live in the utmost comfort and welfare because each individual member of humanity is a member of the body politic and if one member of the members be in distress or be afflicted with some disease all the other members must necessarily suffer. For example, a member of the human organism is the eye. If the eye should be affected that affliction would affect the whole nervous system. Hence, if a member of the body politic becomes afflicted, in reality, from the standpoint of sympathetic connection, all will share that affliction since this (one afflicted) is a member of the group of members, a part of the whole. Is it possible for one member or part to be in distress and the other members to be at ease? It is impossible! Hence God has desired that in the body politic of humanity each one shall enjoy perfect welfare and comfort.[6]

The "close reflection" 'Abdu'l-Bahá says is required to understand this relationship more completely obviously implies something more carefully considered than a guess or two. Furthermore, we might presume that such a study would extend beyond the space or expertise we have at hand to explore in this volume. Yet it is this very quality of reflection that we especially need to rely on at the climax of our study if we are to discover how the soul runs the body.

THE COMMON FACULTY AND THE SYMPATHETIC NERVE

It is doubtful that 'Abdu'l-Bahá's definition of the "common faculty" is also a reference to the "sympathetic nerve" or to the sympathetic nervous system, as some have supposed. It is unmistakably clear that the "common faculty" he discusses is not a physical system. He includes this faculty as one of the five *inner* powers; therefore the common faculty is not a nerve trunk, nor does it have physical properties. However, like the effects that the mind can have on materiality, this communications link is capable of transmitting information bidirectionally. Therefore the brain is capable of sending, receiving, and processing information to and from the inner self.

The "common faculty" thus translates metaphysical ideas into a form that the physical brain can comprehend and subsequently translate into forms of action. This faculty, this "close connection," can thus instantaneously process information bidirectionally. Consequently, while the mind is in a condition of health that enables it to manifest outward expressions of the soul and its powers, we can appreciate that a scientist who does not accept *a priori* a metaphysical reality would not find any meaningful proof that the expression of thought proceeds from a source other than the brain itself.

COMMON SENSE

One other note about 'Abdu'l-Bahá's use of the term "common faculty" is that the words as they appear in the text of *Some Answered Questions* are a translation of the Persian phrase *ḥiss-i-mushtarak,* the equivalent of the English term "common sense," the French *sens commun,* itself a derivative of the Latin *sensus communis.** In Arabic the phrase is rendered *binṭásíyá* or *qinṭásíyá* and refers to "the common characteristics or

---

* The Latin *sensus communis* is a translation of the Greek *koine aesthesis.*

attributes of the various senses; that is, spatiality, temporality, and number."[7] This usage would seem closer to what 'Abdu'l-Bahá describes—a process capable of rendering metaphysical concepts into sensually perceptible characteristics.

The Latin phrase *sensus communis* implies the binding or coordinating of the senses. This same phrase is "used by Aristotle for an aspect of functioning which integrates the various senses and enables a person to perceive such complex interacting qualities as unity, motion, rest, time, and shape. Aristotle thought the integrating organ was the heart." This concept of a common sense has also been used to refer to the "seat of the supposed 'common' or general sensation or perception in which various senses were thought to be united."[8]

The basis for this concept in Aristotelian thought derives from the idea that thinking divides objects of perception into groups. The "special sensibles" are directly perceived by one sense only. "Common sensibles" are directly perceived by more than one special sense, such as shape and movement that may be perceived by sight and touch. To recognize the "common sensibles," one must employ a common mental faculty or power. In the Middle Ages, this power was named *sensus communis,* or "common sense." As Dagobert Runes, author of *The Dictionary of Philosophy,* points out, "It is possible also that Aristotle attributes to this faculty the functions of perceiving and then uniting, coordinating, and organizing data derived from diverse senses into the perception of a single object."[9]

'Abdu'l-Bahá thus speaks in terms of Aristotelian philosophy when he names five outward powers of sight, hearing, smell, taste, and feeling. He similarly names five inner powers: the common faculty (*ḥiss-i-mushtarak),* imagination, thought, comprehension, and memory. The "common faculty," in addition to being one of the five inner powers, "communicates between the outward and inward powers and thus is common to the outward and inward powers."[10] It appears to be the first stage of internalization and perception that integrates the outward stimuli.

In contrast to 'Abdu'l-Bahá's explanation of the five inward powers, Persian and Arab philosophers have advanced complex and sometimes convoluted analyses of this process. Nevertheless, before we can use even the most general concept of the "common faculty" as an allusion to the bridge between the dual aspects of the reality of "self," let us first consider in more detail how the metaphorical self mimics in outward forms the condition of the metaphysical self.

- 15 -

The Brain as Intermediary for the Soul

Know thou that the soul of man is exalted above, and is independent of all infirmities of body or mind. That a sick person showeth signs of weakness is due to the hindrances that interpose themselves between his soul and his body, for the soul itself remaineth unaffected by any bodily ailments. Consider the light of the lamp. Though an external object may interfere with its radiance, the light itself continueth to shine with undiminished power. In like manner, every malady afflicting the body of man is an impediment that preventeth the soul from manifesting its inherent might and power. When it leaveth the body, however, it will evince such ascendancy, and reveal such influence as no force on earth can equal. Every pure, every refined and sanctified soul will be endowed with tremendous power, and shall rejoice with exceeding gladness.

—Bahá'u'lláh, *Gleanings*

In chapter 13 we demonstrated many of the problems inherent in a strict materialist view of the "self" and of "humanness." And yet the astounding capacity of the brain—especially its ability to restore itself to health after injury and to become the ostensible repository of information, ideas, and actions—offers an enticingly simple response to the question of how the gap between spiritual and physical reality is bridged: There is no metaphysical reality; therefore, there is no gap to bridge. The brain is so complex, so utterly remarkable that it is capable of producing the illusion of metaphysical powers, metaphysical experiences, and a metaphysical reality.

To facilitate a discourse and even a possible reconciliation between these apparently divergent and contradictory interpretations of reality (a materialist view versus a materialist-metaphysical view), we can offer a series of observations that provide important clues to the function of the "common faculty" in this process. But to accomplish this, let us begin with a foundational theory of the brain.

THE COMPLEMENTARITY OF SCIENCE AND PHILOSOPHY

It is not necessary for us to delve into the minutia of neurological science to establish a theory of complementarity between a scientific and a religious-philosophical solution to the problem of how physical reality emanates and how it is coordinated from the metaphysical realm. Let us first establish that science offers an exact description of reality that is necessarily incomplete because it studies only small portions of reality, while philosophy and religious thought offer complete descriptions of reality that are necessarily inexact because they theorize about the overall structure of reality.

However, if a scientist possesses a valid overview of reality provided by philosophical or religious thought and then applies that vision to an exacting study of reality (the nature of brain function, for example), this scientist might be significantly ahead of those who attempt the same study while rejecting out of hand a holistic vision—a metaphysical component to human reality that incorporates a possible interplay between material and metaphysical reality.

Without this holistic vision—which can have the downside of enticing the scientist to become an ideologue—the exact description of the parts fails to describe the whole. As a result, far too many scientists still become ideologues. And, as we noted earlier in our discussion, often the scientist is still tempted to impose an overview of reality that accommodates his "exact" observations about parts of reality—such theories as those we have discussed about space being limited or the universe having a point of beginning.

Here a redacted version of a traditional fable serves us well. Three blindfolded zoologists* attempt to describe an elephant, each examining a particular part of the great beast. They soon set about quarrelling as they insist on upholding the validity of their individual perceptions about how the beast is shaped. "It is skinny like a whip," says the tailiologist. "No, it is thick, round, and straight like a tree trunk," says the leggiologist. "You are both wrong! It is flat and thick like a blanket," says the earologist.

In time these scientists—from three distinct and contending fields of elephantology—might agree to pool their findings. They might consult, collaborate, and assemble their particular findings eventually to emerge with some consensus about the shape of the elephant. But how much more rapid their progress would be were there to appear among them one who was not blindfolded, who had no vested interested in a particular area of elephantology, and who could actually see the elephant. What is more important, this individual would be all too happy to share his knowledge with the scientists, or, better still, would help them remove their blindfolds that they might behold the reality of "elephantness" firsthand.

This type of integrative and holistic image of reality is what revealed thought, inspired vision, and philosophical discourse can offer the scientist. Since it is not necessary for us to assay all that has been done or that is being done in the rapidly evolving fields of neurological sciences, let us attempt a relatively simple overview of the brain and its function so that we may become a bit more exact in applying our own integrative overview of what we have portrayed as an associational relationship between spiritual and physical reality on the microcosmic or individual level. The application of our holistic vision may help elucidate more completely how communication takes place between the two expressions of "self" and, thereby, how the distinctly different aspects of reality in which they dwell are bridged. Even more particularly, this examination

---

* They are blind in the fable, but let's change it so that there is a matter of willful neglect of methodology involved.

may enable us to reach helpful conclusions about the analogous relationship between how God runs material reality through the intermediary of the Manifestation and how the soul runs the human body through the intermediary of the brain.

Brain Basics

As we noted in our discussion of the near-death experience, Dr. Melvin Morse in *Transformed* speculates that the point of contact between the soul and the brain (or at least the location of activity during the time that the near-death experience occurs) is the right temporal lobe. He writes, "The near-death experience probably takes place in the right temporal lobe, a spot just above the right ear and deep within the brain. My research and that of other scientists going back fifty years confirms this spot as the anatomical location of the NDE."[1]

But instead of accepting this observation as some conclusive indication that this particular area in the right temporal lobe is where the common faculty conjoins the dual expressions of self by creating an interface between soul and brain, let us first determine how likely Morse's theory might be by reviewing the fundamental method by which the brain functions.

The brain is one of the first distinguishing features of the developing human embryo. The neural tube closes after about three weeks of gestation, and the brain and spinal cord can be seen as having developed at about seven weeks. The brain of a fully developed human being weighs about three pounds and contains three major divisions: (1) the cerebrum, which is divided into two hemispheres and which is by far the largest part of the brain; (2) the brain stem, which includes the pons and the medulla and from which the cranial nerves emerge and connect to the spinal cord, thus allowing the body and brain to communicate; and (3) the cerebellum, which controls movement and is involved in learning motor skills.

Obviously, all portions of the central nervous system and the peripheral nervous systems are coordinated and essential. The peripheral nervous system is distributed throughout the body and communicates with extremities and maintains essential bodily functions and homeostasis. But for our purposes, let us focus on the central nervous system and in particular on the cerebrum, which seems to house most of the areas involved in ideation, memory, and all the faculties essential to commanding thought, memory, and willful action. The cerebrum is also related to other functions involved in the communication between the brain and the conscious "self."

THE CEREBRUM

The cerebrum contains the two hemispheres, each of which controls the opposite side of the body: The left hemisphere controls the right side of the body, and the right hemisphere controls the left side. The two hemispheres are connected by the corpus callosum, a thick band of some 200 to 250 million nerve fibers. Each hemisphere is divided into six lobes: the frontal lobe, the parietal lobe, the temporal lobe, the occipital lobe, the central lobe, and the limbic lobe.

We normally envision the brain as a mass of folds or convolutions, rather than as consisting of distinct sections or lobes. But various new technologies such as imaging techniques and surgical procedures have enabled researchers to map the brain and understand its structure more completely and to appreciate more precisely the coordinated function among its various parts. Even so, we are only beginning to understand the complexity of this magnificent organ.

The lobes in each of the two hemispheres can be subdivided into particular folds called ridges or "gyri." In turn, each of these gyri is separated by fissures called valleys or "sulci." Researchers now are beginning to understand not only the basic function of each lobe, but also what each *gyrus* (fold) does within the overall function of a particular lobe.

THE CEREBRAL CORTEX

Because the brain is constructed on the outer surface with gray folds that constitute the outer mantle—the cerebral cortex—the brain actually contains a vast surface area that is compressed into the protective shell of the skull. This surface is more expansive still because it surrounds the entirety of each hemisphere, including the inside area between the two hemispheres of the cerebrum.

The cerebral cortex is about an eighth of an inch thick and covers an interior white mass called "white matter." The interior of this white matter is composed of nerve fibers that fan out, connecting and presumably helping coordinate the different lobes. These connections integrate the regions or lobes of the cerebral cortex, and they connect one hemisphere to the other as the nerves pass through the corpus callosum (the trunk of nerves between the hemispheres).

Since our analysis of the brain is ultimately aimed at one particular objective—to understand how ideation takes place, how memory is retained, how self-consciousness is conceived—we need not go into detail about the individual function of each gyrus, but it would be helpful to have a general sense of how brain function within the cerebrum is divided among the four main lobes.

THE FUNCTION OF THE LOBES

The *frontal lobe* as a whole seems to control reasoning, planning, speech, movement, and emotion. And while portions of this lobe also contribute to the physical senses (eye movements, smell, sexual urges) and skilled physical movements (physical reaction, muscle movement, and coordination), the most important functions of the frontal lobe are abstract thought, problem solving, creative thought, reason, recollection, judgment, will, and general behavior.

The *temporal lobe* is perhaps the next most important area insofar as ideation is concerned because it is associated with memory, language, and identity, as well as with other related functions such as aspects of learning and visual imagery. If, then, these crucial functions of thought seem specialized to these two lobes, do we necessarily conclude that the metaphysical self must have contact with the physical self at these particular areas of the brain?

The answer is that no such conclusion is implied. We cannot discuss this infinitely intriguing central processing system as if it were easily divisible into categories of function like the various modular systems of a computer. Instead, the more we study the brain, the more we discover how adaptable this organ is and how far we are from even a cursory knowledge of its total complexity.

THE AMAZING ADAPTABILITY OF THE BRAIN

The functions of the central and the peripheral nervous systems are integrated so that there is an immense amount of "sharing" in the brain with regard to faculties and functions. This observation is particularly true among different areas of the brain—we are discovering increasingly that the brain is an amazingly adaptable instrument. Memories, emotions, and even motor skills that had been thought to be completely localized have been found to be capable of being assisted, or even taken over, by other parts of the brain when pathology or trauma induces dysfunction in a particular area of the brain.

This adaptability has certain limits, especially with degenerative neurological pathologies such as cerebral palsy, muscular sclerosis, amyotrophic lateral sclerosis, and Alzheimer's disease. Therefore, without going into any case studies, let us note a few important examples of the type of "sharing" or creative "compensation" that can occur.

EXAMPLES OF SHARING

In some instances of severe and unrelenting epileptic seizures, surgeons have resorted to separating the two hemispheres of the cerebrum. This is a radical alteration of brain structure, yet in some cases this procedure has succeeded in stopping seizures without causing extensive loss of general brain function.

A more common demonstration of the brain's ability to adapt to structural change occurs in cases of stroke. When a stroke causes partial paralysis of limbs, rehabilitation can sometimes retrain one part of the brain to take over the function that had been performed by the now injured area. In effect, rehabilitation and an increasing array of intricate surgeries demonstrate that the brain is capable of what amounts to rewiring itself.

Perhaps the brain is not so totally adaptable that one lobe can take over the gross function of another. And yet there have been cases of people surviving and even functioning relatively well after losing large portions of the brain to injury or disease. In some instances patients have survived and functioned adequately after the removal of an entire hemisphere, even though we have come to think of the two hemispheres as exceedingly specialized.

CREATING METAPHYSICAL ILLUSIONS?

As intricate and adaptable as the brain is now increasingly understood to be, it is no wonder at all that the materialist perspective pervades much of the research into this infinitely complex system, this miracle of miracles. If the brain can help heal itself, then it is not hard for scientists to conclude that the brain is capable of contriving the illusion of "self," the illusion of "will," the OBE (out-of-body experience), or the NDE (near-death experience).

Science writer Joel L. Swerdlow writes, "Infinitely more complex than any machine ever invented, the brain is the essence of what makes us human. Its blood vessels . . . nourish three pounds of delicate tissue. Its billions of cells mysteriously regulate the body, learn from a lifetime of experiences, and summon the memories and thoughts unique to each of us."[2] But a further examination of brain function demonstrates that the relationship between the two expressions of self through the intermediary of the brain is more generalized and more subtle than Swerdlow's machine model could possibly allow.

FUNDAMENTAL PROCESSING OF INFORMATION WITHIN THE NERVOUS SYSTEM

A logical alternative to modular brain theory has emerged—the "holographic" theory of brain function. But before we can appreciate the "holographic" theory versus the conventional "modular" theory, we need to review briefly how information is processed at the most basic level— from neuron to neuron.

FROM CELL TO CELL

Neurons (nerve cells) have the specialized function of carrying electrochemical messages throughout the body. The brain itself is comprised of some hundred billion such cells. All nerve cells are similar to other cells in that they contain a nucleus, are surrounded by a membrane, contain cytoplasm, synthesize protein, and produce energy. But because they are constructed to communicate, neurons have specialized extensions that bring information to the cell (dendrites) and specialized extensions that take information from the cell (axons). Because of these extensions, a nerve cell can communicate with other nerve cells across the *synapse,* the junction between the dendrites and the axons.

Communication from cell to cell occurs when an electrical impulse travels down the axon to the synaptic terminal (also called the presynaptic ending). When the impulse reaches the terminal, spherical vesicles (sacs within the cell) containing a neurotransmitter chemical are sent towards the membrane of the cell. There the vesicles fuse with the membrane and release the neurotransmitter chemical across the synapse, where they are received by the dendrites of the adjacent receiving cell.

This process of communication from cell to cell is completed when the axon of the transmitting cell then reabsorbs or neutralizes the neurotransmitters and enzymes remaining in the terminal, and the recipient cell—or the *postsynaptic* cell—becomes stimulated. If the excitation of the receiving cell is sufficient, the process will continue so that the "message" will be sent to the next cell.

SSRIs AND HUMAN EMOTION

The neurotransmitter with which many people are most commonly familiar is serotonin because it has been discovered to play a crucial role in regulating mood. Commonly known psychoactive drugs such as Prozac and Zoloft can alter the transmission process by changing the rate of the release of the neurotransmitter serotonin and by altering the availability of receptor sites. These drugs are thus designated SSRIs (selective serotonin reuptake inhibitors) because they reduce the insufficiency of serotonin by slowing down the process by which the chemical is transmitted across the synaptic cleft. Consequently, when someone is suffering from an imbalance or insufficiency of serotonin (sometimes the explicit cause of depression or anxiety disorders), these drugs can be employed to reintroduce a normal or sufficient level of serotonin.

The capacity to alter our moods with various drugs is as ancient as civilization. But this sort of specific alteration of a single neurotransmitter indicates how intricate the relationship is between our emotions or feelings about our self and the proper functioning of our brain and even our peripheral nervous system. Are we to conclude that all of our emotions are merely the result of biochemical events? To what extent is our sense of well-being based on reality, as opposed to how our brain is processing various neurotransmitters? An even more worrisome prospect for those who affirm belief in the continuation of consciousness in the afterlife is the question of whether or not we will be able to experience emotion if we have no association with this delicate instrument that can so influence what we feel. When we are dissociated from the brain and its panoply of neurotransmitters, will we be unfeeling zombies existing in some ethereal goop with other equally humorless souls?

The answer that we find in the Bahá'í writings is clear: The emotional aspect of our conscious self is an inseparable expression of our existence. Indeed, dissociated from those incidental and sometimes defective influences, our emotional responses will more accurately reflect the reality of our condition. In this vein Bahá'u'lláh states that those who "are the followers of the one true God shall, the moment they depart out of this life, experience such joy and gladness as would be impossible to describe."[3] To put the matter in the simplest of terms, emotions are the inner response to our experience and perception of reality. The brain as intermediary allows that inner affect to become evident to the external world while we exist in association with the human temple. Once the associative relationship is severed, the experiencing and sharing of inner feeling will be instantaneous because no intermediary connection will be required.

THE SENSE OF "SELF" ACCORDING TO MODULAR BRAIN THEORY

Without memory, the "self" as we know it would not exist because we would have no continuous sense of ourselves. We would exist from moment to moment. The conventional view of the brain recognizes in the composition of the nervous system a hierarchy of modular components in the retention of our memories—our sense of "self."

As we have noted, according to the Bahá'í theory of "self," memory is a power or faculty of the soul. Therefore, from the Bahá'í view, a loss of memory because of brain dysfunction or traumatic injury is temporary, even if this loss endures for the remainder of one's physical existence. The intermediary relationship between the soul and the body may have been severed because the common faculty can no longer link the soul with the body through the intermediary of the brain.

However, according to this same Bahá'í perspective, the memory of self—even the recollection of specific events—will be retained by the soul and regained once the constraints of the associative relationship with the body are severed and the soul is released from its periscopic and indirect connection to reality. Therefore, while one so afflicted must struggle with the loss of self-consciousness or a coherent inner narrative of "self," this individual will regain the "self" once there is a transition to the "unveiled reality" that is the world of the spirit.

Because the brain as intermediary is, during our physical lives, the means by which memory is transmitted to the soul so that self-consciousness and self-reflection can take place, it may seem to those observing someone suffering from a brain disorder or disease that the "self" of the individual has vanished. In those cases where the process is irreversible, this conclusion is accurate insofar as the remainder of the physical experience is concerned.

Consequently, for those who have no belief in the continuation of life beyond physical experience, this type of loss of a loved one is often worse than had the individual died. After all, the physical aspect or metaphorical "self" still exists, still moves about, even though the metaphysical self, the personality, gradually becomes eclipsed and lost. This process would even be easier to bear if it occurred suddenly, as it does with a traumatic injury. But with a pathology like Alzheimer's, we see all the physical evidence that death has not occurred, yet we are faced with the pain of being unable to communicate with the personality or "self" that was associated with the physical being we see before us.

In short, we must endure the company of a living physical reminder of the personhood of one we love, but without any of the true indices of the relationship: recognition, shared memories, affection, meaningful conversation, and so on. Finally, when the conscious mind of the patient totally loses the capacity to conceive of "self," the individual not only loses the sense of "self," but also loses the sense that the loss of self has occurred.

HOW IS MEMORY CONSTRUCTED?

In an article titled "What Is a Memory Made Of?" Joannie Schrof states, "In order to know anything at all, we are utterly dependent on the enigmatic process by which the brain stores and retrieves information." She observes that however this is done, it is nothing like any hardware we can presently imagine: "Where a computer encodes data in strings of 0's and 1's, the brain forms ephemeral patterns of chemical and electrical impulses. Where computers record information in serial order like an index-card file, the human brain creates sprawling interconnections; more than a hundred billion nerve cells each connected to hundreds of thousands of others to form a billion connections." She describes how brain scans are able to chart what areas process special memories by tracking the increased blood flow to certain parts of the brain when it processes "irregular verbs versus regular verbs, pictures of camels versus pictures of wrenches, an object's color versus an object's use."[4]

To a certain extent, then, this is a process where memory exists in a combination of chemical imprints among a collection of neurons. Thus a memory is both local and nonlocal inasmuch as recollection of an event may be triggered by stimulating any portion of the complex of nerve cells in which the memory is stored. Evoking any part of the memory may result in the recollection of an entire event or sequence of events.

Again, these observations about memory accord with the modular theory where, like our blindfolded elephantologists, we are "poking around" in the single most complex organ in creation, observing what happens, and trying to extrapolate scientific theories from our observations. Therefore, as we poke around or view PET scans, it may seem that parts of the brain are dedicated to particular increments or different sequences of memories.

For example, two parts of the limbic system (the hippocampus and the amygdala) are essential in forming memory. Sensory information seems to pass through these structures from the brain stem on the way to the cerebral cortex. Damage to the hippocampus may cause one to experience loss of memory from the point in time when the trauma occurred, but it may leave unaffected those memories prior to the time of trauma. The memories already resident in the cortex neurons can be evoked, but no further information can be processed into a pattern of memory in the cortex.

But if patients thus afflicted learn new skills, their peripheral nervous system may retain the memory, and they may retain the new skill they have learned. But their conscious mind will not be aware of having learned the new skill—the event is not stored as a memory in the cerebral cortex.

Other sorts of injury to other portions of the brain cause a variety of other types of enigmatic effects on memory, all of which cause us to have incrementally more information about how the brain processes thought, memory, and the sense of self. In fact, one of the oddly fortuitous consequences of modern society is that because of the vast number of car wrecks, the equally vast variety of brain injuries enables researchers to study in detail all the anomalies caused by brain trauma. Each anomaly offers an opportunity to study how the divisions of the process of creating memory function and how they are distributed among the integrated parts of the brain.

THE MODULAR BRAIN AS COMPUTER

Even those who support the modular theory of brain function and affirm that a memory has a distinct locus (a specific location in the cerebral cortex) are increasingly realizing that though divided to some extent into fundamental functions, the brain is so integrated as to be almost beyond any exact descriptions of function.

But there are other obvious problems with viewing the brain as a computational device or as a modular system. For example, for a computer to accomplish any useful tasks, it must be programmed. Someone must create an algorithmic process—a sequential set of commands—for the computer to follow. In addition, if the computer is to perform its tasks successfully, the instructions must be set at the beginning when the program is written. According to Robert Rosen in *Life Itself,* no new information (divergent pathways) can be processed by a computer if the computer has not already been programmed to consider this information.[5] The brain, however, can effectively create new sequences and new pathways.

Another problem with the theory of the brain as a modular or computerlike machine is that while we know information is stored in cortical cells, we do not know exactly how it is stored, and, more importantly, we cannot explain why injury to a specific group of neurons does not seem to destroy a particular memory. Similar to our earlier discussion about consciousness being nonlocal, this anomaly appears to imply that memory (a recalled state of consciousness) is also nonlocal. As an abstraction, consciousness exists solely as a metaphysical reality, even if it can be described by attributes recorded by the brain.

If we think of the brain as modular and portions of the brain as the repository of specific memories (the sensory portions of which are somehow assembled from various other parts of the brain) then it is logical that a specific lesion would result in a discrete loss of a particular memory. We might compare this event to damaging a portion of a hard drive on a computer. If part of a hard drive is erased or damaged, the information it contained is permanently lost.

But discrete memory loss rarely occurs in the brain. Therefore we must infer that somehow the components of a memory are distributed throughout the brain and then assembled—or reassembled—at the point of recollection. And quite possibly the ability to evoke a specific memory by stimulating a particular locus in the brain means only that the particular memory is assembled at that locus only *at that particular point in time*. Stimulating that same locus at another time might reassemble an entirely different memory. Hence it seems clear that a memory is not stored in a single site.

HOLOGRAPHIC BRAIN THEORY

Here is where holographic brain theory seems to come to the rescue. Karl Pribram, a leading scholar of the mind-brain relationship and author of *Language of the Brain,* has been largely responsible for pioneering the concept of the brain as operating in holographic function. According to holographic theory, perception and consciousness are not local and are not assembled from parts or bits of information. The entire thought, memory, or concept is distributed throughout the brain; thus the brain as a whole enterprise becomes the intermediary between the soul and the body, between the soul and the "rational faculty" or "mind."

COGNITION IN HOLOGRAPHIC THEORY

In 1985 Pribram conceived the idea that cognition is holistic in process rather than specific and discrete: It is not stored in a particular lobe or in a particular group of cortical cells within a lobe or gyrus. According to holographic theory, a "hologram" or a complete image of a thought or image derives from more than one perspective. Each perspective contains a complete image, not merely a part of an image, even though the entire memory is "distributed" among various parts of the brain—as opposed to "modular" theory, where various aspects of the memory are divided up, retained distinctly, and then coalesce at the moment of recollection.

The classic and most helpful example of how a "distributed system" or holographic image works is described by C. A. Taylor in his 1978 publication *Images* when he demonstrated how the removal of a lens from a slide projector produced an image that was essentially a nondistinct wash of color on the screen. He determined that the resulting image is created because all points of the screen are receiving information from every point on the image emitted by the slide. But when Taylor placed a lens between the projector and the screen (but not over the entire light and not necessarily at any given point), the complete image appeared on the screen. In every case the image will vary in contrast and intensity according to how much of the light is focused by the lens, but each portion of the light beam captured by the lens contains the entire image. The more light the lens captures, the better the resolution of the image will be.

THE VALUE OF THE HOLOGRAPHIC THEORY

As a concept of how the brain processes ideas or memory, the holographic theory implies that each portion of the brain contributing to the recollected idea would contain the complete thought, not a piece of it. In discussing the fundamentals of Pribram's holographic brain theory, Jeff Prideaux, in his study *Comparison between Karl Pribram's "Holographic Brain Theory" and More Conventional Models of Neuronal Computation,* concludes with a helpful demonstration of why this theory seems substantially more feasible and sensible than other brain theories.

Prideaux explains that the difficulty with other theories derives from trying to extrapolate a vision of the whole by studying through microbiology the exact function of particular parts. In contrast, Pribram devises a theory of brain function—particularly regarding thought, reflection, memory, and self-consciousness—that is materialist in nature, yet ultimately the result of a mysterious combining of holonomic functions. These functions, which the brain uses to recall an event or contemplate a thought, represent the utilization of some "common faculty." This capacity allows for an interface between physical information and metaphysical processing of that information.

To a certain extent the holographic theory would seem to accord with Bahá'í observations about the relationship between the dual expressions of self. For human thought, so long as we perceive reality periscopically through the associative relationship with the human temple, is necessarily grounded in physical or metaphorical referents and allusions. Therefore an idea or event may be distributed among a variety of neurons and lobes because there exist various sensory components, as well as other imagistic indices, for a single thought.

According to Pribram, each portion of the image is complete, and, as with the lens of the slide projector, the assembling or focusing of these images together presents a more vivid, more enhanced, and more detailed recollection of the event or the thought. Therefore, the act of providing "focus" might well be comparable to the willful act of reflection or meditation in which a memory or an idea can become ever more intense and clarified by the conscious pooling of information or the focusing of mental faculties and resources on the thought. Through this reflective process, we can begin perceiving more clearly and effectively aspects of an event or an idea we had not previously considered. The result of this meditation or focused thought is that an entirely new idea (perhaps a theory or an invention) emerges from the experience.

THE SYNTHESIS OF PHYSICS AND METAPHYSICS: THE SOUL AS SOURCE

Another particularly intriguing observation by Pribram regarding his theories of the brain relates to William Hatcher's contention that the synthesis of scientific exactness and the completeness of philosophical or religious hypothesis would be the most useful portrait of reality. Pribram has stated that the more he studies the brain and its functions, the more he feels that there may well be something *outside* the brain that accounts for its activity and capacity!

In effect, neither Pribram nor anyone else can account for how non-random, abstract thought and ideation could occur spontaneously from a strictly material entity, regardless of how complex that entity might be. Somehow there must be a motive force that is not "matter" capable of instigating thought and of commanding the brain to do its work. Furthermore, by scientific principle, the source from which the brain receives its "program" needs to be greater than the brain itself—the cause has to be greater than the effect it produces.

As in our earlier TV analogy, Pribram has observed that when he studies the brain, he feels that in truth he is examining an elaborate transceiver rather than the ultimate repository of memory, the ultimate origin of self-consciousness, the primal engine of creativity, the seminal source of will, or the instigator of action. His idea might be explained by the understandable conclusion on the part of someone examining a TV for the first time that the point on the dial of the TV set which produces a particular type of program is the locus for that program, that the program is somehow resident there, stored in that area of this physical object.

So it is that Pribram's conclusions derive not from his having less respect for the powers of the brain than do those materialist scientists who have decided *a priori* that the brain is the source of thought and who have, therefore, focused their study entirely on attaining a greater understanding of ever more finite functions within the brain. Their hope is in time to assemble their vision of these modular parts into a working model of what they believe to be the source of our humanity.

Pribram, on the other hand, cannot conceive logically that any theory of the brain from a materialist perspective can account for how an entity composed of purely physical properties could spontaneously, of its own accord, bring about willful action (or even the illusion of willful action), create a sense of self, and indulge in willful reflection, meditation, and decision making.

For if these abstractions are the sum total of particular functions of parts of the brain, even in a holographic model where all these diverse parts and capacities are coordinated and distributed, how can this "machine" run itself?

Put another way, how can the sum total of the brain's capacity (if it is a distributed system) or a particular locus in the brain (if it is a modular system) determine what the brain itself will do today? Stated even more ludicrously, how can the brain be in charge of making itself function as a brain? Logically, something other than or higher than the brain must be administering the brain, because it is impossible that will itself is the spontaneous action of cortical cellular activity. If this were so—if the brain or some portion thereof, were responsible for willfully controlling the brain—all human activity would be arbitrary and random, since an autonomous three-pound organ (however replete with cells, circuits, and activity) could have no inherent value system, no moral perspective, no goals, nor would it contain any inherent sense of "self" as such or be inherently desirous of order, let alone morality. One might respond that the brain is trained from birth to accept certain concepts of self, value systems, and objectives. Yet twins raised together may have entirely different value systems and may possess different characters and personalities.

Here again we return to the problem with the computer model of the brain. The most elaborate and most powerful computer we have created or will ever create cannot program itself unless it is programmed to program itself. In short, there must exist for any given machine—or machine model of the brain—some willful input from an outside source for it to have any sense of goals or values, or for it to be capable of evaluating progress towards those goals.

THE CRITICAL NATURE OF THE CLOSE CONNECTION

Even if the real "self," the true seat of consciousness, is elsewhere (or, more accurately, nowhere) operating through this neurological miracle by means of an associative relationship, the brain is no less complex or mysterious, no less magnificent, no less a "miracle of rare device."[6] It is no less a product of divine creation and no less worthy of our study and common awe. For if each part of physical reality is the exact counterpart of something in spiritual reality, then the brain, as the counterpart of the soul and its faculties, and comparable in its function in the microcosm to the function of the Manifestation in the macrocosm, must be capable of mimicking in physical or metaphorical terms everything the soul feels, conceives, decides, or wills. This fact explains why a human soul cannot associate with (operate through) anything less complex or less ingeniously devised than the human brain.

The nature of the associative relationship dictates precisely why, for someone who has incurred brain trauma, who is mentally handicapped, who has a severe mental illness, or who has any other circumstances or pathologies that inhibit the complete function of higher brain activity, the soul cannot fully manifest its powers. Still, in the long run, the soul will be unencumbered by this temporary physical inability to have a full associative relationship, or at least to manifest that associative relationship to the rest of us.

These observations call to mind the importance of two previously mentioned passages from the Bahá'í writings:

> For the mind to manifest itself, the human body must be whole; and a sound mind cannot be but in a sound body, whereas the soul dependeth not upon the body.[7]

> The soul of man should be likened unto this sun, and all things on earth should be regarded as his body. So long as no external impediment interveneth between them, the body will, in its entirety, continue to reflect the light of the soul, and to be sustained by its power. As soon as, however, a veil interposeth itself between them, the brightness of that light seemeth to lessen.[8]

The delicacy and refinement of this absolutely critical relationship also help elucidate the reason that the laws of Bahá'u'lláh mandate total abstention from alcohol and drugs. Any practice or substance that distorts the associative relationship between soul and body or that tampers with the brain endangers our ability to function as complete human beings and, thereby, to fulfill our earthly purpose of attaining the knowledge of abstract reality and, subsequently, translating abstract concept into symbolic expression.

Clearly, then, the bridge between the two realities passes through this complex neurological system so long as the outer expression of self is sufficiently healthy to manifest the powers and faculties of the soul. When the brain is healthy, it enables the entire body to mirror forth, and thereby become the outer expression of, every inner faculty. Therefore we could correctly conclude that while the rational mind is a power employed by the metaphysical reality that is the soul, the brain is complex enough to mimic in physical activity every major function of that inner spiritual reality that is the true source of "self."

Consciousness and the Dysfunctional Brain

At this point, it is important to reaffirm that when the brain malfunctions or when the brain becomes somehow prevented from accurately communicating with the soul and manifesting the soul's powers to others in the physical world, neither the soul nor its powers are adversely affected.

One powerful example of this distinction between consciousness as a function of the soul and consciousness as it is experienced in association with the human temple through the intermediary of the brain is the story of fifteen-year-old autistic Tito Mukhopadhyay. Through the relentless and "unorthodox" training of his mother, Tito has been taught "to add and subtract, to enjoy literature, and eventually to communicate by writing." While unable to overcome his autism, Tito has provided us with an "insider's" perspective of his illness. In his book *The Mind Tree: A Miraculous Child Breaks the Silence of Autism,* Tito has described his attempt to organize the confusion of information his mind receives from his senses and his equally arduous struggle to control the behavior of his own body. He has written of two distinct selves, a thinking self that contains thoughts and feelings and a self that is controlling his body movements and over which his thinking self has no more control than if it belonged to another person altogether. In other words, his conscious mind seems incapable of establishing or maintaining control over the fundamentally autonomous movements of his body. He thus describes in powerful images from the inside of the experience what we observe from the outside when we study someone who is autistic.

Apparently the conscious self emanating from the soul of this young man is trying to comprehend reality through his brain that is dysfunctional in very identifiable patterns—though, as science writer James Shreeve observes, while researchers have pinpointed some of the areas of the brain involved, "It is doubtful that a disorder with such a broad spectrum of symptoms and pathologies has any single cause."[9]

The point is that the inner strength of character and will that the soul of this young man is attaining through the struggle to interpret and interact with reality will, once released from the bonds of this associative relationship, most probably evince a power and strength of will beyond anything he might have accomplished without his determination to work through the constraints of a defective intermediary.

This realization is tremendously important to contemplate when we consider that at some point in our lives each one of us will probably have to assist a family member who has become affected by some form of brain deterioration or dysfunction. This realization is perhaps even more important when we consider that in our own aging, we ourselves will also probably experience some degree of brain deterioration, disorder, or dementia. At such a point, or in the course of such a process, we will be challenged to find comfort in the realization that our inner self, our true self, is ultimately safeguarded from its inability to express itself effectively through a progressively deteriorating metaphorical self.

A related point is particularly comforting in cases of long-term and progressive deterioration. In the realm of the spirit, which is the real abode of the soul, there is no time. We may be tempted to feel that the soul of someone enduring such indignity is being withheld from progress, that it is trapped in its associative relationship with a dysfunctional temple and that we should help that "self" become released. But while witnessing the apparent fading of the personality of a loved one is immensely painful, frustrating, and demanding for us, it is not necessarily painful for the loved one. For even if the associative relationship remains for a period of years, what may be years to us are, in the realm of the spirit, but the blink of an eye. 'Abdu'l-Bahá states, "To be limited to place is a property of bodies and not of spirits. Place and time surround the body, not the mind and spirit."[10] Thus the soul of someone so afflicted does not suffer a sense of captivity nor anxiously await release from the confines of a dysfunctional associative relationship.

But when the conscious self that is a metaphysical reality is in unrelenting association with (or to use a machine metaphor, "plugged in to") the physical system that mimics the soul's faculties and powers, then inner reflection and rational thought are also affected. Therefore, how can we say the soul is unaffected if we simultaneously maintain that spiritually motivated physical activity has a positive influence on the soul's progress, and, conversely, selfishly motivated unspiritual activity has a negative effect on the soul?

BRIDGING THE GAP AND HUMAN PURPOSE

When we speak of the progress of the soul or the true "self," we are describing improvement in spiritual character, in our essential capacity, in the process of a spiritual essence becoming refined. Consequently, only those acts that involve us in a spiritual or internal participation can affect our spiritual essence. Such acts are most often characterized by explicit moral choices. Secondly, when we speak of pathology or trauma that disrupts the associative relationship and communication between the twin expressions of the conscious self, we are describing an impediment that takes place without will and therefore without moral aspect or implication. Such a hindrance can have no impact whatsoever on the spiritual progress of the soul.

But does this temporary impediment mean that on another unseen level our soul is progressing, even though we may be unconscious of it? After all, to a certain extent we are often unaware of our own spiritual progress under normal circumstances, especially when that progress is predicated on altruistic motives. That is the point of spiritual motive— we perform truly "spiritual" actions out of a sincere desire to serve others, not to benefit ourselves. Such actions may have an ancillary reward of making us feel better about ourselves, but the motive itself does not spring from a desire for gratification. Therefore it is possible that in some way our soul may be developing even though our conscious knowledge of such progress is impaired.

But what about those instances in which the brain is damaged or dysfunctional enough that an individual would be incapable of judging such abstract concepts? Can the soul of such a person progress while trying to communicate with and work within the environment of physical reality when the conscious mind cannot communicate these concepts to itself, much less to anyone else? For example, we sense the immense willful struggle of someone who has had a stroke to regain speech or retrain limbs. Undoubtedly, this process is capable of instigating profound internal growth and insight. Experiencing such a trial might cause one to enhance the powers of will, humility, and spiritual strength beyond what this same individual might be able to attain without having had this impairment.

As we have noted, refinement of the soul comes primarily as a result of conscious effort. Could the same process occur for one who must live in association with a brain that is dysfunctional or that becomes subject to trauma? Might not growth occur even though the individual may be unaware of any alternative?

WHAT EXPERIENCES ARE VALUABLE?

A useful analogy might help us appreciate the soul's growth in such a case. If a runner trains with weights attached to the legs, those who watch the athlete attempt to run might think the capacity of such a one as quite limited and pitiable. But this training will cause the muscles struggling against the extra resistance to develop much more rapidly and profoundly than would the muscles of someone not so encumbered. Therefore, only when the weights are released will the runner manifest his or her true capacity—the powers that have been developing as a result of the encumbrance.

Might not this same condition apply to those who must associate with a dysfunctional brain and body? The soul may not be able to make its powers manifest to others or even to the conscious self so long as the associative relationship with reality is constrained by a defective intermediary. But once released from this associative impediment, would not the soul evince its true power, and might it not be all the more refined and powerful for having endured such a challenge? Surely the story of Tito and his amazing strides to overcome such an obstacle provides virtually incontrovertible proof to affirm this concept.

There is an even more subtle point in considering this type of interference in bridging the gap between the spiritual and physical aspects of our human reality. When we are trying to communicate with, teach, or assist someone whose brain is injured or dysfunctional, we do not have the same emotional relationship we might have when we are trying to retrain a stroke victim who is suffering from aphasia. In the case of the stroke victim, we may have the sense that the true "self" is fully operant and willfully struggling to break through, to cross the blocked or maimed intermediary or bridge. But when we are with someone who is severely and congenitally dysfunctional, we may sense that the soul is isolated and cannot communicate through this dysfunctional metaphorical self, nor can it communicate well with its own consciousness, even though Tito's story might cause us to question such a conclusion.

THE CONTINUITY OF "SELF"

When the now deceased Christopher Reeve first had to face the fact that he was entirely paralyzed as a result of his fall from a horse, he entered an understandable state of despair and depression. In conversation with his wife, he questioned what of value was left for him in life. Her response, so simple and obvious, had a profound effect on his determination to live the rest of his life in dignity and usefulness: "You are still you!" she reminded him. He could not move his arms, legs, or even breathe on his own, but the essential person, the "self" of the man was still completely there. That intermediary between his soul and the physical world remained quite intact, and he spent the last ten years of his life as an advocate for spinal cord injury research.

In the same way we may find it painfully difficult to accept the reality that one whose brain is no longer functioning well as an intermediary between the soul and the physical world has simply vanished because with an illness like Alzheimer's the personality evaporates by degrees. What is more, we cannot help sensing that somewhere, in some reality, the "self" or identity or personality of our loved one must still exist. We sense this or "know" this not merely because the physical presence before us is a constant reminder of the individual; our intuitive logic dictates that existence (even a composite existence like the personhood or personality or character of another) cannot become nonexistent. On some level beyond our sense of loss, anger, bewilderment, and frustration, we harbor a hope founded on logic and law that an individual human reality cannot cease to be.

Interestingly, the problem we face in such instances is similar to the problem the intimate followers of the Manifestation face after He ascends from this mortal realm. They begin to wonder if that immaculate "Self," that conscious Being, the essential reality of the Manifestation of God, still abides in an unseen realm and still provides them with spiritual sustenance. Suddenly questions may arise as to exactly who this individual was and whether the attraction and esteem believers had for Him were based on something substantial or were merely the result of some temporary charismatic spell. In time the believers may dispute among themselves as to the spiritual station of the Prophet and what should happen now that He has vanished.

Early in His ministry Bahá'u'lláh penned this memorable verse, perhaps in His anticipation (or foreknowledge) of the disputes that would arise among His followers after His own return to the realm of the Spirit: "O My Children! I fear lest, bereft of the melody of the dove of heaven, ye will sink back to the shades of utter loss, and, never having gazed upon the beauty of the rose, return to water and clay."[11]

Certainly our observations should not be taken to disdain the sincere mourning and profound grief one feels for the loss of the presence of a loved one, especially if the temple of that spirit is still alive. But if we are assured that this perplexing separation is only temporary, we can take some consolation in treating the temple with dignity, even as we do when the spirit or the self has totally disassociated itself from the body at death.

According to Bahá'í law, the family of the deceased must wash the body, wrap it in a shroud, and place on a finger a burial ring with the following inscription: "I came forth from God, and return unto Him, detached from all save Him, holding fast to His Name, the Merciful, the Compassionate."[12]

The body is no longer the temple of the soul. It is a lifeless and rapidly deteriorating form. But according to Bahá'í teachings, respect and reverence are due this dust, this "water and clay," simply because "the body, though now dust, was once exalted by the immortal soul of man!"[13] If we pay this much respect to the deceased body because it was in the past exalted by association with the immortal soul of a human being, it seems only reasonable that we should show no less respect to the physical temple that may presently possess some degree of associative relationship with the soul, however dim the glimmer of the light shining through that temple might be.

Conclusion:
The Longing to Cross Over

O SON OF MY HANDMAID! Didst thou behold immortal sovereignty, thou wouldst strive to pass from this fleeting world. But to conceal the one from thee and to reveal the other is a mystery which none but the pure in heart can comprehend.

—Bahá'u'lláh, *Hidden Words*

Since any variety of herbs, drugs, injuries, and mental or physical diseases can instantly render the conscious mind irrational or incompetent, it is understandable that the idea of the seat of consciousness being "outside" and independent of the physical self would seem ludicrous. If the conscious mind derives its powers and faculties from a metaphysical source, how could that source be so easily conquered, so totally dependent on a healthy brain? If we are indeed essentially human souls and essentially spiritual beings, why is it necessary that we participate in this grand illusion that our powers derive from our body and brain?

WHY REALITY IS VEILED

The rationale for the veil between our conscious self and reality during this period in which we function periscopically through the intermediary of the brain is perhaps the single most confounding enigma we encounter. When understood properly, this same veil or illusion is at the heart of how we become prepared for entrance into the "world of vision" where this same conscious self with which we read these words, so thoroughly convinced of its physical reality during our associative existence, will be freed from this indirect experience with reality.

'Abdu'l-Bahá writes, "As to the question whether the souls will recognize each other in the spiritual world: This fact is certain; for the Kingdom is the world of vision where all the concealed realities will become disclosed. How much more the well-known souls will become manifest. The mysteries of which man is heedless in this earthly world, those he will discover in the heavenly world, and there will he be informed of the secret of truth; how much more will he recognize or discover persons with whom he hath been associated."[1]

Explaining part of the rationale for veiling reality during our physical existence, Bahá'u'lláh states that, were metaphysical reality not disguised as it is, we would be unable to concentrate on our objective here—to focus our attention on the foundational lessons we are meant to learn during this period of physical existence: "We dare not, in this Day, lift the veil that concealeth the exalted station which every true believer can attain, for the joy which such a revelation must provoke might well cause a few to faint away and die."[2]

As we have repeatedly noted, this persistent and virtually impenetrable illusion—that we are material beings—is a teaching method upon which all other teaching methods are based: instruction by means of dramatic, indirect, subjective, analogical exercises. Were this illusion not so convincing, we would not be "stretched" intellectually or spiritually. Both our free will and the sincerity of our motives would remain untested and undeveloped. We would be tempted to relax in the comfort of knowing on a subjective or empirical level that physical difficulties are temporary and that the comfort of the "real" world awaits us.

In an extremely pertinent and powerful justification for this illusion, Bahá'u'lláh observes that if we heed His exhortations, we will indeed develop a sense of detachment, a sense of true comfort with our lives, regardless of what tests and difficulties we must endure. But He also observes that not all would find tranquillity in this certitude about the continuation of life. Since in such a reality all that is hidden will be made plain, all our deeds and motives will likewise be made apparent and unconcealed:

Know thou that every hearing ear, if kept pure and undefiled, must, at all times and from every direction, hearken to the voice that uttereth these holy words: "Verily, we are God's, and to Him shall we return." The mysteries of man's physical death and of his return have not been divulged, and still remain unread. By the righteousness of God! Were they to be revealed, they would evoke such fear and sorrow that some would perish, while others would be so filled with gladness as to wish for death, and beseech, with unceasing longing, the one true God—exalted be His glory—to hasten their end.[3]

Explicit Benefits of Physical Reality

Ultimately, this educational process that is our physical experience has the goal of enabling us to become self-sustained in our quest for growth and development, inspired initially by our inherent love of reality. We achieve the object of our quest as we gradually become increasingly adept at discerning the metaphorical, symbolic, or dramatic exercises that constitute our experience as "physical beings" and at expressing that understanding in equally dramatic or symbolic forms of action derived from our own imagination and invention.

As we have repeatedly asserted, these exercises, when pursued properly, are capable of increasing the powers of our soul and even of refining our essential reality itself. But were we from the beginning subjectively aware in our conscious minds of the essentially metaphorical (symbolic or illusory) nature of physical reality, we would find it difficult, if not impossible, to take these exercises seriously. And even if in this life we attain some degree of certitude about what lies before us, the mystery surrounding our individual transition to the next stage of our existence will foster in us a desire to stay focused on our earthly purpose, even as these objectives are devised and articulated by the Manifestation of God. For as Shoghi Effendi notes, our confidence about our destiny in the afterlife will always remain only relatively secure since we cannot objectively assess the spiritual progress of anyone, especially ourselves: "No one knows what the future holds for him, or to what degree he is spoiling it or creating it; therefore the thing to do is one's daily best and let the future take care of itself. It would be very unwise for you to let this experience of a voice—the origin and purpose of which you have no way of knowing—influence you in any way or to set any store on its observations."[4]

So it is that the actions of the body at the behest of the will can enhance the knowledge and spirituality of the soul. So it is that the soul, as a consequence of this refined enlightenment, can command an enhanced actuation of spiritual principle in symbolic physical actions.

THE INNER LONGING TO CROSS OVER

Allusions to the demise of the physical temple are portrayed in Bahá'í scripture in joyful and exhilarating terms. Bahá'u'lláh describes the transition to the next stage of our existence as a fulfilling experience, as a "messenger of joy." Indeed, this unavoidable destiny that so many of us dread is portrayed as a "return" to the source of our being, as a "reunion" with the Beloved of our hearts.[5]

Yet if our identity begins at conception and if our soul already dwells in the realm of the spirit, even if we are temporarily veiled from perceiving that reality directly during our associative relationship with our physical selves, in what sense is death accurately portrayed with these terms? Stated more clearly, if death is so intensely rewarding, why are we not on some inner level already aware of or in touch with this destiny and longing to cross over instead of constantly fearing that point of transition?

According to Bahá'í scripture, those who have used their physical experience to advantage are, in fact, very much aware of that reality and even desirous of attaining that existence where the veils of illusion are lifted. On some level, most of us are aware of that reality, even as we have noted that "the first emanation from God toward man" is a love of reality, and that love of reality derives from the fact that all reality manifests evidence and signs of the Creator.[6]

In other words, as emanations from God, we are fashioned so that we are, in truth, always seeking a single objective—proximity to God, however unaware we may be that all attraction we feel to *anything* and to *everything* is but a veiled expression of or allusion to attaining the presence of God. This verity pertains to even the most distorted or perverted longing, because however confused our understanding of the source of our passions may become, all desire ultimately derives from this sense of incompleteness, this insatiable thirst that can be quenched solely at the fountain of nearness to the Beloved.

This inherent desire to know reality, this veiled desire for the Beloved, does not abnegate our free will nor detract from our responsibility to discover its true origin, but it does mean that until we respond appropriately to this inherent yearning, this overwhelming desire that is an inextricable part of our nature, we will *always* be haunted by unquenchable desires, by insatiable lusts, by unconquerable anguish.

Bahá'u'lláh writes, "The people of the left hand sigh and bemoan. The people of the right abide in noble habitations: they quaff the Wine that is life indeed, from the hands of the All-Merciful, and are, verily, the blissful." If our desire is not recognized as an ecstatic longing for reunion with the source of our origin, it may be confused with earthly cravings so that our response to this inner quest may assume the form of seeking consolation in the allure of wealth, fame, passion, or adventure, that "untraveled world whose margin fades / For ever and for ever when I move."[7]

But nothing short of proximity to true reality—which is our awareness of the signs of God in all created things—will ever give us more than a few moments of solace. Therefore we can correctly observe that this pervasive attraction, this unconquerable law of love, is integral to the close connection between this "Kingdom of Names" that is physical existence and the source of those names that is the realm of the spirit.

How Much Life Is Enough?

Before we conclude our attempt to understand something about how spiritual and physical reality work in tandem to train us in the love of God, let us return to the original question with which we began this quest, this pilgrimage of the heart: How do we explain why injustice seems to dominate life on our small planet?

Industrial pollutants are destroying our atmosphere so that many of the evergreens atop the highest mountains stand denuded like wrought iron statuary. Our water is foul, our environment cluttered. Our communities lack any shared moral perspective or unified vision of how to bring about a just and nurturing social order. Therefore, regardless of God's benign intent in creating such a beauteous and bountiful classroom for our training, what do we do now that we seem to have damaged it beyond repair or usefulness?

As individuals we do not live in the macrocosm, not in the world of solar systems and galaxies, nor even in a global community. We live our lives one day at a time among a handful of acquaintances in a community. If we are wise, we strive to do the best we can to protect our families and loved ones as we direct our lives towards the attainment of spiritual objectives. Yet even in this microcosmic reality, we are often thwarted in our quest for some degree of safety, sanity, justice, and order.

THE "GOOD LIFE"

What we long for is nothing less than the "good life" because the "good life" is paraded before us image upon image, minute by minute. We see it and we see ourselves in it on billboards, in movies, on television, in magazines. It is there for the taking, we are told, if only we buy the right products, do the right exercises, get the right car, build the right house, save for our golden years, and finish with a life of ease and decorum. If we are relentless and follow the rules, we are assured that at some point in our future we will be happy. We will have the "good life"!

It is not as though we can go somewhere else on the planet to escape the "good life." The "good life" has become a universal paradigm with which the world at large has become infected. If we are searching for a shared universal perspective, we have found it. Because the "good life" promises that if we are more or less moral, work hard, make careful choices, get a good education, find the right persons to marry (one to get the family started and a second to fulfill our dreams), succeed by degrees in a profitable vocation, raise at least two children, buy two houses (a beginner for the kids and later the home of our dreams), send the kids to college, maintain an active social life, eventually retire and live in an extended care facility where we need never fear depending on others to take care of us when (or *if*) we become incapacitated, then we will be happy!

The Good Death

True, in time we *may* die, but it will be a decorous and painless affair. Our children and grandchildren will be sitting bedside. They will express in turn their eternal appreciation for all we have accomplished for their sakes. Our body will be in decent enough shape so that the funeral parlor cosmetologist will need to do only minimal repairs. Yes, we are now ready to experience "the good death"!

At the funeral, friends and family will be at a loss for words to praise the contributions we have made to our progeny, to the community, to the world at large. Members of the city council will speak of naming a street after us, or at least a park bench. And as we watch from above in our soft white cloak of Egyptian cotton, our white feathery wings holding us suspended in the aether, we will be confident that our reputation is assured! Yes, this is our immortality—to hover and watch and reflect on how well we did. And we did do well, didn't we?

The Problem with the "Good Life"

But wait! There's a problem here. Just how many people have we ever met or known or heard about who actually experienced the "good life"? And if we think we have known such individuals, are we sure they were happy? Might they have had some secret tragedies in life, some sequestered pain, some unfulfilled longing they took to the grave? Would we right this moment be willing to trade places with them, knowing only as much as we do about them, especially knowing that right now they are dead?

This whole scenario is ludicrous, and on some level we all know it. No one has "the good life," at least not the one that assaults our senses and somehow gains access to every waking moment of our lives—this paradisial Disney World of material ease and rapture. For even if we were to have a painless and perfect existence, we would quickly discover it to be as unsatisfying as a Heaven—the "good Afterlife"—where we need not labor or worry or . . . do . . . anything at all.

In short, we cannot be sure if this "good life" would be worth anything because clearly it is only through effort, struggle, and suffering that we ever acquire anything lasting, anything worth preserving. 'Abdu'l-Bahá observes,

The mind and spirit of man advance when he is tried by suffering. The more the ground is ploughed the better the seed will grow, the better the harvest will be. Just as the plough furrows the earth deeply, purifying it of weeds and thistles, so suffering and tribulation free man from the petty affairs of this worldly life until he arrives at a state of complete detachment. His attitude in this world will be that of divine happiness. Man is, so to speak, unripe: the heat of the fire of suffering will mature him. Look back to the times past and you will find that the greatest men have suffered most.[8]

This passage may seem a somber reality compared to the healthy, slim, young, well-dressed, smiling couples on the screens before us assuring us that we can look like them and be as happy as they seem to be if we invest wisely and do what they do.

Yet a curious thing occurs. While *they* seem to remain ever vibrant and ever youthful, ever strong and smooth and straight and slim, *we* seem to get crooked and old, brittle and wrinkled. What's the matter with us? What have we done wrong? What rules did we ignore or disobey to be so unsightly and unacceptable? Why must we feel so guilty simply because we are unable to counteract the laws of nature?

Surely the secret to the "good life" is not merely longevity? True, we bemoan the early demise of young artists because of what they might have accomplished had they lived a lengthy life. We grieve at the early death of a youth or a child because we understandably lament their lost opportunities, what they might have been. On a spiritual or philosophical level, we may ponder whether or not the infant was properly prepared to enter the next stage of existence, even though on another level we know that a loving God is fully capable of taking care of these souls. Indeed, 'Abdu'l-Bahá was once asked, "What is the condition of children who die before attaining the age of discretion or before the appointed time of birth?" He answered, "These infants are under the shadow of the favor of God; and as they have not committed any sin and are not soiled with the impurities of the world of nature, they are the centers of the manifestation of bounty, and the Eye of Compassion will be turned upon them."[9] On a rational level, we are well aware that the true loss at the death of a friend or loved one belongs to us who are temporarily bereft of their presence.

But what about those who do not live "the good life" or anything close to it, those who must endure intense suffering and deprivation? We are forced to accept that we will never know who has lived well and who has not. In fact, what do we know about how well we ourselves have responded to the opportunities that have been ours and whether or not we have become sufficiently detached and refined?

Perhaps There Is No Bridge To Cross

Clearly there is no set quality or quantity of life that is required in order for our physical experience to prepare us adequately for the continuation of the "self" in the realm of the placeless. If it were otherwise, then this physical existence would be the "real" life, and the afterlife but a recollection of this existence, an evaluation of our performance here and nothing more—what some have called the "Protestant heaven."

Perhaps we can take a lesson from those who have had near-death experiences who testify that a few seconds in the spiritual realm provide enough insight into the nature of that reality that they would much prefer not to return to this existence. That should tell us something about where the "good life" really exists. Those who have experienced such a brief release from the constraints of physicality come to understand the truth about reality—that this brief stage of our eternal existence is a period of gestation in preparation for our second birth, our true awakening to the real world.

Perhaps, then, there is no minimum amount of time required for us to fathom the essential nature of this reality, to learn the fundamental lesson it has to teach us. After all, how many minutes in a prison cell would it take for us to decide that we would rather not spend much time there? And yet we are constantly being coerced into accepting what 'Abdu'l-Bahá terms "this rubbish heap, the world," as the epitome of our existence and the afterlife merely as a theoretical possibility that is largely irrelevant to our daily lives.[10]

If the Bahá'í portrayal of reality is correct, the good life we seek is found only in the solace and satisfaction we derive from gaining knowledge of our true nature—understanding that we are essentially spiritual beings operating temporarily through the vehicle of a physical temple. After achieving that realization, do we then long to attain the presence of the Beloved and escape the bonds and fetters of this mortal coil?

If we learn only one thing from this exploration of ideas, it should be that however illusory physical reality may be, it is quite as much a divine creation as is the spiritual realm. Therefore, while we may be comforted by knowledge of the reality that awaits us, we should consider this physical aspect of creation no less divine and no less essential for our inherent purposes than any other part of our eternal journey. The fact that physical reality and our brief association with it are endowed with spiritual lessons to teach us does not make this foundational portion of our journey any less real, any less worthy of our attention.

Evelyn Underhill is probably correct when she defines "the good life" in terms of a "union with reality" and the enlightened and happy individual as one who pursues the mystic quest for this union: "Mysticism is the art of union with Reality. The mystic is a person who has attained that union in greater or less degree; or who aims at and believes in such attainment."[11]

So, what do we conclude about how the gap between realities is bridged? In one sense, there is no need to bridge the gap because the gap does not exist. Reality is one integral organism with infinite dimensions, only two of which we are slightly aware of, and both of which define aspects of our own reality. Therefore, the union we seek with reality is not so much an escape from where we are, or a pilgrimage to some other place, as it is an awakening of ourselves to the verities governing our total integration with both aspects of reality.

Spiritual growth or development is thus little more than waking from a dream, a dream that we are something other than spirit, a dream that we are something besides a divine emanation from the Creator, an illusion that our own special happiness lies anywhere other than gathering the friends of God to celebrate His praises and emulate His saints and servants—whoever they may be and wherever we may find them.

Notes

Chapter 1

The epigraph for chapter 1 is from Bahá'u'lláh, *Gleanings*, p. 127.
1. 'Abdu'l-Bahá, *Promulgation of Universal Peace*, p. 181.
2. Shoghi Effendi, *World Order of Bahá'u'lláh*, p. 202.
3. Bahá'u'lláh, *Gleanings*, p. 214.
4. 'Abdu'l-Bahá, *Selections from the Writings of 'Abdu'l-Bahá*, no. 12.1.

Chapter 2

The epigraph for chapter 2 is from Bahá'u'lláh, *Prayers and Meditations*, pp. 48–49.
1. Bahá'u'lláh, *Gleanings*, p. 46.
2. 'Abdu'l-Bahá, *Paris Talks*, nos. 58.4, 58.6; Bahá'u'lláh, *Gleanings*, p. 341.
3. 'Abdu'l-Bahá, *Paris Talks*, no. 58.6.
4. Hadíth cited in *Kitáb-i-Aqdas*, note 23.
5. Bahá'u'lláh, *Prayers and Meditations*, pp. 48–49.
6. Luke 12:6–7. All citations of the Bible refer to the Revised Standard Version.
7. Koran 5:72. All citations of the Koran refer to the Abdullah Yusuf Ali translation.
8. Bahá'u'lláh, *Kitáb-i-Íqán*, ¶149.
9. Ibid.
10. Bahá'u'lláh, *Gleanings*, p. 46.
11. Bahá'u'lláh, *Gleanings*, p. 52.
12. 'Abdu'l-Bahá, *Some Answered Questions*, p. 162.
13. Bahá'u'lláh, *Gleanings*, p. 184.
14. Ibid., p. 177.
15. Bahá'u'lláh, *Kitáb-i-Íqán*, ¶104.
16. Bahá'u'lláh, *Hidden Words*, Arabic, no. 3.
17. Ibid., no. 4.
18. Ibid., no. 5.
19. Bahá'u'lláh, *Tablets of Bahá'u'lláh*, p. 70.
20. 'Abdu'l-Bahá, *Promulgation of Universal Peace*, p. 140.

CHAPTER 3

The epigraph for chapter 3 is from the Báb, *Selections from the Writings of the Báb,* p. 196.

1. Bahá'u'lláh, *Gleanings,* p. 160.
2. Shoghi Effendi, *High Endeavors,* pp. 49–50.
3. 'Abdu'l-Bahá, in *Bahá'í Scriptures,* p. 482.
4. Extract from a letter dated 14 November 1947 written on behalf of Shoghi Effendi to an individual, in *Lights of Guidance,* no. 703.
5. Bahá'u'lláh, *Gleanings,* p. 49.
6. Shoghi Effendi, *World Order of Bahá'u'lláh,* p. 112.
7. Bahá'u'lláh, *Kitáb-i-Aqdas,* ¶176.
8. Bahá'u'lláh, *Hidden Words,* Arabic, no. 67.
9. Bahá'u'lláh, *Kitáb-i-Íqán,* ¶106.

CHAPTER 4

The epigraph for chapter 4 is from Bahá'u'lláh, *Gleanings,* p. 213.

1. Shoghi Effendi, *Promised Day Is Come,* ¶303.
2. Shoghi Effendi, *God Passes By,* p. 213.
3. Shoghi Effendi, *World Order of Bahá'u'lláh,* p. 112.
4. 'Abdu'l-Bahá, *Selections from the Writings of 'Abdu'l-Bahá,* no. 24.3.
5. 'Abdu'l-Bahá, *Some Answered Questions,* p. 203.
6. Ibid.; Bahá'u'lláh, *Kitáb-i-Aqdas,* ¶129, ¶175.
7. Bahá'u'lláh, *Epistle to the Son of the Wolf,* p. 155.
8. Bahá'u'lláh, *Kitáb-i-Íqán,* ¶104–05.
9. Luke 22:41–42.
10. Bahá'u'lláh, quoted in Shoghi Effendi, *God Passes By,* p. 126.
11. Bahá'u'lláh, *Gleanings,* pp. 87–88.
12. John 14:10; Bahá'u'lláh, *Summons of the Lord of Hosts,* Súriy-i-Haykal, ¶192.
13. Bahá'u'lláh, *Kitáb-i-Íqán,* ¶263; the Báb, *Selections from the Writings of the Báb,* pp. 167–68.
14. The Báb, *Selections from the Writings of the Báb,* p. 167.
15. Bahá'u'lláh, *Kitáb-i-Íqán,* ¶193, 196.
16. Ibid., ¶196.
17. Shoghi Effendi, *God Passes By,* p. 138.
18. 'Abdu'l-Bahá, *Some Answered Questions,* p. 127.
19. 'Abdu'l-Bahá, *Some Answered Questions,* p. 145.
20. Bahá'u'lláh, *Kitáb-i-Aqdas,* ¶4.

CHAPTER 5

The epigraph for chapter 5 is from Bahá'u'lláh, *Gleanings,* p. 150.

1. John 6:48–52, 60.

2. Extract from a letter dated 28 October 1949 written on behalf of Shoghi Effendi to an individual, in *Lights of Guidance,* p. 508.

3. Matthew 23:34–39.

4. 'Abdu'l-Bahá, *Some Answered Questions,* p. 123.

5. Bahá'u'lláh, *Prayers and Meditations,* p. 295.

6. Bahá'u'lláh, *Kitáb-i-Íqán,* ¶26, ¶185.

7. 'Abdu'l-Bahá, *Promulgation of Universal Peace,* p. 181.

8. Robert Frost, "Mending Wall," in *Norton Anthology,* pp. 1121–22, ll. 35–45.

9. Bahá'u'lláh, *Hidden Words,* Arabic, no. 31.

10. 'Abdu'l-Bahá, *Some Answered Questions,* p. 283.

11. Bahá'u'lláh, in *Bahá'í Prayers,* p. 172.

CHAPTER 6

The epigraph for chapter 6 is from 'Abdu'l-Bahá, *Some Answered Questions,* p. 177.

1. Edgar Allan Poe, "Sonnet—To Science," *Norton Anthology of Poetry,* 4th ed., p. 879.

2. Walt Whitman, "When I Heard the Learn'd Astronomer," ibid., p. 969.

3. Thomas Hardy, "Hap," ibid., p. 1049.

4. Archibald MacLeish, "End of the World," *College Book of Modern Verse,* p. 379.

5. Ernest Hemingway, "A Clean Well-Lighted Place," *Riverside Anthology of Literature,* p. 332.

6. William Harmon and C. Hugh Holman, *Handbook to Literature,* p. 308.

7. W. B. Yeats, "The Second Coming," *Norton Anthology,* 4th ed., p. 1091.

8. 'Abdu'l-Bahá, *Promulgation of Universal Peace,* p. 303; 'Abdu'l-Bahá, *Some Answered Questions,* p. 217.

9. Ibid., p. 198.

10. Ibid., p. 199.

11. Ibid.

12. Extract from a letter dated 14 July 1943 written on behalf of Shoghi Effendi to an individual, in *Lights of Guidance,* no. 1646.

CHAPTER 7

The epigraph for chapter 7 is from 'Abdu'l-Bahá, *Some Answered Questions,* p. 130.

NOTES

1. Ibid., pp. 178–79.
2. John Milton, *Paradise Lost*, 1:939, 10:959–7.
3. Shakespeare, "Troilus and Cressida," *Complete Works of William Shakespeare*, I, iii, 78–110.
4. 'Abdu'l-Bahá, *Some Answered Questions*, p. 230.
5. 'Abdu'l-Bahá, *Promulgation of Universal Peace*, pp. 81–82.
6. Ibid., pp. 80–81.
7. Bahá'u'lláh, *Gleanings*, p. 65.
8. Ibid., p. 177.
9. 'Abdu'l-Bahá, *Some Answered Questions*, p. 231.
10. 'Abdu'l-Bahá, *'Abdu'l-Bahá in London*, pp. 23–24.
11. 'Abdu'l-Bahá, *Paris Talks*, no. 5.15–16.
12. Bahá'u'lláh, *Summons of the Lord of Hosts*, Súriy-i-Haykal, ¶44.
13. 'Abdu'l-Bahá, *Promulgation of Universal Peace*, p. 225.
14. Ibid., p. 10.

CHAPTER 8

The epigraph for chapter 8 is from 'Abdu'l-Bahá, *Foundations of World Unity*, p. 52.

1. 'Abdu'l-Bahá, Tablet of the Universe, unpublished provisional translation, *Bahá'í Library Online,* http://bahai-library.com/?file=abdulbaha_lawh_aflakiyyih.html.
2. 'Abdu'l-Bahá, *Some Answered Questions*, p. 3.
3. Leon Lederman, *The God Particle*, p. 101.
4. Leon Lederman, *The God Particle*, p. 101.
5. James Rees, *The Unit Nature of Matter,* Starlight Publishing Company, www.starlight-pub.com.
6. Leon Lederman, *The God Particle*, p. 375.
7. 'Abdu'l-Bahá, *Some Answered Questions*, p. 190.
8. 'Abdu'l-Bahá, *Auguste Forel and the Bahá'í Faith*, pp. 15–16.
9. 'Abdu'l-Bahá, *Auguste Forel and the Bahá'í Faith*, p. 16.
10. J. E. Esslemont, *Bahá'u'lláh and the New Era*, p. 202.
11. 'Abdu'l-Bahá, Tablet of the Universe, unpublished provisional translation, *Bahá'í Library Online,* http://bahai-library.com/?file=abdulbaha_lawh_aflakiyyih.html.
12. Ibid.

CHAPTER 9

The epigraph for chapter 9 is from 'Abdu'l-Bahá, Tablet of the Universe, unpublished provisional translation, *Bahá'í Library Online*, http://bahai-library.com/?file=abdulbaha_lawh_aflakiyyih.html.

1. David Bohm, *Wholeness and the Implicate Order*, p. 123.

2. Timothy Ferris, *The Whole Shebang*, p. 73.

3. Ibid., p. 44.

4. 'Abdu'l-Bahá, *Some Answered Questions*, p. 281.

5. David Bohm, *Wholeness and the Implicate Order*, p. 192.

6. 'Abdu'l-Bahá, Tablet of the Universe, unpublished provisional translation, *Bahá'í Library Online*, http://bahai-library.com/?file=abdulbaha_lawh_aflakiyyih.html.

7. Ibid.

CHAPTER 10

The epigraph for chapter 10 is from Bahá'u'lláh, *Tablets of Bahá'u'lláh*, p. 156.

1. 'Abdu'l-Bahá, Tablet of the Universe, unpublished provisional translation, *Bahá'í Library Online*, http://bahai-library.com/?file=abdulbaha_lawh_aflakiyyih.html; *Some Answered Questions*, p. 182.

2. 'Abdu'l-Bahá, *Some Answered Questions*, p. 182.

3. Ibid., p. 183.

4. Ibid., p. 151.

5. Ibid., p. 152.

6. Ibid., pp. 85–86.

7. Shoghi Effendi, *God Passes By*, p. 244.

8. 'Abdu'l-Bahá, *Some Answered Questions*, p. 155; Shoghi Effendi, *Unfolding Destiny*, p. 449.

9. Bahá'u'lláh, *Epistle to the Son of the Wolf*, p. 155.

10. Bahá'u'lláh, *Prayers and Meditations*, p. 321.

11. Shoghi Effendi, *God Passes By*, pp. 54–55.

12. Shoghi Effendi, *World Order of Bahá'u'lláh*, p. 202.

CHAPTER 11

The epigraph for chapter 11 is from 'Abdu'l-Bahá, *Some Answered Questions*, pp. 239–40.

1. Bahá'u'lláh, *Tablets of Bahá'u'lláh*, p. 156.

2. Bahá'u'lláh, *Kitáb-i-Íqán*, ¶107.

3. 'Abdu'l-Bahá, *Selections from the Writings of 'Abdu'l-Bahá*, no. 206.9; Bahá'u'lláh, *Hidden Words*, Persian, no. 45.

4. Shakespeare, *Hamlet*, 3:1, 70–71.

5. 'Abdu'l-Bahá, *Promulgation of Universal Peace*, pp. 421–22.

6. Stephen Priest, *Theories of the Mind*, p. 214.

7. See Joseph B. Verrengia, "Brain Misfiring May Explain Out-of-Body Experience," *Tampa Tribune*, Nation / World section, September 19, 2002, p. 6.

8. Larry Dossey, *Recovering the Soul*, p. 24.

9. Ibid., pp. 28–29.

10. Ibid., pp. 45–46.

11. Ibid., p. 162.

12. Larry Dossey, *The Healing Words*, p. 162.

13. Lothar Schäfer, *In Search of Divine Reality*, p. 86.

14. Ibid., p. 90.

15. Ibid.

16. David Chalmers, *The Conscious Mind*, pp. 170.

17. Ibid., p. 171.

18. Ibid., p. 214.

19. Julian Jaynes, *Origin of Consciousness*, p. 302.

20. Ibid., p. 135.

21. Ibid., p. 140.

22. Extract from a letter dated 9 October 1947 written on behalf of Shoghi Effendi to an individual, in *Lights of Guidance*, no. 1699; 'Abdu'l-Bahá, *Some Answered Questions*, p. 240.

23. 'Abdu'l-Bahá, in *Divine Philosophy*, p. 132; extract from a letter dated 23 August 1984 written on behalf of the Universal House of Justice to an individual.

24. 'Abdu'l-Bahá, *Some Answered Questions*, pp. 239–40.

25. 'Abdu'l-Bahá, *Some Answered Questions*, pp. 205–06.

26. Extract from a letter dated 20 November 1937 written on behalf of Shoghi Effendi to an individual, in *Lights of Guidance*, no. 392.

27. 'Abdu'l-Bahá, *Some Answered Questions*, p. 210.

28. Extract from a letter dated 5 January 1948 written on behalf of Shoghi Effendi to an individual, in *Lights of Guidance*, no. 1699.

29. Extract from a letter dated 5 August 1969 written on behalf of the Universal House of Justice to the National Spiritual Assembly of Monaco, in *Lights of Guidance*, no. 1820.

30. Extract from a letter dated 22 April 1954 written on behalf of Shoghi Effendi to an individual, in *Lights of Guidance*, no. 1826.

31. 'Abdu'l-Bahá, *Promulgation of Universal Peace*, p. 307.

32. 'Abdu'l-Bahá, in *Bahá'í Scriptures*, p. 405.

CHAPTER 12

The epigraph for chapter 12 is from Bahá'u'lláh, *Gleanings*, p. 165.

1. Bahá'u'lláh, *Gleanings*, pp. 158–59.

2. Bahá'u'lláh, *Kitáb-i-Íqán*, ¶107.

3. Bahá'u'lláh, *Gleanings*, p. 165.

4. 'Abdu'l-Bahá, *Some Answered Questions*, p. 73; 'Abdu'l-Bahá, *Paris Talks*, no. 29.4; 'Abdu'l-Bahá, *Some Answered Questions*, p. 233.

5. 'Abdu'l-Bahá, *Promulgation of Universal Peace*, p. 49.

6. Ibid., p. 50.

7. Shoghi Effendi, *Arohanui*, p. 89.

8. 'Abdu'l-Bahá, *Paris Talks*, no. 31.7–8.

9. Ibid., no. 28.14.

10. Bahá'u'lláh, *Tablets of Bahá'u'lláh*, p. 127.

11. 'Abdu'l-Bahá, *Some Answered Questions*, p. 295.

12. Ibid., p. 242.

13. 'Abdu'l-Bahá, in *Auguste Forel and the Bahá'í Faith*, p. 8.

14. Bahá'u'lláh, *Gleanings*, p. 164.

15. Ibid.; extract from a letter dated 26 September 1943 written on behalf of Shoghi Effendi to an individual, in *Lights of Guidance*, no. 1722.

16. 'Abdu'l-Bahá, in *Auguste Forel and the Bahá'í Faith*, p. 8.

17. Bahá'u'lláh, *Gleanings*, pp. 153–54.

18. 'Abdu'l-Bahá, in *Auguste Forel and the Bahá'í Faith*, p. 9.

19. Ibid., pp. 8–9.

20. 'Abdu'l-Bahá, *Promulgation of Universal Peace*, p. 157.

CHAPTER 13

The epigraph for chapter 13 is from 'Abdu'l-Bahá, *Some Answered Questions*, p. 226.

1. 'Abdu'l-Bahá, in *Bahá'í Prayers*, p. 302.

2. 'Abdu'l-Bahá, *Some Answered Questions*, p. 162.

3. Bahá'u'lláh, *Gleanings*, p. 164.

4. 'Abdu'l-Bahá, *Some Answered Questions*, p. 157.

5. Ibid., pp. 157–58.

6. Ibid., p. 157.

7. Ibid., pp. 157, 210.

8. Bahá'u'lláh, *Tablets of Bahá'u'lláh*, p. 149.

9. Bahá'u'lláh, *Kitáb-i-Íqán*, ¶28; Koran 21:30, 21:33.

10. 'Abdu'l-Bahá, *Some Answered Questions*, p. 210.

11. Bahá'u'lláh, *Kitáb-i-Aqdas*, pp. 96–97.

12. 'Abdu'l-Bahá, *Promulgation of Universal Peace*, p. 121.

13. Bahá'u'lláh, *Gleanings*, p. 149.

14. Jeffrey Satinover, *Quantum Brain*, pp. 220–21.

15. Ibid., p. 221.

16. Daniel M. Wegner, *Illusion of Conscious Will*, p. ix.

17. Ibid., pp. 3, 49, 325, 317.

18. Robert Jahn and Brenda Dunne, *Margins of Reality*, p. 277.

19. Ibid.

CHAPTER 14

The epigraph for chapter 14 is from Oliver Wendell Holmes, "The Chambered Nautilus," *The Norton Anthology of Poetry*, 4th ed., p. 878.

1. 'Abdu'l-Bahá, *Some Answered Questions*, p. 144.

2. John 14:9; Bahá'u'lláh, *Gleanings*, p. 315.

3. 'Abdu'l-Bahá, *Some Answered Questions*, p. 210.

4. 'Abdu'l-Bahá, *Tablets of Abdul-Baha Abbas*, vol. 2, p. 309.

5. Ibid.

6. 'Abdu'l-Bahá, *Foundations of World Unity*, p. 38.

7. S. M. Afnán, *A Philosophical Lexicon in Persian and Arabic*, p. 73; J. P. Chaplin, *Dictionary of Psychology*, p. 101.

8. Raymond J. Corsini, *Dictionary of Psychology*, p. 888; J. M. Baldwin, ed., *Dictionary of Philosophy and Psychology*, vol. 1, p. 200.

9. A. P. Iannone, *Dictionary of World Philosophy*, p. 390; Dagobert D. Runes, *Dictionary of Philosophy*, p. 59.

10. 'Abdu'l-Bahá, *Some Answered Questions*, p. 210.

CHAPTER 15

The epigraph for chapter 15 is from Bahá'u'lláh, *Gleanings*, pp. 153–54.

1. Melvin Morse, *Transformed*, p. 195.

2. Joel L. Swerdlow, "Quiet Miracles of the Brain," *National Geographic* 187:6:10.

3. Bahá'u'lláh, *Gleanings*, p. 171.

4. Joannie M. Schrof, "What Is a Memory Made Of," *U.S. News and World Report*, 18 August 1997, pp. 71–73.

5. See Robert Rosen, *Life Itself*, p. 86.

6. Samuel Taylor Coleridge, "Kubla Khan," *Norton Anthology*, p. 742, 1.35.

7. 'Abdu'l-Bahá, in *Auguste Forel and the Bahá'í Faith*, p. 8.

8. Bahá'u'lláh, *Gleanings*, pp. 154–55.

9. James Shreeve, "Beyond the Brain," *National Geographic*, March 2005, p. 23.

10. 'Abdu'l-Bahá, *Some Answered Questions*, p. 241.

11. Bahá'u'lláh, *Hidden Words*, Persian, no. 13.

12. Bahá'u'lláh, *Kitáb-i-Aqdas*, note 149.

13. Extract from a letter dated 13 November 1944 written on behalf of Shoghi Effendi to an individual, in *Lights of Guidance*, no. 650.

CONCLUSION

The epigraph for the conclusion comes from Bahá'u'lláh, *Hidden Words*, Persian, no. 41.

1. 'Abdu'l-Bahá, in *Bahá'í World Faith*, p. 367.

2. Bahá'u'lláh, *Gleanings*, pp. 9–10.

3. Ibid., p. 345.

4. Extract from a letter written on behalf of Shoghi Effendi to an individual believer, in *Lights of Guidance*, no. 1744.

5. Bahá'u'lláh, *Hidden Words*, Arabic, no. 32.

6. 'Abdu'l-Bahá, *Promulgation of Universal Peace*, p. 49.

7. Bahá'u'lláh, *Gleanings*, pp. 40–41; Wordsworth, "Ulysses," *Norton Anthology*, p. 896, 11. 20–21.

8. 'Abdu'l-Bahá, *Paris Talks*, no. 57.1.

9. 'Abdu'l-Bahá, *Some Answered Questions*, p. 240.

10. 'Abdu'l-Bahá, *Memorials of the Faithful*, no. 23.8.

11. Evelyn Underhill, *A Little Book for Normal People*, p. 3.

Bibliography

WORKS OF BAHÁ'U'LLÁH

Epistle to the Son of the Wolf. 1st pocket-size ed. Translated by Shoghi Effendi. Wilmette, IL: Bahá'í Publishing Trust, 1988.

Gleanings from the Writings of Bahá'u'lláh. 1st pocket-size ed. Translated by Shoghi Effendi. Wilmette, IL: Bahá'í Publishing Trust, 1983.

The Hidden Words. Translated by Shoghi Effendi. Wilmette, IL: Bahá'í Publishing, 2002.

The Kitáb-i-Aqdas: The Most Holy Book. 1st pocket-size ed. Wilmette, IL: Bahá'í Publishing Trust, 1993.

The Kitáb-i-Íqán: The Book of Certitude. Translated by Shoghi Effendi. Wilmette, IL: Bahá'í Publishing, 2003.

Prayers and Meditations. Translated by Shoghi Effendi. 1st pocket-size ed. Wilmette, IL: Bahá'í Publishing Trust, 1987.

The Seven Valleys and the Four Valleys. New ed. Translated by Ali-Kuli Khan and Marzieh Gail. Wilmette, IL: Bahá'í Publishing Trust, 1991.

The Summons of the Lord of Hosts: Tablets of Bahá'u'lláh. Haifa: Bahá'í World Centre, 2002.

Tablets of Bahá'u'lláh revealed after the Kitáb-i-Aqdas. Compiled by the Research Department of the Universal House of Justice. Translated by Habib Taherzadeh et al. Wilmette, IL: 1988.

WORKS OF THE BÁB

Selections from the Writings of the Báb. Compiled by the Research Department of the Universal House of Justice. Translated by Habib Taherzadeh et al. Haifa: Bahá'í World Centre, 1976.

WORKS OF 'ABDU'L-BAHÁ

'Abdu'l-Bahá in London: Addresses and Notes of Conversations. London: Bahá'í Publishing Trust, 1982.

Foundations of World Unity: Compiled from Addresses and Tablets of 'Abdu'l-Bahá. Wilmette, IL: Bahá'í Publishing Trust, 1972.

Paris Talks: Addresses Given By 'Abdu'l-Bahá in Paris in 1911. 12th ed. London: Bahá'í Publishing Trust, 1995.

The Promulgation of Universal Peace: Talks Delivered by 'Abdu'l-Bahá during His Visit to the United States and Canada in 1912. Compiled by Howard MacNutt. 2d ed. Wilmette, IL: Bahá'í Publishing Trust, 1982.

Selections from the Writings of 'Abdu'l-Bahá. Compiled by the Research Department of the Universal House of Justice. Translated by a Committee at the Bahá'í World Center and Marzieh Gail. 1st pocket-size ed. Wilmette, IL: Bahá'í Publishing Trust, 1996.

Some Answered Questions. Compiled and translated by Laura Clifford Barney. 1st pocket-size ed. Wilmette, IL: Bahá'í Publishing Trust, 1984.

Tablets of Abdul-Baha Abbas. 3 vols. New York: Bahai Publishing Society, 1909–16.

Will and Testament of 'Abdu'l-Bahá. Wilmette, IL: Bahá'í Publishing Trust, 1944.

WORKS OF SHOGHI EFFENDI

Advent of Divine Justice. 1st pocket-size ed. Wilmette, IL: Bahá'í Publishing Trust, 1990.

Arohanui: Letters from Shoghi Effendi to New Zealand. Suva, Fiji: Bahá'í Publishing Trust, 1982.

God Passes By. New ed. Wilmette, IL: Bahá'í Publishing Trust, 1974.

High Endeavours: Messages to Alaska. [n.p.]: Bahá'í Publishing Trust, 1976.

The Promised Day Is Come. 1st pocket-size ed. Wilmette, IL: Bahá'í Publishing Trust, 1996.

The Unfolding Destiny of the British Bahá'í Community: The Messages from the Guardian of the Bahá'í Faith to the Bahá'ís of the British Isles. London: Bahá'í Publishing Trust, 1981.

The World Order of Bahá'u'lláh: Selected Letters. 1st pocket-size ed. Wilmette, IL: Bahá'í Publishing Trust, 1991.

COMPILATIONS OF BAHÁ'Í WRITINGS

Bahá'u'lláh, the Báb, and 'Abdu'l-Bahá. *Bahá'í Prayers: A Selection of Prayers Revealed by Bahá'u'lláh, the Báb, and 'Abdu'l-Bahá.* New ed. Wilmette, IL: Bahá'í Publishing Trust, 2002.

Bahá'u'lláh and 'Abdu'l-Bahá. *Bahá'í Scriptures: Selections from the Utterances of Bahá'u'lláh and 'Abdu'l-Bahá.* Edited by Horace Holley. 2d ed. New York: Bahá'í Publishing Committee, 1928.

Bahá'u'lláh and 'Abdu'l-Bahá. *Bahá'í World Faith: Selected Writings of Bahá'u'lláh and 'Abdu'l-Bahá.* 2d ed. Wilmette, IL: Bahá'í Publishing Trust, 1976.

Helen Hornby. Compiler. *Lights of Guidance*. New ed. New Delhi, India: Bahá'í Publishing Trust, 1994.

Other Works

['Abdu'l-Bahá and Auguste Forel]. *Auguste Forel and the Bahá'í Faith*. Translated by Hélène Neri. Commentary by Peter Mühlschlegel. Oxford: George Ronald, 1978.

Afnán, Soheil M. *Vázhih Námih Falsafí* (A Philosophical Lexicon in Persian and Arabic). Iran, Nashri-Nuqrih, n.d.

Baldwin, J. M., ed. *Dictionary of Philosophy and Psychology*, vol. 2. Gloucester, MA: Peter Smith,1960.

Bohm, D., and B. J. Hiley. *The Undivided Universe: An Ontological Interpretation of Quantum Theory*. New York: Routledge, 1993.

_____. *The Wholeness and the Implicate Order*. London: Routledge, 1980.

Brown, Keven, editor. *Evolution and Bahá'í Belief: 'Abdu'l-Bahá's Response to Nineteenth-Century Darwinism*. Los Angeles: Kalimát Press, 2001.

Chalmers, David J. *The Conscious Mind: In Search of a Fundamental Theory*. New York: Oxford University Press, 1996.

Chaplin, J. P. *Dictionary of Psychology*. New York: Bell Publishing, 1968.

Chamberlain, Isabel Fraser. *Abdul Baha on Divine Philosophy*. Boston: Tudor Press, 1918.

Corsini, Raymond J. *The Dictionary of Psychology*. Philadelphia: Brunner/Mazel, 1999.

Cousins, Norman. *Anatomy of an Illness as Perceived by the Patient: Reflections on Healing and Regeneration*. New York: W. W. Norton, 1979.

De Rougement, Denis. *Love in the Western World*. Translated by Montgomery Belgion. Princeton, New Jersey: Princeton University Press, 1983.

Dihkhudá, 'Alí Akbar. *Lughat-Námih 'Alí Akbar Dihkhudá*, 50 vols. Tehran: Tehran University, 1337 Shamsí.

Dossey, Larry, M.D. *Healing Words: The Power of Prayer and the Practice of Medicine*. San Francisco: Harper San Francisco, 1993.

_____. *Recovering the Soul: A Scientific and Spiritual Search*. New York: Bantam Books, 1989.

Esslemont, J. E. *Bahá'u'lláh and the New Era: An Introduction to the Bahá'í Faith*. 5th rev. ed. Wilmette, IL: Bahá'í Publishing Trust, 1980.

Ferris, Timothy. *The Whole Shebang: A State-of-the-Universe(s) Report*. New York: Simon and Schuster, 1997

Feynman, Richard P. *Six Not-So-Easy Pieces: Einstein's Relativity, Symmetry and Space-Time*. Cambridge, MA: Perseus Books, 1997.

Greene, Brian. *The Elegant Universe: Superstrings, Hidden Dimensions, and the Quest for the Ultimate Theory*. New York: Random House, 2000.

Gundersen, P. Erik. *The Handy Physics Answer Book*. Canton, MI: Visible Ink Press, 1999.

Hatcher, John S. *The Arc of Ascent: The Purpose of Physical Reality II*. Oxford: George Ronald, 1994.

_____. *The Divine Art of Revelation*. Wilmette, IL: Bahá'í Publishing Trust, 1998.

_____. *The Purpose of Physical Reality: The Kingdom of Names*. Wilmette, IL: Bahá'í Publishing Trust, 1987.

_____. *A Sense of History: A Collection of Poems by John S. Hatcher*. Oxford, England: George Ronald, 1990.

Hatcher, John S., and William S. Hatcher. *The Law of Love Enshrined: Selected Essays by John Hatcher and William Hatcher*. Oxford: George Ronald Publishers, 1996.

Hatcher, William S. *Love, Power, and Justice: The Dynamics of Authentic Morality*. Wilmette, IL: Bahá'í Publishing Trust, 1998.

Hayden, Robert E. *Collected Poems*. Edited by Frederick Glaysher. New York: Liveright Publishing Corporation, 1985.

Hemingway, Ernest. "A Clean Well-Lighted Place." *The Riverside Anthology of Literature*. Edited by Douglas Hunt. Boston: Houghton Mifflin Company, 1988.

Holman, C. Hugh, and William Harmon. *A Handbook to Literature*. 6th ed. New York: MacMillian Publishing Company, 1992.

Hunt, Douglas. *The Riverside Anthology of Literature*. 3d edition. New York: Houghton Mifflin, 1997.

Iannone, A. Pablo. *Dictionary of World Philosophy*. London: Routledge, 2001.

Jahn, Robert G. and Brenda J. Dunne. *Margins of Reality: The Role of Consciousness in the Physical World*. New York: Harcourt Brace and Company, 1987.

Jaynes, Julian. *The Origin of Consciousness in the Breakdown of the Bicameral Mind*. Boston: Houghton Mifflin Company, 1990.

Lederman, Leon. *The God Particle: If the Universe Is the Answer, What Is the Question?* New York: Dell Publishing, 1993.

Milton, John. *The Complete Poetical Works of John Milton*. Edited by H. F. Fletcher. Cambridge, MA: Houghton Mifflin Company, 1941.

Momen, Wendi, ed. *A Basic Bahá'í Dictionary*. Oxford: George Ronald, 1989.

Morse, Melvin, M.D. *Closer to the Light: Learning from the Near-Death Experiences of Children*. New York: Ivy Books, 1991.

_____. *Transformed by the Light: The Powerful Effect of Near-Death Experiences on People's Lives*. New York: Villard Books, 1992.

Moyers, Bill. "The Mind Body Connection." *Healing and the Mind,* vol. 2. New York: Ambrose Video Publishing, Inc., 1993.

Norton Anthology of Poetry. 4d. ed. Edited by Ferguson, Salter, and Stallworthy. New York: W. W. Norton & Company, 1996.

Peat, F. David. *Infinite Potential: The Life and Times of David Bohm.* Reading, MA: Addison-Wesley, 1997.

Plato. *The Dialogues of Plato.* 2 vols. Translated by B. Jowett, M. A. New York: Random House, 1937.

_____. *The Republic of Plato.* Translated by Francis M. Cornford. New York: Oxford University Press, 1958.

Prideaux, Jeff. *Comparison between Karl Pribram's "Holographic Brain Theory" and more conventional models of neuronal computation.* Virginia Commonwealth University. http://www.acsa2000.net/bcngroup/jponkp/.

Priest, Stephen. *Theories of the Mind.* New York: Houghton Mifflin, 1991.

Rees, James. *The Unit Nature of Matter.* Hermosa Beach, CA: Starlight Publishing Company, 2004. http://www.starlight-pub.com/UnitNatureofMatter/UnitNatureofMatter.html.

Robinson, James K., and Walter B. Rideout. *A College Book of Modern Verse.* Evanston, IL: Row, Peterson, 1977.

Rosen, Robert. *Life Itself: A Comprehensive Inquiry into the Nature, Origin, and Fabrication of Life.* New York: Columbia University Press, 1991.

Runes, Dagobert D. *Dictionary of Philosophy.* Totowa, NJ: Littlefield, Adams, 1962.

Satinover, Jeffrey. *The Quantum Brain: The Search for Freedom and the Next Generation of Man.* New York: John Wiley and Sons, Inc., 2001.

Schäfer, Lothar. *In Search of Divine Reality: Science as a Source of Inspiration.* Fayetteville, Arkansas: University of Arkansas Press, 1997.

Schrof, Joannie M. "What Is a Memory Made Of?" *U.S. News and World Report,* 18 August 1997, pp. 71–73.

Shakespeare, William. *The Complete Works of Shakespeare.* Edited by Hardin Craig. Chicago: Scott, Foresman and Company, 1951.

Shreeve, James. "Beyond the Brain." *National Geographic,* 197, no. 3 (March 2005): pp. 2–31.

Swerdlow, Joel L. "Quiet Miracles of the Brain." *National Geographic* 187, no. 6 (June 1995): 2–41.

Taylor, C. A. *Images.* London: Wykeham Publications, 1978.

Tillyard, E. M. W. *The Elizabethan World Picture.* New York: Random House, 1959.

Underhill, Evelyn. *Practical Mysticism: A Little Book for Normal People.* London: J. M. Dent and Sons, Ltd., 1914.

BIBLIOGRAPHY

Verrengia, Joseph B. "Brain Misfiring May Explain Out-of-Body Experience." *Tampa Tribune,* 19 September 2002, Nation / World section.

Vitale, Barbara M. *Free Flight: Celebrating Your Right Brain.* Rolling Hills Estates, CA.: Jalmar Press, 1986.

Wegner, Daniel M. *The Illusion of Conscious Will.* Cambridge, MA: The MIT Press, 2002.

Wilber, Ken. *The Spectrum of Consciousness.* Wheaton, IL: Quest Books, 1993.

Wolf, Fred Alan, Ph.D. *The Spiritual Universe: How Quantum Physics Proves the Existence of the Soul.* New York: Simon and Schuster, 1996.

Zukav, Gary. *The Dancing Wu Li Masters: An Overview of the New Physics.* New York: William Morrow and Company, Inc., 1979.

Index

For more information about the Bahá'í Faith,
or to contact the Bahá'ís near you, visit
http://www.us.bahai.org/
or call
1-800-22-UNITE

Bahá'í Publishing
and the Bahá'í Faith

Bahá'í Publishing produces books based on the teachings of the Bahá'í Faith. Founded nearly 160 years ago, the Bahá'í Faith has spread to some 235 nations and territories and is now accepted by more than five million people. The word "Bahá'í" means "follower of Bahá'u'lláh." Bahá'u'lláh, the Founder of the Bahá'í Faith, asserted that He is the Messenger of God for all of humanity in this day. The cornerstone of His teachings is the establishment of the spiritual unity of humankind, which will be achieved by personal transformation and the application of clearly identified spiritual principles. Bahá'ís also believe that there is but one religion and that all the Messengers of God—among them Abraham, Zoroaster, Moses, Krishna, Buddha, Jesus, and Muḥammad—have progressively revealed its nature. Together, the world's great religions are expressions of a single, unfolding divine plan. Human beings, not God's Messengers, are the source of religious divisions, prejudices, and hatreds.

The Bahá'í Faith is not a sect or denomination of another religion, nor is it a cult or a social movement. Rather, it is a globally recognized independent world religion founded on new books of scripture revealed by Bahá'u'lláh.

Bahá'í Publishing is an imprint of the National Spiritual Assembly of the Bahá'ís of the United States.

Other Books Available from Bahá'í Publishing

THE HIDDEN WORDS
by Bahá'u'lláh

A collection of lyrical, gem-like verses of scripture that convey timeless spiritual wisdom "clothed in the garment of brevity," the Hidden Words is one of the most important and cherished scriptural works of the Bahá'í Faith.

Revealed by Bahá'u'lláh, the founder of the religion, the verses are a perfect guidebook to walking a spiritual path and drawing closer to God. They address themes such as turning to God, humility, detachment, and love, to name but a few. These verses are among Bahá'u'lláh's earliest and best-known works, having been translated into more than seventy languages and read by millions worldwide. This edition will offer many American readers their first introduction to the vast collection of Bahá'í scripture.

THE KITÁB-I-ÍQÁN: THE BOOK OF CERTITUDE
by Bahá'u'lláh

The Book of Certitude is one of the most important scriptural works in all of religious history. In it Bahá'u'lláh gives a sweeping overview of religious truth, explaining the underlying unity of the world's religions, describing the universality of the revelations humankind has received from the Prophets of God, illuminating their fundamental teachings, and elucidating allegorical passages from the New Testament and the Koran that have given rise to misunderstandings among religious leaders, practitioners, and the public. Revealed in the span of two days and two nights, the work is, in the words of its translator, Shoghi Effendi, "the most important book written on the spiritual significance" of the Bahá'í Faith.

ADVANCEMENT OF WOMEN: A BAHÁ'Í PERSPECTIVE
by Janet A. Khan and Peter J. Khan
Advancement of Women presents the Bahá'í Faith's global perspective on the equality of the sexes, including:
- The meaning of equality
- The education of women and the need for their participation in the world at large
- The profound effects of equality on the family and family relationships
- The intimate relationship between equality of the sexes and global peace
- Chastity, modesty, sexual harassment, and rape

The equality of women and men is one of the basic tenets of the Bahá'í Faith, and much is said on the subject in Bahá'í writings. Until now, however, no single volume created for a general audience has provided comprehensive coverage of the Bahá'í teachings on this topic. In this broad survey, husband-and-wife team Janet and Peter Khan address even those aspects of equality of the sexes that are usually ignored or glossed over in the existing literature.

Tactfully treating a subject that often provokes argumentation, contention, polarization of attitudes, and accusations, the authors elevate the discussion to a new level that challenges all while offending none.

THE BAHÁ'Í FAITH: THE EMERGING GLOBAL RELIGION
by William S. Hatcher and J. Douglas Martin
Explore the history, teachings, structure, and community life of the worldwide Bahá'í community—what may well be the most diverse organized body of people on earth—through this revised and updated comprehensive introduction (2002).

Named by the *Encylopaedia Britannica* as a book that has made "significant contributions to knowledge and understanding" of religious thought, *The Bahá'í Faith* covers the most recent developments in a Faith that, in just over 150 years, has grown to become the second most widespread of the independent world religions.

An excellent introduction. [*The Bahá'í Faith*] offers a clear analysis of the religious and ethical values on which Bahá'ism is based (such as all-embracing peace, world harmony, the important role of women, to mention only a few)."
—Annemarie Schimmel, past president, International Association for the History of Religions

"Provide[s] non-Bahá'í readers with an excellent introduction to the history, beliefs, and sociopolitical structure of a religion that originated in Persia in the mid-1800s and has since blossomed into an international organization with . . . adherents from almost every country on earth."—*Montreal Gazette*

THE CHALLENGE OF BAHÁ'U'LLÁH:
DOES GOD STILL SPEAK TO HUMANITY TODAY?
by Gary L. Matthews
One person examines the astonishing claims made by the Prophet who founded the Bahá'í religion.

Author Gary Matthews documents why he believes that the revelation of Bahá'u'lláh is divine in origin, representing a unique summons of unequaled importance to humanity. The book contains discussions of Bahá'í prophecies concerning historical events and scientific discoveries. Among the events and discoveries discussed are the fall of the Ottoman Empire, the worldwide erosion of ecclesiastical authority, the Holocaust, and the development of nuclear weapons. A new and updated edition. The previous edition (George Ronald, ISBN 0-85398-360-7) was a limited release and not offered to the U.S. trade/consumer market.

GOD SPEAKS AGAIN: AN INTRODUCTION TO THE BAHÁ'Í FAITH
by Kenneth E. Bowers
Written by an internationally known member of the Bahá'í community, *God Speaks Again* is the first comprehensive introduction to the Bahá'í Faith written for general readers that includes many important and beautiful passages of Bahá'í scripture to both illustrate and explain the Faith's history, teachings, and distinctive relevance for life on our planet today. The book contains 30 chapters covering all aspects of the religion, as well as notes, a glossary, a bibliography, and a suggested reading list. The history and teachings of the Bahá'í Faith center around the inspiring person of its Prophet and Founder, Bahá'u'lláh (1817–1892). The extraordinary qualities that Bahá'u'lláh displayed throughout the course of His life, the voluminous and comprehensive body of His written works, and the impact they continue to have around the globe undeniably qualify Him as a major figure in world religious history.

IT'S NOT YOUR FAULT: HOW HEALING RELATIONSHIPS CHANGE YOUR
BRAIN & CAN HELP YOU OVERCOME A PAINFUL PAST
by Patricia Romano McGraw
Simply put, you can't think your way to happiness if you're suffering the effects of trauma or abuse. Yet every day, millions receive this message from a multi-billion-dollar self-help industry. As a result, many think it's their fault when their efforts to heal themselves fail. Far too many sincere, intelligent, and highly motivated people who have followed popular advice for self-healing still feel depressed, anxious, unloved, and unlovable. Why is this? If popular pathways

for self-healing don't work, what does? How can those who suffer begin to find relief, function better, and feel genuinely optimistic, relaxed, loved, and lovable? This engaging and highly readable book, based on the author's professional experience in treating those who suffer from the devastating effects of emotional trauma, offers hope for those who suffer and those who care about them. McGraw describes how trauma affects the brain and, therefore, one's ability to carry out "good advice"; explains the subtle and largely hidden processes of attunement and attachment that take place between parents and children, examining their impact on all future relationships; tells what is needed for healing to occur; discusses the profound health benefits of spirituality and a relationship with God in assisting and accelerating the healing process; and suggests how members of the helping professions can begin to tap the deepest, most authentic parts of themselves to touch the hearts of those they seek to help.

MARRIAGE BEYOND BLACK AND WHITE: AN INTERRACIAL FAMILY PORTRAIT
by David Douglas and Barbara Douglas
A powerful story about the marriage of a Black man and a White woman, *Marriage beyond Black and White* offers a poignant and sometimes painful look at what it was like to be an interracial couple in the United States from the early 1940s to the mid-1990s. Breaking one of the strongest taboos in American society at the time, Barbara Wilson Tinker and Carlyle Douglas met, fell in love, married, and began raising a family. At the time of their wedding, interracial marriage was outlawed in twenty-seven states and was regarded as an anathema in the rest.

Barbara began writing their story to record both the triumphs and hardships of interracial marriage. Her son David completed the family chronicle. The result will uplift and inspire any reader whose life is touched by injustice, offering an invaluable perspective on the roles of faith and spiritual transformation in combating prejudice and racism.

PROPHET'S DAUGHTER: THE LIFE AND LEGACY OF BAHÍYYIH K͟HÁNUM, OUTSTANDING HEROINE OF THE BAHÁ'Í FAITH
by Janet A. Khan
The first full-length biography of a member of Bahá'u'lláh's family, an important woman in world religious history.

A biography of a largely unknown yet important woman in world religious history—the eldest daughter of Bahá'u'lláh, founder of the Bahá'í religion—who faithfully served her family and the early followers of a then completely new faith through nearly seven decades of extreme hardship. During the mid-nineteenth and early twentieth centuries, when women in the Middle East were largely invisible, deprived of education, and without status in their communities, she was an active participant in the religion's turbulent early years and contributed significantly to its emergence as an independent world religion. The example of her life and her remarkable personal qualities have special relevance to issues confronting society today.

THE REALITY OF MAN
compiled by Terry J. Cassiday, Christopher J. Martin, and Bahhaj Taherzadeh
An important new collection of Bahá'í writings on the spiritual nature of human beings.

This compilation provides a sample of the Bahá'í religion's vast teachings on the nature of man. Topics include God's love for humanity, the purpose of life, our spiritual reality, the nature of the soul, how human beings develop spiritually, and immortality and life hereafter. The writings are from Bahá'u'lláh and His appointed successor, 'Abdu'l-Bahá.

"Men at all times and under all conditions stand in need of one to exhort them, guide them and to instruct and teach them. Therefore He hath sent forth His Messengers, His Prophets, and chosen ones that they might acquaint the people with the divine purpose underlying the revelation of Books and the raising up of messengers, and that everyone may become aware of the trust of God, which is latent in the reality of every soul." —Bahá'u'lláh

"The mission of the Prophets, the revelation of the Holy Books, the manifestation of the heavenly teachers and the purpose of divine philosophy all center in the training of the human realities so that they may become clear and pure as mirrors and reflect the light and love of [God] . . . Otherwise, by simple development along material lines man is not perfected. At most, the physical aspect of man, his natural or material conditions, may become stabilized and improved, but he will remain deprived of the spiritual or divine bestowal. He is then like a body without a spirit, a lamp without the light. . . ." —'Abdu'l-Bahá

REFRESH AND GLADDEN MY SPIRIT:
PRAYERS AND MEDITATIONS FROM BAHÁ'Í SCRIPTURE
Introduction by Pamela Brode
Discover the Bahá'í approach to prayer with this uplifting collection of prayers and short, inspirational extracts from Bahá'í scripture. More than 120 prayers in *Refresh and Gladden My Spirit* offer solace and inspiration on themes including spiritual growth, nearness to God, comfort, contentment, happiness, difficult times, healing, material needs, praise and gratitude, and strength, to name only

a few. An introduction by Pamela Brode examines the powerful effects of prayer and meditation in daily life, outlines the Bahá'í approach to prayer, and considers questions such as "What is prayer?" "Why pray?" "Are our prayers answered?" and "Does prayer benefit the world?"

RELEASE THE SUN
by William Sears

Millennial fervor gripped many people around the world in the early nineteenth century. While Christians anticipated the return of Jesus Christ, a wave of expectation swept through Islam that the "Lord of the Age" would soon appear. In Persia, this reached a dramatic climax on May 23, 1844, when a twenty-five-year-old merchant from Shíráz named Siyyid 'Alí-Muḥammad, later titled "the Báb," announced that he was the bearer of a divine revelation destined to transform the spiritual life of the human race. Furthermore, he claimed that he was but the herald of another Messenger, who would soon bring a far greater revelation that would usher in an age of universal peace. Against a backdrop of wide-scale moral decay in Persian society, this declaration aroused hope and excitement among all classes. The Báb quickly attracted tens of thousands of followers, including influential members of the clergy—and the brutal hand of a fearful government bent on destroying this movement that threatened to rock the established order.

Release the Sun tells the extraordinary story of the Báb, the Prophet-Herald of the Bahá'í Faith. Drawing on contemporary accounts, William Sears vividly describes one of the most significant but little-known periods in religious history since the rise of Christianity and Islam.

SEEKING FAITH: IS RELIGION REALLY WHAT YOU THINK IT IS?
by Nathan Rutstein

What's your concept of religion? A 2001 Gallup Poll on religion in America found that while nearly two out of three Americans claim to be a member of a church or synagogue, more than half of those polled believe that religion is losing its influence on society. *Seeking Faith* examines today's concepts of religion and the various reasons why people are searching in new directions for hope and spiritual guidance. Author Nathan Rutstein explores the need for a sense of purpose, direction, and meaning in life, and the need for spiritual solutions to global problems in the social, economic, environmental, and political realms. Rutstein also discusses the concept of the Spiritual Guide, or Divine Educator, and introduces the teachings of Bahá'u'lláh and the beliefs of the Bahá'í Faith

The Story of Bahá'u'lláh: Promised One of All Religions
by Druzelle Cederquist
An easy-to-read introduction to the Prophet and Founder of the Bahá'í Faith.

The Story of Bahá'u'lláh presents in a clear narrative style the life of the Prophet from His birth into a wealthy merchant family, through His transforming spiritual experience while incarcerated in the infamous Black Pit of Tehran, and over the decades of harsh and increasingly remote exile that followed. Woven into the story are Bahá'u'lláh's principal teachings and references to historical events and persons that place the development of the new religion in a global perspective. This book chronologically follows the story told in *Release the Sun* (Bahá'í Publishing, 2003).

As explained in such resources as *The Oxford Dictionary of World Religions* and the *Encyclopaedia Britannica*, members of the Bahá'í Faith believe that all the Founders of the world's great religions have been Messengers of God and agents of a progressive divine plan for the education of the human race. According to Bahá'u'lláh (1819–1892), the Prophet and Founder of the Bahá'í religion, the teachings of the divine Messengers—including Abraham, Moses, Buddha, Christ, Muḥammad—vary with the receptivity and maturity of the people of their era, but all represent one single "religion of God." Bahá'u'lláh, Whom Bahá'ís accept as the divine Messenger for the present age, taught that the unity of all the peoples of the earth is the spiritual destiny of this period in human history.

A Wayfarer's Guide to Bringing the Sacred Home
by Joseph Sheppherd
What's the spiritual connection between self, family, and community? Why is it so important that we understand and cultivate these key relationships? *A Wayfarer's Guide to Bringing the Sacred Home* offers a Bahá'í perspective on issues that shape our lives and the lives of those around us: the vital role of spirituality in personal transformation, the divine nature of child-rearing and unity in the family, and the importance of overcoming barriers to building strong communities—each offering joy, hope, and confidence to a challenged world. Inspiring extracts and prayers from Bahá'í scripture are included. This is an enlightening read for anyone seeking to bring spirituality into their daily lives.